A NATION'S UNDESIRABLES

INTERSECTIONAL RHETORICS
Karma R. Chávez, Series Editor

A NATION'S UNDESIRABLES

MIXED-RACE CHILDREN AND WHITENESS IN THE POST-NAZI ERA

Tracey Owens Patton

THE OHIO STATE UNIVERSITY PRESS
COLUMBUS

Copyright © 2024 by The Ohio State University.
All rights reserved.

Library of Congress Cataloging-in-Publication data available online at https://catalog.loc.gov
LCCN: 2023057264
Identifiers: ISBN 978-0-8142-1561-6 (hardback); ISBN 978-0-8142-5907-8 (paperback); ISBN 978-0-8142-8344-8 (ebook)

Cover design by Brad Norr
Text composition by Stuart Rodriguez
Type set in Minion Pro

For Lilli and Lore

CONTENTS

List of Illustrations		ix
Acknowledgments		xi
INTRODUCTION	Challenging the Historical Narrative: Braiding Memory, Postmemory, and Critical Imagination	1
CHAPTER 1	Construction of Race and Nation: A History of Black Germany	29
CHAPTER 2	Jim Crow in the European Theater: Institutionalizing Anti-Blackness in Germany	60
CHAPTER 3	Womb Wars: Interracial Relationships and the Historical Construction of White German Identity	88
CHAPTER 4	Aborted out of Germany: Born, Kept, and Abandoned	112
CHAPTER 5	The Transatlantic Appeal of Jim Crow: Reclaimed, Abandoned, and Adopted	145
CHAPTER 6	A Family Reunion and Generational Trauma: A Conclusion	176
Bibliography		209
Index		219

ILLUSTRATIONS

FIGURE 0.1	Three generations of family	4
FIGURE 0.2	*Ebony* magazine, October 1948	5
FIGURE 0.3	Author's German family tree	23
FIGURE 1.1	"Happy Easter" German colonial postcard	41
FIGURE 1.2	"Another city, another girl!" German colonial postcard	43
FIGURE 1.3	German propaganda, 1920	48
FIGURE 1.4	Two Dachau survivors	53
FIGURE 2.1	German World War I military dinner	68
FIGURE 2.2	Bund Deutscher Mädel parade, ca. 1933–39	73
FIGURE 2.3	US 92nd Infantry Division, ca. 1944	77
FIGURE 2.4	Great-grandfather Robert walking in Germany	80
FIGURE 3.1	US Army propaganda poster, ca. 1918	93
FIGURE 3.2	A German woman's public shaming, 1942	97
FIGURE 3.3	Postwar socializing	104
FIGURE 3.4	Stollenwörthweiher See, Mannheim, Germany	105

FIGURE 4.1	The twins as infants, 1948	115
FIGURE 4.2	Greta and her mother playing a board game	116
FIGURE 4.3	The twins as toddlers in matching outfits	119
FIGURE 4.4	A scene from *Toxi*	125
FIGURE 4.5	The twins with Greta	126
FIGURE 4.6	The twins in school	136
FIGURE 5.1	Lore and Greta reunite	153
FIGURE 5.2	Greta becomes a US citizen	155
FIGURE 5.3	Twins at the Wasserturm	163
FIGURE 5.4	Lilli after her return to the US	173
FIGURE 6.1	The author and Greta meet for the first time	187
FIGURE 6.2	German family reunion	188
FIGURE 6.3	The author and Greta examine stitchery	191
FIGURES 6.4A AND 6.4B	Comparing time periods at the Wasserturm	205
FIGURE 6.5	Tracey and Lore	206

ACKNOWLEDGMENTS

I could not have begun or completed this journey without the help and support of many individuals. Most importantly, I am thankful for the trust and bravery of my mother, Lore, and her twin, Lilli, in sharing stories that not only brought me greater understanding of our German roots and family but also brought me closer to them. Without their self-disclosure, there would be no book. I am grateful to the other *afrodeutsche Nachkriegskinder* for sharing such intimate life experiences and welcoming me into their world of scholarship. Thank you to Susanna Martinez and Prof. Dr. Hans-Peter Schwoebel for the tour of Mannheim, and thank you to Susanna for sharing her story.

I am grateful for the guidance, patience, and wisdom that my wonderful acquisitions editor, Tara Cyphers, and Intersectional Rhetorics series editor, Dr. Karma Chávez, provided throughout this project. Tara helped bring my vision of this book to fruition, and both Tara and Dr. Chávez see the value and importance of intersectional research. A big thank you to The Ohio State University Press production team, as well as a thank you to book cover designer Brad Norr and indexer Shannon Li.

I am filled with love for my family, who have always been there for support: John and Lore Owens Jr. (my parents) and Sam Patton (my husband). I also thank my colleagues and friends who listened to my research ideas and read drafts of chapters: Dr. Darrell Jackson, Dr. Kerry Pimblott, and Dr. Marcus Watson. A special thank you to my dear friend, Dr. Mindi Golden, who provided encouragement and support as I embarked on this writing journey. I would also like to thank my former students and former student researchers who assisted in this project over the years in a myriad of ways: Dr. Sam Allen, Dr. Richelle Clifton, Esther Adeyemo, Christine Henschler, and Sydney Stein. I have a debt of gratitude for the insights, humor, skillful editing, wisdom, and unwavering support and enthusiasm that Sam Patton and my co-conspirator, Dr. Nancy Small, provided, which added greater depth to my book and pushed me beyond what I knew I could do. I am forever grateful.

Finally, I am appreciative of the academic research grants I received from the following entities within the University of Wyoming, which provided funds that enabled me to engage in this research: the African American and Diaspora Studies Program, College of Arts & Sciences; the Department of English; the Devine Excellence Fund in the School of Culture, Gender, and Social Justice; the Faculty-Grant-in-Aid Program; the Flittie Sabbatical Award; the Gender and Women's Studies Program; the International Programs Office, International Travel Grant; the Caitlin Long Excellence Fund; the McNair Scholars Program, Research and Economic Development Division; the Social Justice Research Center Committee; and the Wyoming Institute for Humanities Research. Thank you to the US Holocaust Memorial Museum and the archivists in Germany who aided me in this project, particularly those at the Bundesarchiv in Koblenz, the Marchivum Mannheim City Archive in Mannheim, and the Stadtmuseum (SAM—City Museum at Market) in Wiesbaden. I am particularly thankful to the archivists at the Institut für Stadtgeschichte, in Frankfurt, and to the private meeting with the archivist at the BallinStadt (Emigration Museum) in Hamburg.

Portions of this book have appeared previously in earlier versions and are used by permission of the publishers: "'Weil Wir Uns Schämen': Memory, Postmemory und Reflektionen uber Errinnerung, 'Rasse' und Zurückweisung," in *Kinder der Befreiung Transatlantische Erfahrungen und Perspektiven Schwarzer Deutscher der Nachkriegsgeneration,* ed. Marion Kraft (Münster, Germany: Unrast-Verlag, 2015): 192–222; "That Was the Worst Day of My Life: Recrafting Family through Memory, Race, and Rejection in Post-WWII Germany," *Genealogy Journal* 1, no. 11 (June 9, 2017): 1–25; "'Because We're Embarrassed': Memory, Post-Memory, and Reflections on 'Race' and Rejection," in *Children of the Liberation: Transatlantic Experiences and Perspectives of Black Germans of the Post-War Generation,* ed. Marion Kraft (Oxford, UK: Peter Lang, 2020): 209–42; and "I Want to Show You My New Family: Race, Rejection, and Reunion in Postwar Germany," in *Adoption across Race and Nation: US Histories and Legacies,* ed. Silke Hackenesch (Columbus: The Ohio State University Press 2022).

INTRODUCTION

Challenging the Historical Narrative

Braiding Memory, Postmemory, and Critical Imagination

> My search for you, Greta, began approximately four years ago, and my research began with [US] Homeland Security [which detailed my German heritage] and adoption history. You, Greta, are remembered with much love, kindness, and respect. Through the decades, so many fond memories come to mind of Germany, i.e., my loving grandmother, our uncle who used to carry me on his shoulders through a Mannheim parade, our motorcycle rides with him, walks along the Rhine River with family and stopping to peer in store windows—especially the town chocolatier. I remember going to Catholic Church every Sunday. Enclosed is my verification of my authenticity.
> —Lore's reintroduction letter to Greta, 2012

INTRODUCTION

After fifty-two years of separation, Lore,[1] my mother, was reunited with her birth mother in July 2012. The search for my biological German grandmother, Greta, began two years prior to that reunion and was an international affair because my mother and her twin, Lilli, are German. As a first-generation American,[2] I grew up haunted by the ghost whom I would later call Greta, or *oma*, and I longed to unveil the mysteries she held. Greta slowly came into focus as I navigated city, state, and federal archives in Germany; the mayor's office in Mannheim, Germany; US Homeland Security; the state of California court systems; the Children's Home Society of California; and the Ming Quong Home in Los Gatos, California. After a closed adoption in 1960, the destruction of paperwork on the part of the adoptive parents, and the passage

---

1. *Lore* is pronounced like *Laura* in English and is the German spelling for *Lora*.
2. Here I am referring to myself as a "first-generation American," as I am the first person on the German side of my family to be born in the US.

of fifty-two years, I doubted that Greta would be found—and that she wanted to be. I was wrong. She answered Lore's letter, and what I found was a ninety-year-old woman living a regimented life in California.

Greta, whom you will come to know better as this book progresses, was born in Mannheim, Germany, in 1922 and lived her childhood, teens, and twenties during and in between two world wars. As a child during the post–World War I era, she was afraid of the African French colonial soldiers who remained in Germany, and during World War II she found herself conscripted into the Hitler Maidens and working for the Hitler regime between the ages of seventeen and twenty-three. Anyone who had a job in Germany during World War II essentially worked for Hitler. It can be argued that Greta's formative years (youth through her twenties), as related to the nation-state, were awash in issues of race, racism, and hatred. After World War II, Greta worked in Heidelberg, Germany, on the US military base and found herself in love with, living with, and pregnant with Albert Flowers's twin daughters. Albert was a Black American GI who broke her heart. Eventually Greta, leaving Lilli and Lore behind in Mannheim, immigrated to the US in 1955, coming through Ellis Island and settling in California. Like many immigrants, Greta was first employed in the food industry (she worked for a bakery) and then later found administrative work for an engineering firm. Later in 1955, Greta sent for Lilli and Lore to join her, and it was in 1958, when the twins were ten years old, that Greta signed away her parental rights and married an American man who informed her, "I'll marry you, but I won't take another man's children." My grandmother dropped the twins off at the steps of an orphanage and married the man. Greta visited the twins monthly, but once they were adopted, at almost twelve years old in 1960, she stopped all contact.

Lilli and Lore were not immediately identified by Greta as *afrodeutsche Nachkriegskinder* (Black German postwar children), or "colored occupation children."[3] There were "approximately 95,000 children born in Germany shortly after WWII,"[4] and of that number my mother and her twin represent "an estimated three to four thousand Black German children born between 1946 and 1953"[5] who were either raised in Germany, adopted by German families, or adopted outside of Germany (e.g., in Denmark, England, or the United States). This purging of biracial German children through international adoption did not begin to subside until 1955. In the past, multiracial Black German

---

3. It is important to note that not all children born of Black US GIs and white German women during and after World War II were "occupation children" who were placed for adoption.
4. "German Brown Babies."
5. Sollors, *Temptation of Despair*, 222.

children have been vilified and called horribly racist names such as "child of mixed blood," "half-blood," "n—— child," "occupation children," and "*Mischlingskinder*."[6] In reclaiming an identity for themselves, *afrodeutsche Nachkriegskinder* refer to themselves Afro-German, or Black German.

Color, the appearance of color (imagined or not), and colorism were very important in Greta's life because after experiencing twelve years of Nazi rule, and before that the racist colonial fabric of Germany, Greta's life was saturated with white supremacy and racism. This form of white identity bled into her beliefs about white womanhood, her representation of self, and her attitudes toward her twin daughters. Black-and-white baby photos of the twins (see figs. 4.1, 4.3, 4.5, and 4.6) make them appear darker in phenotypic hue than they really are due to the age of the photos, poor lighting, and shadows.[7] However, because Lilli and Lore's visible phenotype is actually white, and because the twins were not up for adoption in Germany like some mixed-race postwar German children were, Greta exercised what little power she had and never labeled them *afrodeutsche Nachkriegskinder*. Rather, Greta kept the twins' "racial" categorization in limbo while in Germany. Only after the twins were out of Germany and eventually thrust into the California foster care system from 1958 to 1960 did Greta take advantage of the racist "one drop" of Black blood rules prevalent in the US[8] and identify her twin daughters as Black and the biological father of Lilli and Lore as African American.[9] With Greta's decision to racially mark the twins as something other than white, Lilli and Lore were suddenly wrapped up in the diasporic exodus that purged *afrodeutsche Nachkriegskinder* out of Germany and into seemingly more diverse locales in a desire to keep Germany "white." Upon Greta's "outing" the twins as biracial Black children, the California social worker to whom Greta and the

---

6. These are racist, harmful terms to Black people and particularly to the Black German community. Therefore, these terms are placed in quotation marks to indicate their status as white supremacist social concepts and language, not biological constructs or truth.

7. Cameras from the late 1940s and 1950s are vastly different from the advanced cameras made today, and where Lilli and Lore appear to have a darker phenotype in the older black-and-white photos in this book, the photographic difference is more likely due to shadows and lighting (overexposure or underexposure), shading and white balance, and the optical illusions a camera creates depending upon the wavelengths available from various light sources (e.g., indoor versus outdoor lighting) than a change in phenotype or skin color.

8. To be classified as Black under the one-drop rule, a person had to have 1/32 or more Black ancestry, or a Black ancestor as recently as five generations ago. As a result, such a person would not benefit from whiteness or any of the privileged notions that come with being white. The one-drop rule in the US applied as a racial qualifier to Black / African American people. See J. Davis, *Who Is Black?*

9. The terms *African American* and *Black* are used interchangeably. *African American* or *Black American* specifically refers to people from the United States, whereas *Black* is used as a diasporic term referring to Black peoples worldwide.

FIGURE 0.1. Three generations of family reunited after fifty-two years. Lore (*left*), Greta (*center*), and Tracey (*right*). Family photo.

twins were assigned once she made the decision to have Lilli and Lore adopted praised Greta for finally getting rid of the "two mistakes" she was saddled with to the detriment of her own career and life advancement.[10] Once the twins were suddenly declared Black, Greta was absolved from the responsibility of her children and her expected role as mother, and she simultaneously regained and reclaimed her whiteness and white womanhood in the United States. Fifty-two years later, my grandmother, my mom, and I (see fig. 0.1) were reunited and began the process of redefining what family is and how family can be constructed and reconstructed over decades.

In the United States, Black German children were covered in the mass media of the day such as *Ebony* magazine, where they made the cover of the October 1948 issue, "Homes needed for 10,000 Brown Orphans" (see fig. 0.2), and *Jet* magazine, which featured several Black German children available for adoption in 1951. The goal of this mediated coverage was to have Black German children brought to the US and adopted by African American families.

---

10. Social worker, Children's Home Society of California, accessed 2012.

FIGURE 0.2. *Ebony* magazine, October 1948.

The adoption of the twins was enabled by a racist, white supremacist German system that encouraged international removal of mixed-race German children, and it represents the embodiment of generational trauma. Lilli and Lore were haunted by an erased past and placed in a liminal existence by Greta, Germany, and the US through the stereotypes of Blackness. As Avery Gordon aptly notes, "to be haunted is to be tied to historical and social effects."[11] The twins were haunted by the racist stereotypes that kept them in liminality in Germany and then further cloaked in racist stereotypes in the Jim Crow US.

All people inherit and develop their understanding of memories not only through their own mental processes but also through seemingly external, shareable phenomena such as artifacts, attitude and behaviors, cultural narratives, and history.[12] As the daughter of an *afrodeutsche Nachkriegskind*, I inherited the unspoken, the unknown, the hidden, and the erased. When I

---

11. Gordon, *Ghostly Matters*, 190.
12. See Hirsch, *Generation of Postmemory*.

examine the trauma my mother and her twin, along with many of the *afrodeutsche Nachkriegskinder*, went through, I am left with an incomplete story. I can see glimpses of their history, their trauma, and their rejection. I inherited snapshots of memories that are not included in the official historical record. How does one tell a story of race, racism, adoption, and rejection, and how does one do it as the indirect recipient, as the bearer not of direct memories of this history but of postmemories? I am a mixed-race first-generation American, and what I thought was going to be a unique personal story turned out to place my mother and her twin right in the middle of an international expulsion. My eventual discovery of the *afrodeutsche Nachkriegskinder* diaspora placed my personal story in conversation with a much larger, largely erased narrative.

Scholar Marita Sturken addresses such issues of "absent presence" in her scholarship on remembering Japanese and Japanese Americans who were imprisoned in US concentration camps.[13] Sturken specifically invokes aspects of memory, presence, and absence in her discussion of how that World War II event is remembered and retold for generations to come. What we as societies remember, and how, involves both active and passive acts of memory and erasure. Tangible records of time such as monuments and documents are places where identity can be claimed. But when such physical reminders are invisible or do not exist, they are no less significant, their very absence speaking powerfully to the processes of memory making. And sometimes tangible records, such as the historical documents associated with Lore and Lilli's adoption, are a record of liminality, invisibility, and absence. As Paul Ricoeur notes, these invisible places suddenly become marked with and for significance.[14] What happens when a place, a moment, a time in history marks your place and your presence with liminality, invisibility, and absence? How do you write yourself into visibility?

Popular and scholarly research situates World War II as a watershed moment in the progression of Western racial ideology. There is a sense that World War II, and the horrors of the Holocaust especially, forced a pivotal change in the role of race-thinking by state agencies and popular institutions, particularly in the US, but also in European countries like Germany. However, my research challenges this popular assumption, as well as the fantasy of the decline of scientific racism in its wake. My book and research do not uncover examples of colorblind racism but rather examples of direct racism sponsored by the nation-state and supported and reified by the populace. My research highlights how families experienced and resisted these racial

---

13. Sturken, "Absent Images of Memory," 692.
14. See Ricoeur, *Memory, History, Forgetting*.

parameters and their intersections with citizenship, sex, and sexism. Thousands of books have been written about World War II from multiple angles and perspectives, but relatively few about Black German discourses and narrative experiences that elaborate on what it means to be both German and Black in ways that challenge the stereotypical assumptions about "white" Germany. This personal experience plunged me into a world of scholarship that has guided this research as it relates to race, citizenship, family, and memoried erasure and that altered how I see World War II in terms of the ordinary lives lived. This research adds to the fields and disciplines of adoption studies, African American studies, communication, German studies, genealogical studies, history, and information studies, particularly as it concerns complicating the communicative and historical notions surrounding race, racism, adoption, and rejection regarding white German women, Black American soldiers, and mixed-race children of the postwar generation.

In looking back to look forward, this book puts into practice Jeffrey Olick's claim that "memory makers don't always succeed in creating the images they want and in having them understood in the ways they intended. Social actors are often caught in webs of meaning they themselves participate in creating though not in ways they necessarily could have predicted."[15]

Lilli and Lore's personal narratives are important additions to the existing scholarship on *afrodeutsche Nachkriegskinder*, and the overall understanding of identity and identity formation, during this postwar era. I use my family as an example in this case study because many Black German children, if they were adopted, tended to be adopted as infants or toddlers. This was not the case for Lilli and Lore, who have longstanding German familial connections and detailed memories of these connections. Thus Lilli and Lore's personal narratives illuminate the experience of being born into liminality and ultimately erased from their German biological family. The lived rejection and racism these preteens experienced was transnational, spanning two continents, and ultimately affected the next generation.

In conducting a close read of the testimony of Auschwitz survivors, Giorgio Agamben found that language was incapable of bearing witness to such trauma because the language used was the language of the oppressor.[16] Both Dylan Trigg and Ana Lee have since extended Agamben's notions of language,

---

15. Olick, introduction to *States of Memory*, 7.
16. Agamben, *Remnants of Auschwitz*. Also, see research on critical race theory, which addresses issues of language and oppression (e.g., the work of Derrick Bell, Kimberlé Crenshaw, Richard Delgado, Mari Matsuda, and Jean Stefancic); standpoint feminist theorists (e.g., Patricia Hill Collins, Sandra Harding, and Dorothy Smith); and muted group theory (Cheris Kramarae), which asserts that language is culture bound and steeped in power with an explicit patriarchal bias. For the latter, see "Muted Group Theory."

trauma, and representation. Trigg, in "The Place of Trauma," focuses on how traumatic memory takes up space and residence both in the physical site and in the haunting of the memoried experience. Lee considers collective memory-making and meaning-making and how "visual testimonies can occupy the place of non-place and transform haunting into a site for collective memory building."[17] Lee states that "visual testimonies . . . are . . . strategic memory sites."[18] I echo Agamben, Trigg, and Lee and argue that a rhetorical critique of language coupled with interview, oral communication (storytelling), and visual rhetoric serves my goal of centering and listening to liminal and erased voices that require delving into memoried and postmemory hauntings.

I also echo the work of rhetoricians Carole Blair, Greg Dickinson, and Brian L. Ott, who remind readers that "memory was in the founding works of the rhetorical tradition—memory was, after all, one of the five ancient canons of rhetoric—[and] rhetorical studies has for years relegated memory to a background issue."[19] White German women and Black German children's lives after World War II tend to be underexplored in juxtaposition to men's war efforts. My research explores memory and postmemory through an autoethnographic centering of women and children's lives, particularly as they relate to race, citizenship, family, and memoried erasure. Like Hirsch, my use of postmemory includes the next generation in addition to those who directly experienced a trauma. It is important to center disenfranchised and erased voices and memories not included in the memoried/historical accounting and in particular to analyze and understand the way these traumas are passed down generationally through memories. In this book, I not only demonstrate the powerful connection between memory and postmemory, but I also extend that correlation to Afrofuturism. Afrofuturism helps move postmemory into critical imagination.[20] Afrofuturism is about centering, examining, and understanding Black representation, Black histories, Black futures, and most importantly, Black imagined futures through reframing the (memoried) past (i.e., history) in favor of a postmemory retelling. This makes room for Black agency and Black futures, which are needed in the face of continued Black oppression, violence, and erasure because they challenge the collective "official" remembrance. Afrofuturism challenges the fantasy of freedom and fights to curate a life, to curate new knowledge, and to cultivate subjectivity.

In this book, I weave together memory, postmemory, Afrofuturism, and the legacy of forgetting/erasure to argue that although they were former World War II enemies, Germany and the US collaborated to remove Black

---

17. Lee, "Memory and Non-Place," 99.
18. Lee, "Memory and Non-Place," 103.
19. Blair, Dickinson, and Ott, "Introduction: Rhetoric/Memory/Place," 1.
20. See Kirsch and Royster, "Feminist Rhetorical Practices."

German children conceived after World War II in order to maintain the myth of Germany as a "white" nation. In importing Jim Crow to West Germany, both nations suggested that mixed-race children were the dross that must be removed from women, the nation's wombs, to make room for a future Aryan child. At the intersection of these transnational threads, the experiences of citizenship, race, racism, sex, and sexism are illuminated and problematized, and I ask: What happens when we view these Black German children of the postwar generation not only through the actions of the biological mother but also through the experiences of the children affected? How do we better understand the experiences of postwar Black German children through memory, "race," and rejection? In meeting this rhetorical moment, I argue that place, space, and country are embedded in people's actions and lived experiences, which they then carry with them, making memories transnational and as such "a set of theoretical stances and critical tactics that offer ways of understanding, evaluating, and intervening in a broad range of human activities."[21] This autoethnographic story is a public telling that cannot be untold, but it is also a scholarly endeavor told through the lens of a critical cultural rhetorical scholar. As Karma Chávez states, "doing this work in this way is important because rhetoric constitutes how issues are framed, how people are imagined, and which public memories endure over time."[22] Afrofuturism then comes to the imaginative forefront due to its existence in the space of creative imaginings. Afrofuturism utilizes the transformative power of imagining and reimagining Black people to challenge memoried spaces of silence, which allows me to center, and at times, reimagine the lived realities of Albert, Greta, Lilli, Lore, and myself.

I move visually through time from the Crusades Era to the present day to explore the legacy of the past and its impact upon memoried erasure, to better understand the present and the future through a postmemory lens. Summarizing a large volume of commonalities as related to memory research across multiple academic disciplines are six common memory stances that I have embedded in each chapter, which I borrow from Blair et al.: "1) memory is activated by present concerns, issues, or anxieties; 2) memory narrates shared identities, constructing senses of communal belonging; 3) memory is animated by affect; 4) memory is partial, partisan, and thus often contested; 5) memory relies on material and/or symbolic supports; [and] 6) memory has a history."[23] I put these six positions into practice in addressing the three concepts that provide the foundation of this book—gender, place, and race.

---

21. Blair, Dickinson, and Ott, "Introduction: Rhetoric/Memory/Place," 3.
22. Chávez, *Borders of AIDS*, 5.
23. Blair et al., "Introduction: Rhetoric/Memory/Place," 6.

In reflecting on German society, I find that the issues confronting Germany today—citizenship, immigration, the rise of anti-immigrant sentiment, race, racism, radical right extremism / identity movement, and who is and can be considered German—are the same issues haunting Germany's forced forgetting of the past. For example, the continual liminality of Black Germans today was remarked on by scholar Michelle Wright, who notes, "many white Germans, especially those from rural areas, seem psychologically incapable of conceiving of someone who is both Black and German. White Germans, even after a detailed explanation from their nonwhite interlocutor, still attempt to determine what African country the subject comes from. In short, the Afro-German identity is not the *antithesis* in the dialectic of (white) German subjectivity: it is *simply nonexistent*."[24] Reynaldo Anderson challenges the Eurocentric framing of Black and mixed-race Black people in his argument about a 2.0 Afrofuturism that encapsulates my goal for the use of the term in this book:

> Afrofuturism 2.0 is the beginning of both a move away and an answer to the Eurocentric perspective of the twentieth century's early formulation of Afrofuturism that wondered if the history of African peoples, especially in North America, had been deliberately erased. Or to put it more plainly, future-looking Black scholars, artists, and activists are not only reclaiming their right to tell their own stories, but also to critique the European/American digerati class of their narratives about cultural others, past, present and future . . . , challenging their presumed authority to be the sole interpreters of Black lives and Black futures.[25]

In juxtaposition to Germany's haunted past, this book employs Afrofuturism 2.0 as a tool to examine the resistant and enduring way white supremacy operates. My Afrofuturistic use of postmemory reimagining is more than a mere correction to the memoried narrative that is regurgitated and consistently retold despite its many historical gaps. As Kodwo Eshun argues, "Afrofuturism may be characterized as a program for recovering the histories of counter-futures created in a century hostile to Afrodiasporic projection and as a space within which the critical work of manufacturing tools capable of intervention within the current political dispensation may be undertaken."[26] In putting Anderson's and Eshun's arguments into practice, I am actively employing Afrofuturism to expose and correct for these past absences and erasures.

---

24. Wright, *Becoming Black*, 191.
25. R. Anderson, "Afrofuturism 2.0," 228.
26. Eshun, "Further Considerations on Afrofuturism," 288.

In addition, I put forth a new possible future as told through and imagined through those minoritized people.

MEMORY, POSTMEMORY, AND AFROFUTURISM

Binding diasporic experiences together is a form of meaning-making wherein memory and postmemory can be used as cognitive tools to challenge the hegemonic hierarchies often supported by language, thought, and interaction. Given that communities and nation-states, as well as individuals, participate in identity formation, we must examine how forces such as the retrenchment and static remembering of race and power, forgiveness, image repair, individual and group trauma, and imagined futures function in such formations. In our discursive and socially constructed world, language shapes thought, and thought shapes interaction and language, thereby "teaching us that reality is . . . a product of group and cultural life."[27] What we know about ourselves through our relationship with others, as well as our perception of self, affects how we see, interact, and communicate with one another. What we know or think we know about other people, cultures, and events is typically based on what is recorded or remembered (visually or through storytelling), not what is placed in liminality, forgotten, or erased. My monograph centers what has been erased by including over a decade of first-person interviews (2012–23) and incorporating a three-generation approach in which I weave my own family's experience into an examination of the legacy of both sexism and racism in determining who counts as German. I argue that Black American GIs, German women, and mixed-race German children suffer due to the nation-state's narrow conception of who is German, and this multigenerational racism follows and further fractures families of these mixed-race children in the United States.

Memory

My research is a case study that engages with the memoried (official) historical past of Germany and the US and the ways in which fixed articulations of gender, race, and racism allow for only a surface understanding of the effects of World War II and the postwar era on the bodies of women and children. Once out of the confines of official histories and situated into diasporic

---

27. Littlejohn, *Theories of Human Communication*, 34.

frames, the use of alternative histories and memories makes sense because we now have the tools to redefine and reconceptualize "original history." The nefarious effect of memory is that it is treated as fact. Memory has the ability to engage and center narrative hegemonic structures, often in favor of a story that can be neatly packaged—one that has a beginning, middle, and end with no outliers or outlier effects to make the story less pristine. Tina Campt argues that "particular representations of memory and history that have come to be institutionalized as narratives of 'official history' and national or collective identities . . . leave out alternative forms of memory that have yet to be recorded."[28] This means that only the storied events of official history, usually white and male, comprise our national and/or collective identities. Often societies celebrate men's achievements in theaters of war, but rarely do we celebrate or even recognize women's achievements during that time, and long forgotten are the ways in which postwar events are experienced as living history by children. Because of this gendered erasure, documented official histories "by definition, render [women's and Black, Indigenous, and people of color's histories] invisible and unrecognizable by virtue of the fact that they are seen as unintelligible in relation to these official histories."[29]

Events on a global scale are often reduced to the "winners" and the "losers," and those who do not fit neatly into this binary divide are easily erased from the official memoried (historical) recounting. Frances Yates argues that "the artificial memory is established from places and images (*Constat igitur artificiosa memoria ex locis et imaginibus*), the stock definition to be forever repeated down the ages,"[30] and it is these official memories that become collective cultural frameworks.

> The past is not preserved but is reconstructed on the basis of the present. . . . The collective frameworks of memory are not constructed after the fact by the combination of individual recollections; nor are they empty forms where recollections coming from elsewhere would insert themselves. Collective frameworks are, to the contrary, precisely the instruments used by the collective memory to reconstruct an image of the past which is in accord in each epoch, with the predominant thoughts of the society. . . . One may say that the individual remembers by placing himself [*sic*] in the perspective of the group, but one may also affirm that the memory of the group realizes and manifests itself in individual memories.[31]

---

28. Campt, *Other Germans*, 14.
29. Campt, *Other Germans*, 14.
30. Yates, *Art of Memory*, 6.
31. Halbwachs, *On Collective Memory*, 40.

In affirming memory through erasure of one group over another, institutionalized hegemonic societal structures are formed, and thus the narratives of an "official history" become naturalized and normalized. Critically examining the memoried and memorialized history becomes a threat to hegemony, because questioning exposes and makes visible the gaps in an otherwise "complete" history. In the case of this research, memory, race, and rejection are complicated in all societies, but particularly so in Germany, where the illusion of an all-white society remains a prominent narrative in the historical and social constructions of the country in spite of the multicultural groups who have long existed within its borders.[32] Therefore, if Maurice Halbwachs is correct, memory can be conceived of as an artifact—remembered, reproduced, and reinterpreted to function as an aspect of one's lived experiences, both collectively and individually. Thus, both the root and the routes of these narratives become part of our collective memories. The question then becomes what kind of present do we hope to make out of strategically remembering the past? How does one tell a story of race, racism, adoption, and rejection in ways that make visible liminal and erased experiences? Postmemory may be one way.

Postmemory

Marianne Hirsch created the concept of postmemory and argued that it can be applied to traumatic events. She also argued that postmemory affects the lives of those who did not directly experience the trauma itself, for example, descendants of Holocaust survivors.[33] Postmemory is not perfect, nor is it representative of the "truth," but postmemory is a powerful weapon in the desire to craft, shape, or reshape an individual's life. As Sara Ahmed argues, memory and postmemory studies "become sticky, or saturated with affect, as sites of personal and social tension. Emotions are after all moving, even if they do not simply move between us."[34] Such stickiness and its residue are to be found in this book within the critical examination of discourses, events, group memberships (or denial of them), identity construction, interviews, memoried/historical erasures, narratives, objects (e.g., letters, legal paperwork), postmemory/critical imaginings, and visual images. Many of the aforementioned items can evoke affective emotions such as "pride, contempt, anxiety, anger,

---

32. See Partridge, "Occupying American 'Black' Bodies."
33. Hirsch, *Generation of Postmemory*.
34. Ahmed, *Cultural Politics of Emotion*, 11.

horror, shame, guilt, confidence, gratitude, or compassion,"[35] which may not be related to "truth" but rather more akin to identity formation and how one sees themselves in memoried and imagined construction of the stories that are told and their place in them. As Mark Roseman argues, "the postwar world would accept only certain kinds of stories, making it doubly hard to render a truly authentic account,"[36] and this includes postwar descendants of children from Black American GIs and white German women. The adoption of the twins served Greta well as she constructed her new identity and embraced her postmemory future through "prescriptive forgetting," whereby forgetting or erasing a past is a gain. In some case, as Paul Connerton notes, "not to forget might . . . provoke too much cognitive dissonance: better to consign some things to a shadow world."[37]

Therefore, the use and recovery of postmemory experiences are action-oriented in design because their articulation of the memories allows for an alternative way of knowing, which in turn allows space for disenfranchised narratives to take root. As Barbie Zelizer aptly notes, a "basic premise in our understanding of collective memory concerns its partiality. No single memory contains all that we know, or could know, about any given event, personality, or issue."[38] Postmemory meaning-making, as a result, can be used as a cognitive tool to challenge the hegemonic hierarchies often supported by language, thought, and interaction.

The narrative I share here is a collection of stories and experiences that are subjective. In this composite narrative, there is no "official history" recounted, and as such, my narrative experiences are postmemory. I have termed my narrative experiences "postmemory" because I specifically include experiences that are erased from the official, historical (memoried) recounting, and the "truths" shared here allow for the juxtaposition of my familial truths alongside the official recounting. Per Tina Campt, "the most difficult part of beginning any story, any project, or any study but especially any history lies in the choices and decisions we make with regard to context,"[39] and postmemory allows me to reshape, situate, and categorize transformative and powerful images and experiences of life in ways that create meaning and guide lived and communicative processes. It is important to understand that meaning-making identity formation occurs as we situate ourselves in our lived experiences in ways that are reimagined for the narratives we tell ourselves, and the narra-

---

35. Blair et al., "Introduction: Rhetoric/Memory/Place," 16.
36. Roseman, *Lives Reclaimed,* 8–9.
37. Connerton, "Seven Types of Forgetting," 63.
38. Zelizer, "Reading the Past," 224.
39. Campt, *Other Germans,* 1.

tives we tell others about ourselves. As the centered heroes of our stories, what matters most is how we are situated in and juxtaposed against others in our lives and in our meaning-making in order that our memory and postmemory make sense. Therefore, as a challenge to hegemonic hierarchies, one's story and the sharing of the story create space for experiences that are often left on the margins and/or erased and forgotten altogether. Through postmemory, Greta, Lilli and Lore, and I are able to make meaning of both significant and nonsignificant events in our lives.

While some groups and communities may be resistant to an examination of the past for fear they may be complicit in or benefit from past discriminations, not understanding the past weaponizes white patriarchal heterosexual hegemony, makes static any understanding of the present, and inhibits a critical imagining of the future. At its surface, one may find that this book is an individual account of historical transnational and transgenerational trauma, but that thinking does not allow for a deeper examination of the ways individual, group, and nation-state actors operate in order to have their actions live on, narrated in public memory. This book shows how these antiquated memories are written upon bodies presently. A memoried/historical situating may signal past remembrances, but through a dialectical perspective (thinking through multiple perspectives with a both/and rather than an either/or lens), what is produced is a greater understanding of how collective memory is mapped onto people, spaces, and places. In postmemory (which also includes intentional forgetting), the anchoring of roots and routes traveled makes room for the transformative potential of creative imagining. At the same time, postmemory lives in a space of restraint, resistance, and reinscription of marginalization and erasure. Using my family and other first-person accounts, what develops is a more complex understanding of the generational trauma of race, racism, and exclusion and how aspects of racism and Jim Crow wash over Black people generationally in spite of social justice movements like the 1950s and 1960s civil rights movements and the Black Lives Matter and Afrofuturism narrative fantasies. Also shown in this case study are the limits of Afrofuturism due to the resistance measures put in place in favor of white hegemony and support of a racial caste system.

Afrofuturism

The term *Afrofuturism* was coined in 1993 by cultural critic Mark Dery. In his 1994 edited collection, *Flame Wars: The Discourse of Cyberculture*, Afrofuturism is defined as "speculative fiction that treats African-American themes and addresses African-American concerns in the context of 20th century technoculture—and more generally, African-American signification that appropriates images of technology and a prosthetically enhanced future."[40] Writer Jordi Oliveres builds on this conception of Afrofuturism, defining it as "a sweeping, cultural aesthetic that examines issues around black representation, the black future and black agency using music, novels, visual media, history and myth to create something else entirely."[41] This book takes a transnational and interdisciplinary approach to Afrofuturism. I like to think of Afrofuturism as a place of emergence, a terrain for reimaginative postmemoried existence, a place where Kevin Quashie challenges what we think we know about Black people and culture when he states, "What would it mean to consider black aliveness, especially given how readily—and literally—blackness is indexed to death? To behold such aliveness, we have to imagine a black world ... we have to imagine a black world so as to surpass the everywhere and every day of black death."[42] Afrofuturism then becomes a place where ancestors of Afrofuturism, before it was labeled and defined as such, lived: iconic orators like Frederick Douglass, W. E. B. Du Bois, Sojourner Truth, and Ida B. Wells; artistic movements like the Harlem Renaissance; musicians like George Clinton and Parliament-Funkadelic; writers like Ralph Ellison (*Invisible Man*, 1952) and Octavia E. Butler (*Kindred*, 1979); and even comic book superheroes like Black Panther (1966 in *Captain America: Civil War*), John Stewart / Green Lantern (1971, first Black superhero in DC Comics), Luke Cage (1972, Marvel Comics), and Black Lightning (1977, first Black superhero with own origin and storyline in DC Comics). These forbearers of Afrofuturism speak to the framework of social justice and reimagining that has been a lantern of light and a beacon of hope for Black people in the diaspora and paved the way for the continuation of fighting against the nation-state in order for our shared cultures to exist against the facade of democracy and equality.

Afrofuturism articulates new knowledge and subjectivity with a focus on liberation, empowerment, and Black agency, but this does not guarantee that one can always achieve these goals in imagined or actualized ways. Confining Afrofuturism to focus only on the future is a perfect way for people to embrace forgetting and erasing the Black past, because then one is not bogged down by the racist past that has yet to be reconciled, which effectively reifies a forced forgetting. As memory scholar Paul Connerton noted in his article "Seven Types of Forgetting," forgetting includes "repressive erasure, prescriptive forgetting, forgetting that is constitutive in the formation of a new

---

40. Dery, *Flame Wars*, 136.
41. Oliveres, "Watch: What Is Afrofuturism?," para. 1.
42. Quahie, *Black Aliveness*, 1.

identity, structural amnesia, forgetting as annulment, forgetting as planned obsolescence, and forgetting as humiliated silence."[43] What these kinds of forgetting mean is that to forget is not necessarily a sign of failure but rather a way in which one can protect their identity and/or create a new identity in the restructuring of power in a dynamic world. Forgetting can also be a way to reinscribe white supremacy and enforce power and instill silence.

An archivist I interviewed in Germany (who wished to remain anonymous) had this to say about German history that is destroyed daily:

> We have different retention periods for different files. If personal matters are concerned [documents are retained for] 30 years. After those 30 years [the documents] might go into an archive—if the content is relevant for judicial questions or historical interest. Once the documents have become archival files they are not allowed to be destroyed. However, with the Jugendamt [Youth Welfare Office] the documents [between 1945] and 1953 are supposed to be held. With regard to *afrodeutsche Nachkriegskinder*, archivists are not taught this history. They have no knowledge of what exists. If you don't know about it and don't study it in school, you can't tell patrons and can't catalogue the material, so in essence it doesn't exist. That's why a lot of documents [concerning this era] never make their way to any archives at all. (Personal interview, November 2018)[44]

When these documents are not included in the archives, they are destroyed, allowing for a white supremacist version of history that results in an additional layer of Black identity erasure and a new language of absence, loss, and liminality for Black people, and in this case, Black Germans.

Decolonialism also connects to Afrofuturism and postmemory, and at the intersection of these concepts, marginalized, peripheral experiences can be granted agency, critical imagining, empowerment, and visibility. Decolonialism exposes how some people are excluded and is also, like Afrofuturism, concerned with futurity, not a return to the historical (memoried) past. Afrofuturism imagines a future yet to be lived, a futuristic reality that colonialism cannot contaminate and one that allows postmemory to be used in critical imagining;[45] it is a way to insert the self into pasts, presents, and imagined, postmemoried futures that failed to include the self in the first place.

---

43. Connerton, "Seven Types of Forgetting," 59.
44. The Jugendamt is the Youth Welfare Office and is designed to promote the welfare of children. Postwar children in orphanages in Germany had files in these offices, which were set up around the country.
45. See Kirsch and Royster, "Feminist Rhetorical Practices."

Therefore, a postmemory critical imagination coupled with Afrofuturism allows for the study of marginalized and erased pasts, "especially those whose voices have rarely been heard or studied by rhetoricians" and allows me to consider questions posed by Gesa Kirsch and Jacqueline Royster about the aims of feminist rhetorical practice: "How do we render their work and lives meaningfully? . . . How do we transport ourselves back to the time and context in which they lived, knowing full well that it is not possible to see things from their vantage point? How do *they* frame (rather than *we* frame) the questions by which they have navigated their own lives?"[46]

I use the aforementioned concepts in the same spirit as Kirsch and Royster, who state, "We support the idea of keeping the imagination engaged as we keep boundaries fluid and being willing to shift operational paradigms in the interest of functioning with greater interpretive power."[47] A memory, postmemory, and Afrofuturistic accounting of my topic is important where the voices of women and the orphaned and adopted, particularly during iconic events like world wars, are often erased. Rhetoric has a rich history that allows me to engage in this communicative endeavor. It is my hope that this book will broaden what we think we know about postwar eras through the centering of voices that are captured and retained the least—those of women, children, and people of color.

INTERVIEWS AND AUTOETHNOGRAPHY

The methodological frame chosen for this study involves autoethnographic reflections from Greta (my grandmother), Lore (my mother), Lilli (my mother's twin), and myself (as the third generation). Autoethnography allows for the turning of a critical cultural lens on oneself. This methodology fosters a critical examination of one's lived experiences and allows personal narratives and experiences to be treated as primary data,[48] which is paramount in understanding, analyzing, and voicing the experiences of marginalized groups.[49] As a scholar with this area of specialization, discourse and audience are key as is the use of multiple sources, which provide me with my interdisciplinary

---

46. Kirsch and Royster, "Feminist Rhetorical Practices," 648.
47. Kirsch and Royster, "Feminist Rhetorical Practices," 644.
48. See Jackson, *Paths toward a Clearing*; and Van Maanen, "End to Innocence."
49. For more information on autoethnography as primary data, see Ashcraft and Pacanowsky, "Woman's Worst Enemy"; Denzin, *Interpretive Ethnography*; Geist and Gates, "Poetics and Politics of Re-Covering"; and Murphy, "Hidden Transcripts."

approach. In this study, I use the fields of Black studies, communication, cultural studies, gender studies, history (US and German), and rhetoric. I use artifacts collected from over a decade of research in archives and museums located in Germany and the US. I rely on conversations, field notes, interviews, government documents, news reports, political propaganda, speeches, and visual images. As a critical cultural studies rhetorician, I critically analyze the nonverbal, verbal, and visual as well as the absent and erased. My methodological choice is what Kirsch and Liz Rohan describe as "a lived process . . . [moving] back and forth between past and present, between visiting historical sites and bring them into the present, between searching archives and walking the land."[50] This methodological approach actively engages in postmemory counterstory. According to Aja Martinez, "counterstory . . . is a method of telling stories by people whose experiences are not often told. Counterstory . . . serves to expose, analyze, and challenge stock stories of racial privilege [and gender privilege] and can help to strengthen traditions of social, political, and cultural survival and resistance."[51] The written narrative is coupled with images throughout each chapter, with the visual rhetoric illuminating and expanding the written argument. I am particularly interested in how people construct their own identity framing, which guides both how they see themselves in the world as well as their cultural way of being and affects their past, present, and future. The narratives people tell themselves have the ability to affect their memoried past (history/memory), as well as their imagined future (Afrofuturistic postmemory). Enclosed here is not the "truth" but rather the marginalized and erased narratives of Black American GIs, children, and women made visible and centered, because knowing more about the experiences of these marginalized groups helps shape and broaden what we know about nations, war, and postwar periods.

My interviews were collected during two time periods, 2012–15 and 2017–23. Answers to questions I posed were gathered over months and years of phone calls, in-person visits, and emailed responses. In addition, I was able to include statements from Greta's youngest sister, who was present at our initial reunion in 2012 and again during a visit in 2013. Greta has a middle sister, whom I was unsuccessful in meeting when I lived in Germany in the summer of 2014. I sent the middle sister a letter, and she did not respond to my request to meet in person and get to know one another. My interviews with my family were rather informal, and the questions I asked were posed during social

---

50. Kirsch and Royster, "Feminist Rhetorical Practices," 657. See also Kirsch and Rohan, *Beyond the Archives*.

51. Martinez, "Plea for Critical Race Theory," 38.

interactions such as conversations, meals, and shopping.[52] The interviews in this study do not exemplify the stereotypical social science interview style in which there is a designated time for the interview and a specific set of questions. There were no recording devices, but notes were taken at the conclusion of our interaction. There was sometimes resistance and suspicion to questions I asked, and delay tactics and strategies such as "I don't understand, my English isn't very good," "Oh, you speak German, I can't language switch," or "I don't want to talk about it" were often used. Greta deemed some memories sacred, protected remembrances but sought to forget others. What I, as the researcher, learned is that this story depended on what my family chose to share, when and if they decided to share it. Most of my interviews were over the phone, but twice I visited my German family in person: once in 2012 and again in 2013 with an onsite visit to Hidden Villa Ranch in Los Altos, California, where Greta and the twins temporarily lived upon entry into the United States (see chapter 5). A visit to the Ming Quong orphanage, where the twins once resided in Los Gatos, California, was attempted; however, the orphanage no longer exists and has since been turned into a historical museum focused on Chinese American orphaned girls (also see chapter 5).

Also analyzed for this research were official documents obtained from the state of California written by the social worker involved in the adoption of the twins. These documents aid in the analysis of memory and postmemory and illuminate the space of liminality and loss the twins occupied. Participant observation and interview data allowed for a privileging and centering of memories and postmemories that might otherwise have remained unknown and undiscovered. Given these conditions, the theoretical and methodological choices made in this study are those best suited to examining memory, postmemory, and Afrofuturism as they concern memory, race, and rejection as related to this specific *afrodeutsche Nachkriegskinder* experience. The storytelling in my research often functions as a counternarrative whereby marginalized postmemory experiences are given equal standing with historically sanctioned (memoried) scripts.

---

52. In 2010, when Lore and I first began our search for Greta, I did not know if I had a book or a research project. After attending both the Black German Heritage and Research Association conference and the German Studies Association conference, meeting other Black Germans, and meeting with Greta in 2012, I knew I would be working on a research project. With all people interviewed (family or not), I shared that I was writing a book and asked clarifying questions about the field notes I collected. I also allowed all interviewees the opportunity to read, edit, and delete the transcripts and every single quote I attributed to them. Further, I had Lore read not only the quotes attributed to her but also the entire manuscript, as she became the spokesperson for both Greta and Lilli after they died during the writing of this book. In addition, Lore was present at the first reunion with Greta and could confirm and fill in gaps in my field notes.

SELF-REFLECTION AND JUSTIFICATION

Self-Reflection and Postmemory Positioning

When engaging in this scholarship, I thought of Tara Westover, who once asked herself, "Who writes history?" and then answered, "I do."[53] I also thought of Svend Brinkman, Michael Jacobsen, and Søren Kristiansen, who note that "history writing is not just about the past but also about the present and the future."[54] I am a scholar who represents the next generation born of the *afrodeutsche Nachkriegskinder*. I am the daughter of a woman who has gone through such labeling, the daughter of a German woman who was eventually stripped of her language, culture, and citizenship. What happened to my mother is trauma, what happened to her twin is trauma, and what happened to me is transgenerational trauma. In this book, I primarily retrace the histories of three generations of German women—Greta, Lilli, and Lore, and myself—as they concern memory, race, and rejection. The twins had had no contact with their biological mother after the adoption; however, due to my curiosity and interest in my German heritage, my mother and I began the search for Greta in 2010.

The German government has never issued an apology to or officially recognized those children who suffered in this way. In fact "children born in wedlock between Jan. 1, 1914 and Dec. 31, 1974, acquired German citizenship only if the father was a German citizen at the time of their birth. . . . Children born in wedlock between April 1, 1953 and Dec. 31, 1974 to a German mother and a non-German father did not become German citizens by birth."[55] In other words, in cases of married couples where a child's mother was a German citizen but their birth father was not, citizenship was not passed on. This German law implied that German women would be the ones to transgress with Others (men who are not white), whereas German men would not. It could be argued that this law was an effort to keep Germany white, for white Germans, and a way to address interracial coupling after World War II and the mixed-race children produced, the *afrodeutsche Nachkriegskinder*. Not until August 20, 2021, did Germany correct for this restrictive law.

My mother and her twin, once their adoptive family applied for their US naturalization at nineteen years old, lost their German citizenship. Children who were adopted acquired the citizenship of the adoptive parents once they filled out the proper paperwork—the citizenship of the adoptive parents was not automatic. In addition to Lilli and Lore being born in Germany, and into

---

53. Westover, *Educated*, 318.
54. Brinkman et al., "Historical Overview," 18.
55. "Obtaining German Citizenship."

a long documented German heritage that goes back to 1766, the three of us also possess one of the hallmarks of German identity, the *Familienstammbuch* (family genealogy book),[56] but Greta never filled in our names—only blank pages await our arrival in such a precious family heirloom, which even after our reunion in 2012 remain empty. In my own transnational childhood, I grew up in a bicultural world. I grew up learning and speaking both English and German, I attended a German university on student exchange, and I have spent many years traveling back and forth between Germany and the US. I earned two bachelor's degrees as an undergraduate student, one being a German degree, and I hoped to live in Germany permanently as a citizen, particularly given the change in German citizenship law. Most recently, I applied for German dual citizenship since as of August 20, 2021, I was finally able to make a citizenship declaration: "Anyone who was excluded from birth due to earlier gender-discriminatory parentage regulations can acquire German citizenship by declaration (declaration of acquisition according to § 5 StAG),"[57] but this applies only to children who were born "after May 23, 1949."[58] I submitted eighty-seven pages of documented German citizenship proof in June 2022 and only recently received a reference number indicating acknowledgement of my materials along with a message that my application is being processed in the order in which it was received.

In keeping with the renewed focus on memory and communication that some scholars such as Carole Blair, Edward S. Casey, Greg Dickinson, Brian L. Ott, Kendall Philips, and Barbie Zelizer have offered to the communication and rhetoric fields, my research aims to add further depth to this scholarship through the inclusion of an often-erased group, Black Germans, and the postwar experiences of this group through a combination of scholarship, storytelling, and images. As Rosemarie Peña aptly points out, "No ethnographic study exists that examines the diverse childhood experiences by the thousands of Black German children comprising the finite cohort of adoptees that Yara-Colette Lemke Muniz de Faria identifies in her seminal texts about Afro-German 'occupation children.'"[59] In answering this call to continue to fill historical gaps and liminalities, I use my family as an example, particularly since Lilli and Lore, and likely other adoptees during this time period, felt the effects of and lived the close connection between race and nation in Germany,

---

56. The *Familienstammbuch* was a family document introduced in Germany on January 1, 1871, with the official opening of the Standesämter (Bureaus of Vital Statistic or Registry Office). My family began their *Familienstammbuch* in 1895.

57. "Nationality Law Changed."

58. "Declaration Acquisition."

59. Peña, "Stories Matter," 244.

CHALLENGING THE HISTORICAL NARRATIVE • 23

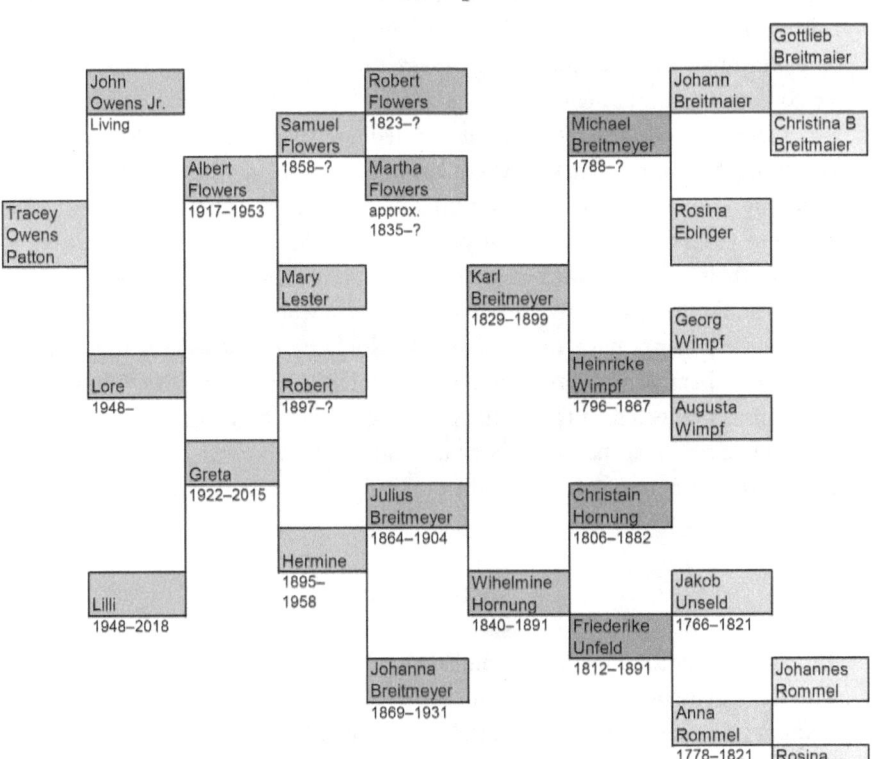

FIGURE 0.3. The author's German family tree documented back to at least 1766. The source used to assist this data gathering was Ancestry.com.

as well as the connection between nationalism, nation-building, and whiteness. It is the goal of this book to join other scholars in documenting the presence of *afrodeutsche Nachkriegskinder* and share the story of their experiences in order to rescue this history from the abyss of silence and the destruction of historical evidence.

An intimate look at the lives of a few people often left out of the official memoried events of World War II adds to postwar significance, because it is in their storytelling that we learn of lives lived. Additionally, using my family as a window into other marginalized experiences is apt for the following reasons: (1) The women who gave birth to the *afrodeutsche Nachkriegskinder* are aged into their nineties or already deceased. It is important to preserve their voices regardless of how small the sample size. (2) Most of the women who birthed *afrodeutsche Nachkriegskinder* refuse to talk about such a private experience due to shame. And (3), in the case of adoption, most adoptions during this time were closed. Therefore, finding birth mothers is extremely rare and involves time-consuming research to which most people have little or no access as well as considerable expense. Using my family as an example provides a rare glimpse into the often closed and silent world of *afrodeutsche Nachkriegskinder,* particularly where I am able to include the voices of three generations of German women and their life experiences. Further, my mother and her twin were adopted at nearly twelve years old, and over the first twelve years of their lives they formed genealogical bonds and memories with their biological family that most children from this era who were adopted as babies and toddlers do not have, thus making this study unique. As I seek to tell the stories of others, I aim to reclaim my own stolen German identity. I, too, am German. As reflected in the family genealogy chart shown in figure 0.3, my German ancestry, so far, dates back to 1766. *Wenn ich nicht Deutsch bin, ist es niemand* (If I am not German, then no one is). I am the insider without.[60]

Justification

This book is unique in that it centers the experiences of postwar children who have their own detailed memories of liminality, erasure, adoption, *and* reunion with their German biological mother after fifty-two years. Most books about World War II and the postwar period that exist today largely focus on war theaters and soldiers. These are all important foci, but lost are women's and mixed-race children's voices, which lend a greater understanding of ordinary lives lived in Germany and the sexist and racist repercussions of merely existing in a way that violated Hitler and the Third Reich's constructions of *ein Volk* (a people, or one people), defined by white supremacy and homogeneity. In Mark Roseman's book, *Lives Reclaimed: A Story of Rescue and Resistance in Nazi Germany,* he shows the need to capture the voices and experiences of Jewish survivors of the Holocaust because most of the narratives were about the rescuers. Scholars like Roseman show that sharing narratives and the act of remembering changes as circumstances in life change: "Immediately after the war when memories were still fresh, the way you had to respond to an arrest in 1933 was no longer valid in 1939 and different again in 1942."[61] As a

---

60. See Small, *Rhetoric of Becoming,* 167.
61. Roseman, *Lives Reclaimed,* 8.

result, Roseman argued that a "disquisition on the relationship between memory and experience"[62] is needed.

According to Peña, herself a Black German adoptee, Black German "adoptions . . . hav[e] been successful overall; but these are not necessarily those who are inclined to write memoirs, allow themselves to be featured in documentaries, or even express interest in identifying as Black Germans or to participate in the discussion in Black German social media forums."[63] Lilli and Lore represent the average German adoptees Peña refers to who are not writing memoirs or appearing in documentaries. On the other hand, I have chosen to center their stories because these personal narratives are important additions to the existing scholarship on *afrodeutsche Nachkriegskinder* and the overall understanding of identity and identity formation during the postwar era. Black Germans born after World War II, along with their memoried accounts of family and adoption, visually signify and orally challenge the official and historical narratives of that war and its victims.

This living history is important because the voices of the orphaned and adopted, particularly during and immediately after iconic events like world wars, are often erased in favor of recounting a packaged narrative. This research explores memory and postmemory through an autoethnographic centering particularly as it relates to race, citizenship, family, and memoried erasure. After all, it was memory, postmemory, and curiosity that led Greta my grandmother to respond to a letter from us after fifty-two years.

OVERVIEW OF BOOK

A Nation's Undesirables: Mixed-Race Children and Whiteness in the Post-Nazi Era argues that governmental policing of interracial coupling functioned as another form of state-sponsored eugenics in the postwar era, in which mixed-race people had no value in the state's vision of society. These mixed-race children were not seen as German but rather were viewed as foreign to the German nation-state and antithetical to the goals for the nation's wombs, which were reserved for the future white child. With families shattered, German women had no rights over their womb as it became property of the nation-state, African American soldiers were viewed through screens of racism and sexualized stereotypes, and mixed-race children were seen as future

---

62. Roseman, *Lives Reclaimed*, 8–9.
63. Peña, "Stories Matter," 249.

threats to the imagined white nation of Germany's memoried past. German women, Black American GIs, and their mixed-race children had no power, and they endured racism, sexism, and exclusion that had transnational implications stretching from Germany to the United States.

Everyone in this book (unless they declined) has been given an alias except members of my family: my *oma* (Greta), Greta's boyfriend (Albert), my mother (Lore), and my mother's twin (Lilli). With permission of the living, I named the people centered in this story because I wanted to lift the veil of anonymity, and as some interviewees told me, they "have nothing to hide and want their story told." Our family stories are entangled with loss, shame, racism, upheaval, and erasure, and I no longer wanted a shroud put between reality, family, and myself.

Chapter 1, "Construction of Race and Nation: A History of Black Germany," is foundational to understanding the importance of postmemory and Afrofuturism as it relates to Black German history from the Crusades forward. If there is no knowledge about Black diasporic history and influences in Europe and Germany, then there continues to be no understanding and no space for Black Europeans today. This historical undertaking is an Afrofuturistic endeavor because I engage in a historical revision by *including* Black people in Europe and through a postmemory engagement. This challenges the standard communicative identity of Black people in Europe, which is largely told through absence and erasure. I visually highlight how race and racism impacted Germany and German citizenry as related to Black people through an examination of images, and I put into practice Anderson and Eshun's challenge to move away from Eurocentric perspectives and recover the histories of counter-futures through my use of postmemory and Afrofuturism. This chapter highlights how early constructions of race set the stage for racism to be used to justify race-based oppression during the colonial era, World War I, and World War II. It is this racist foundation that later impacts the lives of Greta, Albert, and twins Lilli and Lore.

Chapter 2, "Jim Crow in the European Theater: Institutionalizing Anti-Blackness in Germany," highlights war history as a cross-racial and international affair and offers a postmemory and Afrofuturist lens through which to view Black military experiences in both Germany and the US, showing the importance of Germany as a physical place and space in which Black American soldiers imagined themselves as "free," particularly in juxtaposition to the Jim Crow culture that the US clung to inside its borders and exported to Germany.

Chapter 3, "Womb Wars: Interracial Relationships and the Historical Construction of White German Identity," centers on German women's experiences before, during, and after wars, with a concentration on how white womanhood is earned or taken away, particularly when interracial coupling is involved. Constructing a white homogenous citizenry was a state interest that enveloped all German people, but especially white German women if they happened to interracially couple with Black American GIs. German women's bodies were a state commodity and as such were disciplined in choices of marriage, reproduction, and social support. The statutory restrictions on German women's rights over their wombs and bodies was intimately tied to notions of white male patriarchy. Postmemory and Afrofuturism are utilized to show the impact that historical, societal, and transnational aspects of gender and racism had on Greta and Albert's relationship. In contrast to the lack of choice, along with the transnationalism of Jim Crow the couple faced, this chapter puts postmemory and Afrofuturism into action through creative imagining of "what could have been" and "were it not for" ponderings.

Chapter 4, "Aborted out of Germany: Born, Kept, and Abandoned," questions in what ways, and for what reasons, Black German children have been incorporated or excluded from the German polis. The limits of Afrofuturism are explored here as related to twins Lilli and Lore. The twins become examples of liminal space, as they are minors who have no ability to fight against racist German history or the choices Greta made. Of primary concern is what place Black German children and their mothers were allowed to occupy in the German national ideal and to what extent their individual rights and interests were superseded by the assertion of state interests in managing the German citizenry. There was no space for creative imaginings or postmemory desires for Lilli and Lore, as they were infants dependent upon Greta, who was reeling from her loss of access to white womanhood. Greta felt she was punished for inadvertently challenging the fantasy of an all-white Germany through the birth of the twins, so to begin anew she concentrated on how to free herself from the racism she faced after birthing the twins, and in doing so, eventually left them behind.

Chapter 5, "The Transatlantic Appeal of Jim Crow: Reclaimed, Abandoned, and Adopted," highlights the interview data obtained and relates what happened to the children of these Black German families, focusing on their identity formation and the power of images and communicative rejection. In centering postmemory, this chapter shows how white womanhood, once lost in Germany, could be regained and reclaimed through the maintenance of the US white supremacist system, if one abided by its racist standards. Greta was given the permission to abandon her memoried German past and recoup her lost white womanhood once she left Lilli and Lore behind. Greta's imagined postmemory future could begin in the US since no one cared about her past in Germany, and the visual markers that once prohibited her access to white womanhood (Lilli and Lore) were now part of the California state foster care system. While Lilli and Lore languished in a US system mired in Jim Crow, racism, and rejection and were eventually adopted into a family who abused them, Greta created new memories and a new life. This chapter shows how postmemories can work for some while also showing the limits of Afrofuturistic creative imaginings.

Chapter 6, "A Family Reunion and Generational Trauma: A Conclusion," examines reengaging with the memoried past as a way to challenge and solidify familial actions and highlights transgenerational (cross-generational) trauma. In this chapter, a more complicated and deeper understanding of postmemory and Afrofuturism is provided as they relate to the creative imagining of what could be and the resistance put up against such imagining by an investment in whiteness. Postmemory and Afrofuturism are not static concepts; they are dynamic and move between people who have different desires, goals, and power, as well as between different spaces.

This introduction marks the beginning of our travel into postmemory and creative imagined spaces that naturally lend themselves to an examination through Afrofuturism. This book uncovers German and US transnational actions that had repercussions related to nation, gender, race/racism, and whiteness that continue to reverberate today. Allow yourself to be curious in order to understand the power of memory and postmemory and how actions taken by governments still leave people like Lilli, Lore, and I awash in the racism of the Jim Crow era. This book requires an examination of and makes space for lived experiences on the margins. It also expands what we think we know about so-called settled history as related to colonialism, World War I, and World War II and retells it, reexamines it, and centers those who are often overlooked when the official, memoried histories are written; in this case, the fallout is on women, children, and Black American GIs. To meet this rhetorical postmemoried moment, turn the page and journey back in time with me to better understand how country, place, and imagined spaces are carried forward transnationally.

CHAPTER 1

Construction of Race and Nation

A History of Black Germany

The majority of US Americans simply do not focus on the past when it comes to people of color. There is no tangible understanding of the fact that what was done in the name of white supremacy from 1607, with the founding of Jamestown, to the present day, resulted in benefits that white people take for granted in the twenty-first century. How can we explain this lack of awareness and understanding? For over four hundred years, Indigenous people (Black and Native) have experienced cultural, linguistic, and religious erasure, have been stripped of family, have been stolen from their homelands and enslaved, and have had their lands taken away.[1] This violence continues through a history of being hunted down by slave patrols, military units, and police units, all in the name of white nationalism and white supremacy. Televisual images of state-sanctioned murder of largely Black people are now seen around the world, as nearly everyone has access to an internet connection. I suspect the larger problem as it relates to structural and institutionalized forms of racism and murder of BIPOC (Black, Indigenous, and People of Color) is that white people alive today have not seen and do not grasp the magnitude of the millions of bodies, the people, lost in the name of white supremacy. History and

---

1. *Indigenous* is an umbrella term I use to signal a diasporic transnational identity that has been affected by land dispossession and loss of land. Because African people were stolen, enslaved, and lost land through colonization, Black people are also Indigenous. See Dei, *Reframing Blackness and Black Solidarities*.

the present day show us that many white Americans can express some appreciation for the dead when it comes to places like Arlington National Cemetery and Gettysburg, and even the failed Confederate cause is memorialized in buildings and military bases named after the defeated enslavers who seceded from the Union. To date, there are no memorials, momuments, or national cemetaries dedicated to those Black people whose blood was spilled to further the power, wealth, and generational wealth that benefitted and still benefits multiple generations of white people.

For most people, Europe, the United Kingdom, and the United States are the visual signifiers of whiteness, white people, and white culture. A desperate attachment to this ideal whiteness informs much of the Western world, what we are taught about the West, and who is considered as belonging to the West. How and what we think about ourselves transforms our understanding of the past. We are all in a relationship with past events. Learning new information from a new viewpoint can change our memory and our memoried experiences. Memory is history. Memory affects the present. Memory asks us to hold space. Catching up with an erased past, a marginalized history, can cause cognitive dissonance because we are unearthing layers of complex history that were never allowed to be amplified in the first place.

The emotional white chaos and memoried erasure that often swallows up voices of color is not unique to the United States but is found around the globe and includes a Black Russia, a Black Europe, and, yes, a Black Germany. This chapter is a diasporic glimpse into the establishment of the racist oppression of Black people, primarily Black Germans, from the Crusades forward. This chapter is not a thorough rendering of history in Germany—for that, one can look at historical scholarship that has been published in this area. Rather, in chapter 1, I show that a historical retelling of European history that centers Black Europeans is important by visually highlighting how race and racism impacted Germany and German citizenry. Specifically, I locate Black people through an examination of historical absences, erasures, laws, and images. In making Black German history visible, I utilize the concept of Afrofuturism.

Adriano Elia defines Afrofuturism as "a transnational and transdisciplinary cultural movement based upon the unusual connection between the marginality of allegedly 'primitive' people of the African diaspora and 'modern' technology and science fiction—itself a peripheral literary genre, the 'golden ghetto,' as William Gibson dubbed it."[2] I place Elia's argument in this chapter by connecting Black people and cultures within the Black diaspora to the West. In doing so, I expose and challenge the idea of so-called

---

2. Elia, "Languages of Afrofuturism," 84.

primitive Black people in juxtaposition to the idea of the "modern" which, when attached to people, is by default white. Using Afrofuturism in this way allows me to highlight war history as a cross-racial and international affair and analyze it through the screen of racism, which is often erased. I examine how early formations of race from the Crusades and colonialism set the stage for issues of race and racism against Black people to be weaponized by the German government and white German citizens during and after World War I and World War II. This weaponization constructs the foundation on which all Black Germans stood. In fact, having this historical context about Black people in Europe generally, and specifically in Germany, allows for the example of my family and other *afrodeutsche Nachkriegskinder* to be in conversation with the memoried past, which allows for a more complicated space of racism to be examined and understood.

Afrofuturism means reimagining the past for people erased by global, systemic anti-Black racism. My use of Afrofuturism parallels what Octavia Butler did in her iconic 1979 book, *Kindred*, in which the Black protagonist, Dana, was catapulted back in time to ensure the survival of her ancestors so that she and her family could exist in the future. Traveling back in time, Dana has to write herself into existence as an enslaved woman and endure abuse and enslavement by her ancestor, Rufus, who fathers another of her ancestors by rape, so she can exist in the future. Navigating between past and present, Dana is altered historically (she must walk through the world as a Black woman differently during US enslavement versus her present), mentally (she must learn to operate between the two worlds) and physically (she loses her arm). I am engaging in the same Afrofuturistic act by weaving together the past and the present, centering Black European history and military history (specifically in Germany), and overtly challenging the fantasy of an all-white Germany. Recentering the presence of Black people in Germany is not only an act of creating more accurate historical representation but also an act of making visible the ways in which the communicative identity of Black people in Germany is largely told through absence and erasure and correcting for that fact.

This chapter centers on the idea that communication through visible presence alters how Germany—a nation that has crafted its identity around the myths of white racial purity—is seen, understood, and experienced. By centering Black German lives, Black erasure and liminality is challenged. I argue that if there is no Afrofuturistic understanding of Black history and lives in Europe, if there is no historical revision *including* Black people in a so-called white European space, then there continues to be no space for Black Europeans today. Understanding this history allows for a more informed read of the remainder of this book and the actions taken by and forced onto people like

Greta and Albert as well as the ripple effects that flowed down to Lilli, Lore, and me. This kind of Afrofuturistic gaze exposes the structural, institutional, and foundational elements of white racism that have been intentionally erased in favor of a white supremacist read of Europe. "White" Europe maintained the travel/colonial narrative wherein whiteness was normalized and naturalized and blackness was never internal, always external, and inferior. By highlighting this problem, I present a position that may be hard for some to understand, that of a minoritized gaze upon a historical period that resists such an empowered look. Putting Afrofuturism into practice in a period where it was not named disrupts the artificial flow of time and white supremacist identity.

THE CRUSADES–1700s: MOOR FASCINATION AND RACISM

Germany constructed the image of a "white" nation before the existence of Hitler and the Nazi regime. Germany, like other nations including the US, constructs its identity through what it believes it is not, in this case, Black. However, Black people in Germany have a long history that one can trace back to the Crusades (1095–1291), and in these pre-Enlightenment times, European perceptions of Black people seem less beholden to the racist black/white dichotomies of today. The Western memoried narrative tends to marginalize and erase Black people's presence and contribution to the continent of Europe. White-centered narratives not only make the continent of Africa static but also, tribal, underdeveloped, and backward in juxtaposition to the supposed superiority of white Western Europe. There is little public knowledge in Europe about the twelfth, thirteenth, and fourteenth centuries being dynamic and complex societies that visually contest the black/white binaries and power structures that dominate how the West learns about that period. Societies during this time disrupt and reject Enlightenment ideals about people, culture, and race if by nothing else then by the fluidity, border crossing, and dynamism of place and self.

For example, as Mischa Honeck, Martin Klimke, and Anne Kuhlmann note, "during the twelfth and thirteenth centuries, Africans crossed the Mediterranean to Spain, Sicily, and Italy or made their way to Europe via the Middle East and the Byzantine Empire."[3] In these points of contact, those of African descent successfully navigated their way throughout Europe and experienced cross-cultural, interracial, and interreligious encounters. As Paul

---

3. Honeck et al., introduction to *Germany and the Black Diaspora*, 3.

Kaplan argues, it was "during the reign of Emperor Frederick II of Hohenstaufen (1220–50) [that] people of black African descent had begun to appear in German-speaking lands, and it did not take long for German artists—perhaps encouraged by Frederick's display of his black African retainers—to start creating images of people of color."[4] African people were such a visual phenomenon in Europe as early as the thirteenth and fourteenth centuries that art and literature (e.g., Wolfram von Eschenbach's Arthurian epic novel, *Parzival* [1197–1210])[5] incorporated images of Black people (Moors) in diverse roles, from the black magus or king to saints, medieval court members, and the enslaved. Kaplan notes that St. Gregor Maurus of Cologne "appeared in stained glass from the early 1300s onward [and] by the fifteenth century the black St. Maurice had become a standard element around Magdeburg and in adjoining parts of northern and eastern Germany, where the saint's cult was strongly developed."[6] It is believed that "the earliest known example of a black king may be represented in a wall painting of about 1360 in the Emmaus monastery in Prague. It is certain that by the beginning of the 15th century some European artists had begun to depict one of the kings as black rather than white,"[7] as Audrey Baker points out.

As Kate Lowe notes, as early as 1492, there were white minstrel performances (use of blackface performativity) by journeymen "from the guilds of Konstanz in southwest Germany"; in 1496 in Brussels, Juana of Castile (mother of Charles V) was greeted by a pageant where someone was dressed as an "Ethiopian princess"; and in England a pageant in 1521 featured a white actor in "blackface" with blackened clothing to portray the King of Moors.[8]

While African people who lived in Europe during this time were almost always purchased as slaves, they were connected with the magi. In fact, with color hierarchies then, as Kuhlmann observes, "dark skin did not determine their social rank as a matter of course; both downward and upward social mobility were possible. At the same time, most of the attractive or available posts were located at the highly color-conscious courts scrambling to add the exotic glimmer and cosmopolitan cachet of people of black African heritage to their noble decorum."[9] Their role as magi, even if objectified and later problematized as the Hollywood trope of a "magical Negro," allowed their selves

---

4. Kaplan, "Calenberg Altarpiece," 21.
5. See Honeck et al., introduction to *Germany and the Black Diaspora*, 8.
6. Kaplan, "Calenberg Altarpiece," 21.
7. Audrey Baker, *English Panel Paintings 1400–1558*, cited in Victoria and Albert Museum, "Adoration of the Magi," "Historical Context" section.
8. Lowe, "Black Diaspora in Europe," 39.
9. Kuhlmann, "Ambiguous Duty," 67.

to be presented as visual artifacts of persuasion. Magi, as Honeck et al. note, "were an integral part of courtly representation. By the eighteenth century, a growing number of black Europeans worked and lived in the bourgeois households of merchants, retired colonial officials, and plantation owners. Others made an independent living as seamen or guild members."[10] In their role as magi, depictions of the wise men/kings "have been especially venerated in Cologne, [Germany]. Their relics are contained in a shrine in [the] Cologne Cathedral,"[11] as Baker notes.

To be clear, courts were not a bastion of social equality particularly since, as Kuhlmann stated, there was "no modern concept of individual civil rights and liberties."[12] The presence of positive depictions of Black Europeans in medieval European art and literature does not mean there were no visual or verbal depictions to the contrary. In fact, art and literature make visual, written, and oral appeals to the societal construction of Black place and space that evoke aspects of both memory and history. As Pierre Nora states,

> Memory and history, far from being synonymous, are thus in many respects opposed. Memory is life, always embodied in living societies and as such in permanent evolution, subject to the dialectic of remembering and forgetting, unconscious of the distortions to which it is subject, vulnerable in various ways to appropriation and manipulation, and capable of lying dormant for long periods only to be suddenly reawakened. History, on the other hand, is the reconstruction, always problematic and incomplete, of what is no longer.[13]

As Ruth Mellinkoff found in her exhaustive study of visually marginalized people in medieval Europe, a "white-skinned society could tolerate a black magus and a black St. Maurice because they represented an abstract piety, but more often white society viewed blacks as physically and morally ugly, and therefore inferior and despicable."[14] Germany, like the rest of Europe, was intrigued by the possibility of what Africa presented them and how it could further their economic power, as Honeck et al argues:

> Germans were present as slave traders in Seville and Santo Domingo, plantation owners and merchants in South America and the Caribbean, sailors

---

10. Honeck et al., introduction to *Germany and the Black Diaspora*, 3.
11. See Baker, "English Panel Paintings."
12. Kuhlmann, "Ambiguous Duty," 68.
13. Pierre, "General Introduction," 3.
14. Ruth Mellinkoff, *Outcasts*, cited in Kaplan, "Calenberg Altarpiece," 23.

on slave ships from the coastal regions of the North Sea, travelers in Africa and the Americas, employees of the transatlantic trade companies in Bordeaux and Cádiz with branch offices in Dutch, English, French, Spanish, and Portuguese cities, missionaries in the West Indies, west Africa, and North Americas, and soldiers and settlers in North and South America.[15]

The slide from Moor to dehumanized Black "Other" in Germany's conception of Black people was not a difficult transition, particularly given that, as Lowe notes, "Hanseatic German merchants with black slaves could be the northern European equivalent of New Christians (Iberian Jews who were forced to convert to Christianity) with black slaves. Everywhere that New Christians are recorded, so too are their black slaves, and converted Jews must have taken their Iberian slave-owning mentality with them when they left Portugal."[16] The term *Moor* was replaced with the white supremacist term "'Negro,' which alluded instead to a trading commodity; a childish, cheap, and unskilled hand."[17] By the time society entered the Enlightenment period (1715–89), the curiosity about and valorization of the Black Magi had disappeared, and the creation of the sociological concept of race had hardened into lines of division that we live with today.

THE ENLIGHTENMENT ERA

In the Enlightenment period, according to Maria Diedrich, "scholars of all disciplines were beginning to write systematic and complex natural histories of the human species, determined to 'scientifically' classify humanity and redefine nation in racial terms—Kant, Blumenbach, Herder, and, of utmost importance for Kassel, the anatomist Samuel Thomas Sömmerring"[18] all believed in the inferiority of Black people. Kassel, Germany, for example, had a population of Black citizens since 1664 and once boasted the highest population of Black Germans in the 1700s.[19] But forces like the American Revolution, as Diedrich details, impacted how white Hessian soldiers viewed their fellow black Hessian comrades. Hessian soldiers involved in the American Revolution (1775–83), as Diedrich explains, "had been transported across the Atlantic against their will, in a state of semibondage—a transnational in-betweenness

---

15. Honeck et al., introduction to *Germany and the Black Diaspora*, 7.
16. Lowe, "Black Diaspora in Europe," 49.
17. Honeck et al., introduction to *Germany and the Black Diaspora*, 3.
18. Diedrich, "From American Slaves to Hessian Subjects," 95.
19. See Jones, "'On the Brain of the Negro,'" 138.

these Hessians, in turn, were struggling to negotiate for themselves."[20] Similarly, there were Black American men ("self-liberators" and enslaved) who, as Diedrich continues, "lived side-by-side in the Hessian army camps during the"[21] American Revolution, a fact that exposed the horrors of enslavement and challenged the white propaganda that denigrated Black people. "With their admiration for the black self-liberators now transformed into fellow Hessians,"[22] along with seeing Black people's zeal for freedom, the white Hessian soldiers returned to Germany with conflicting, often incompatible images of blackness and slavery firmly planted in their minds. On one hand, the white Hessian soldiers had the degrading American racial identification of blackness, African, Negro, and slavery as their visual signifiers, and on the other hand, they had their abhorrence of the reality of American chattel slavery. As related to the dehumanization of Black people, this translated into wealth for certain German companies and German families historically and into the present day. For example, "the Welser and Fugger families, both from Augsburg . . . and the Ehinger family from Konstanz . . . helped finance the Portuguese slave trade in the early 1600s, as the Fuggers did, or, held economic titles to slave plantations in today's Venezuela, as the Welsers did,"[23] as Heike Raphael-Hernandez and Pia Wiegmink note. As related to abhorrence, this translated into abolitionist work.

One of the most widely known abolitionists was Alexander von Humboldt (1769–1859), who traveled extensively throughout the Americas witnessing the enslavement of Black people firsthand. In his 1826 book, *Essai politique sur L'isle de Cuba*, as Raphael-Hernandez and Wiegmink relate, Humboldt declared that slavery is "possibly the greatest evil ever to have afflicted humanity."[24] Even with antislavery abolitionists in Europe and the US and the successful fight for freedom during the Haitian Revolution (1791–1804), the continued transatlantic slave trade and the unabated US slave trade (from 1619 until the signing of the Emancipation Proclamation in 1863) had an impact on Black Europeans. As Diedrich argues, the once "exotic *Mohr* would gradually lose out to the *Neger*, and the *Neger* would become identical with the degraded slave, the essentialized racial inferior."[25]

---

20. Diedrich, "From American Slaves to Hessian Subjects," 95.
21. Diedrich, "From American Slaves to Hessian Subjects," 94.
22. Diedrich, "From American Slaves to Hessian Subjects," 95.
23. Raphael-Hernandez and Wiegmink, "German Entanglements in Transatlantic Slavery," 422.
24. Raphael-Hernandez and Wiegmink, "German Entanglements in Transatlantic Slavery," 424.
25. Diedrich, "From American Slaves to Hessian Subjects," 95.

In 1784, as Jeannette Jones points out, Sömmerring wrote a seminal book, "*Über die körperliche Verschiedenheit des Mohren vom Europäer* [*About the Physical Difference of the Black from the European*] which inspired a generation of race thinkers who cited the conclusions to argue for Negro inferiority."[26] In the 1785 edition of his book, Sömmerring ponders, "Do we have the right to treat them [*Neger*] with such coldness?"[27] He posited this rhetorical question to defend himself against the negative criticism of the 1784 version of his book. In 1788 Sömmerring joined the Collegium Carolinum in Kassel as the department chair of "Anatomy Theater." This is where he "and other European anatomists used the bodies of the Kassel blacks first dissected there to establish many of the accepted theories about sexual and racial difference in the eighteenth century."[28] Based on his dissections, he believed that "Negroes resemble simians more than Europeans," but he "denied advocating for the mistreatment of blacks, stating that no matter how much they resemble simians, '*Mohren* still remain human beings who are superior to any species (of simians)' and that 'there are several among the *Schwarze* who are similar to their white brothers, and some even surpass them intellectually."[29] Despite Sömmerring's lament, he still believed in a hierarchy of humans (with Black Europeans beneath white Europeans), and with his dissection and handling of Black bodies along with the title of his books, the physical and communicative exclusion of Black Europeans as an inferior, racialized other was cemented.

This reification of the Black Other continued, and before Germany embarked on its official colonial quest, according to Robbie Aitken and Eve Rosenhaft, "increasing numbers of non-Western European individuals were recruited to appear in exhibitions . . . to perform in German zoos; a 'Nubian Caravan' was even put on display in Berlin's zoological garden in 1878 and 1879."[30] Through visual and physical extermination, it was easy to forget that "for two centuries or more individual Blacks had sojourned at German courts and universities or in German cities as exceptional individuals (though of widely ranging status and provenance)."[31] In fact, in 2005, the Augsburg Zoo in Augsburg, Germany, continued this marginalizing tradition and placed an exhibit about African culture in a zoo. As Charles Hawley reports, the "African

---

26. Jones, "'On the Brain of the Negro,'" 139.
27. Quoted in Jones, "'On the Brain of the Negro.'" Jones further explains that "'the coldness' to which [Sömmerring] referred included the enslavement of Africans in the Americas and the 'prejudices' shown to Negroes in general" (139).
28. Jones, "On the Brain of the Negro," 140.
29. Jones, "On the Brain of the Negro," 140.
30. Aitken and Rosenhaft, *Black Germany*, 53.
31. Aitken and Rosenhaft, *Black Germany*, 2.

Village," complete with "grass huts and 'African' culture[, was] nestled between the monkey and the Savannah exhibit."[32] The exhibit opened to worldwide protests, but not before the zoo director justified the exhibit and its placement by stating that one of the organizers was "born in Africa and has black skin. . . . You can be sure this wasn't a mistake in planning. I think the Augsburg zoo is exactly the right place to communicate an atmosphere of the exotic."[33]

IMPERIAL GERMANY, 1884–1918: ANTI-BLACKNESS IN GERMANY

Imperial Germany offers a valuable point of departure for an analysis of citizenship, race, and gender discourses that surround Black Germans because it represents an initial public discursive intervention into the construction of the raced citizen in Germany. Because Germany claims that its official entrance into colonialism didn't occur until 1884, Germany is able to argue that, unlike Belgium, Denmark, England, France, the Netherlands, Portugal, and Spain, it was one of the last European nations to enter into abhorrent practices such as the international slave trade. Nonetheless, Fatima El-Tayeb and other scholars such as Adam Blackler, Michelle Moyd, Britta Schilling, Helmuth Stoecker, and Susanne Zantop show how race and national belonging are inextricably linked in German history, having their roots in Germany's colonialist politics and practice (1884–1918).[34] German citizenship laws were designed to maintain whiteness as the default Germanness, and the idea that to be German meant to be white deeply impacted *afrodeutsche Nachkriegskinder* in the post–World War II era.

The Berliner Konferenz secured Germany's entrance as a colonial power, and in the 1880s Otto von Bismarck, the first chancellor of the German empire, established five German colonies in Africa (on lands in modern-day Cameroon, Namibia, Rwanda, Tanzania, and Togo) and expanded German colonialism in order to consolidate German political and economic strength relative to other imperial European powers (Britain, Belgium, France, Italy, Portugal, and Spain).[35] As historian Michelle Moyd aptly points out, Germany's colonial power could not have been achieved without the loyalty of

---

32. Hawley, "'African Village.'"
33. Hawley, "'African Village.'"
34. See Axster, "'. . . Will Try to Send You'"; Blackler, "After the Herero 'Uprising'"; El-Tayeb, *Schwarze Deutsche*; Moyd, *Violent Intermediaries*; Stoecker, *German Imperialism in Africa*; Zantop, *Colonial Fantasies*; and Steinmetz, *Devil's Handwriting*.
35. See Stoecker, *German Imperialism in Africa*; and Fatima El-Tayeb, *Schwarze Deutsche*.

African soldiers, *askaris,* who were part of the German East African colonial army. Between 1890 and 1918, these loyal African soldiers were complicitous in Germany's oppressive colonial actions through violent measures as well as everyday activities that made the racist acts of the hegemonic power seem normalized and naturalized; for example, they worked as "tax collectors, messengers, escorts, guards, and executioners" as well as "clerks, interpreters, and teachers."[36] An important part of the often-overlooked German colonial military history, *askari* soldiers in Tanzania, for example, were praised for their loyalty to Germany and hated by the people they oppressed, their fellow citizens. The *askari* served German colonial goals at the expense of the local people and culture.

After World War I, German propaganda used the image of the model African soldier and the racist stereotype of the happy oppressed Black subject to argue for the return of their colonies in the same way the US made the argument for enslavement of Black Americans using the image of the "happy slave." When these racist images of loyalty failed to lift sanctions and bring about the return of the German colonies, the propaganda narrative changed from praising the African soldiers willing to help with Germany's colonial desires to promoting the stereotype of the violent Black Other, similar to the racist trajectory of images of Black people in the US. Just like Black men in the US, the *askari* were seen as sexual threats against which bans on interracial marriages were required in order to protect the boundary and supposed purity of whiteness.

As some white male German colonial settlers and Indigenous African women in those aforementioned countries developed sexual relationships, they also began the creation of family units. For example, as Aitken and Rosenhaft note, an article found in the *Teltower Kreisblatt* newspaper in April 1882 reported that "Berlin had a 'Neger colony' of sixty people both from the United States and Africa. . . . Many of [the people] were not only fluent in German, but even spoke in a Berlin dialect; three men were married to 'white girls' and their children were said to be doing well at school."[37] In order to better control, or at least discourage, interracial unions in an effort to maintain German "white purity," the German colonial governments began to implement functional bans on interracial marriages throughout colonial Germany. In 1907 Paul Rohrbach, the *Ansiedlungskommissar* (Settlement Commissary) in Germany made clear the lines between white racial purity and the colonized Black other when, according to Blackler, he "articulated the specific intentions

---

36. Moyd, *Violent Intermediaries*, 4.
37. Aitken and Rosenhaft, *Black Germany*, 1.

behind *Rassentrennung* (racial segregation)."³⁸ German colonial officials began to refuse the registration of interracial unions as early as 1890, and by 1912 interracial marriages were banned by colonial gubernatorial decree in Southwest Africa (now known as Namibia), German East Africa, and Samoa.³⁹

Restrictions on marriage rights offered an important constraint on the notion of the German citizen, because it was through marriage that white German men extended the rights of the polis to their wives and children. As fear of interracial coupling and mixed-race children emanated from within and outside the borders of Germany, the rhetoric of replacement and white supremacist hegemonic inversion reigned, thus making space for these racist laws to take hold. As Jonathan Hyslop notes,

> mixed-blood children produced by a native woman become German citizens and are thereby subject to the laws valid for Germans. The male mix-bloods will be liable for military service, capable of holding public offices, and will assume the right to vote sometime in the future, as well as other rights tied to citizenship. Not only is the preservation of purity of the German race and German civilization here substantially impaired because of them, but also the white man's position of power is altogether endangered.⁴⁰

These are the same racist fears that later materialize in the post–World War I and post–World War II eras. To reinforce these laws, a public relations campaign using postcards presented a visual way to show insiders versus outsiders as Germany tried to hold and reinforce white racial divisions and a white racial caste system. These postcards also provided a way for colonialists to ensure a connection to Germany, a connection to whiteness, and a connection to supposed white superiority through visual images like postcards.

Postcards were extremely popular in Germany. Felix Axster notes that "a billion picture postcards were sent from the German Empire in 1900," and because of this ubiquity, they became a very important rhetorical symbol of colonialism: "the postcard becomes a symbol for everything foreign."⁴¹ Postcards showcased the exotic and erotic in juxtaposition to oneself, in this case white Germany against the colonized brown Other. As shown in figure 1.1, the "brown eggs," a referent for African people, are running for their lives from the "white eggs," a referent for the supposedly superior white German colonizers, who are armed with swords, while the so-called inferior African has

---

38. Blackler, "After the Herero 'Uprising.'" See also Pugach et al., *After the Imperialist Imagination*.
39. See Campt, "Converging Specters."
40. Hyslop, "White Working-Class Women," 65.
41. Axster, "'... Will Try to Send You,'" 55–56.

FIGURE 1.1. "Happy Easter" German colonial postcard. Rare Historical Photos, public domain image, https://rarehistoricalphotos.com/colonial-postcards-pictures-1890-1914/.

no technological advancement or weaponry to wield in protection. The white eggs possess the artifacts of advancement with hats, belts, boots, and superior weapons. The brown eggs have nothing and are essentially naked, rhetorically signifying they have achieved nothing. The white eggs symbolized the wave of the future, which can only be achieved through the extermination of the "inferior" and cowardly brown eggs.

Postcards allowed for the emerging colonial power to keep close connections to Germany, and in many, these visual tropes recur, showing how white Germans, as Bradley Naranch argues, "entertained their own fantasies of colonial rule in Africa," whereas Africans "were rendered more savage, indolent, and threatening."[42] Through these racist and entertaining postcards, it was easier to construct an imagined white space as superior.

This postcard visually depicts what historians now refer to as General Lothar von Trotha's extermination (*zerstörung*) order. Blackler describes von Trotha's order as "the most destructive German effort," one that began "in 1904 during the so-called *Herero-Aufstand* (Herero Uprising) [and] . . . instigated the first genocide of the twentieth century."[43] Von Trotha commanded the following:

---

42. Naranch, "Global Proletarians," 170–71.
43. Blackler, "After the Herero 'Uprising.'"

> The Herero are no longer German subjects [and] must now leave the country. If it refuses, I shall compel it do so with the [great cannon]. Any Herero found inside the German frontier, with or without a gun, with or without cattle, will be shot. I shall spare neither women nor children. Such are my words to the Herero people.[44]

Using the word "it" to refer to Herero people, Trotha simultaneously dehumanized Herero people and justified the genocide of them, because they were seen as nonhuman. Ultimately, as Britta Schilling aptly notes, "the war against the Herero and nama [sic] from 1904 to 1907 . . . claimed the lives of at least one-third, but perhaps as much as 75 to 80 per cent of the indigenous Herero population. . . . The nama, who had joined the fighting shortly after the Herero, saw their numbers reduced to approximately half of their population."[45]

The postcard, as a visual signifier / image, became an additional way for communicating white supremacy and dominance through violence and technology. The postcards also show military might and a unified Germany claiming their part of the African continent—an enormous territory that was believed to be up-for-grabs by the white Western colonial world—as well as reinscribing Enlightenment ideals of so-called racial superiority. As Axster details, "postcards played a major role in communicating the mental cohesion between people and army. . . . The fear of an impending *Verkafferung*, a 'going native' of the settlers far away from home and without sufficient contacts, was a prominent topic in the colonial discourse in the German Empire."[46] The fear of going *Verkafferung* was related to the persuasive messaging and propaganda of postcards. *Verkafferung* was a label used in the colonial era to discourage interracial coupling and the potential for mixed-race children. The fear of *Verkafferung* was the nation-state fear of losing the privilege of being a so-called white nation by racially mixing with the so-called Black Other. To be marked as *Verkafferung* placed someone outside the compact of Germanness and whiteness, and this belief continued into the post–World War II era with *afrodeutsche Nachkriegskinder* children, like twins Lilli and Lore.

For example, postcards such as one reading, "Another city, another girl" (see fig. 1.2), highlighted the racist fear of interracial coupling and mocked the possibility of interracial attraction and love between white German men and African colonized women as absurd. Throughout the debates, colonial officials constructed an image of the racially mixed children as a threat to the

---

44. Blackler, "After the Herero 'Uprising.'"

45. Schilling, *Postcolonial Germany*, 3. Some scholars like Schilling mark the end of this war as 1908, "when the last Herero and nama prisoners of war were released from concentration camps," 3. See also Zimmerer, "Krieg, KZ, und Völkermord."

46. Axster, "'. . . Will Try to Send You,'" 60.

FIGURE 1.2. A postcard related to Germany's fear of interracial sexual relations developing between Indigenous Black women and white German men during Germany's colonial era. The translated text reads "Another city, another girl!" Rare Historical Photos, public domain image, https://rarehistoricalphotos.com/colonial-postcards-pictures-1890-1914/.

recognizable German family. Colonial Secretary Solf, speaking in favor of the ban on interracial marriage, warned of the risk of German men coming back from the colonies with, as Fitzpatrick notes, "wooly-haired grandchildren"[47] who would bastardize the white German race and rupture the fundamental division between the white civilizing cultural force and the backward Black colonial subject.

The African woman depicted in the postcard becomes a trope for all Black women and attempts to negatively highlight her Blackness as unattractive (e.g., thick lips, dark skin, Rubenesque body shape, and tightly coiled hair complete with feather) in juxtaposition to white womanhood, which is the absent enthymeme of beauty, Germanness, and womanhood with the implied narrow lips, light skin, straight hair, thin body shape, and no feather. Tina Campt argues the colonial decrees against interracial marriages resulted in objections that culminated in the Reichstag debates of 1912 which were, "one of the first important sites of public articulation for Germany's response to its Black German population."[48]

---

47. Fitzpatrick, "'Threat of 'Wooly-Haired Grandchildren.'"
48. Campt, "Converging Specters," 327.

The 1912 Reichstag debates over interracial marriage in Germany drew on a gendered discourse that positioned white German women's bodies as the protective barrier of the white German citizenry and constructed the bodies of women of color as threatening to pollute German genetic stock with intrinsically deficient mixed-raced children. This colonial fear about mixed-race children foreshadows debates about place, space, and belonging for *afrodeutsche Nachkriegskinder*, who were the embodiment of the fear of "going native" and thus born into a liminal German/non-German existence. This racist attitude speaks to similar fears that cultural studies scholar Martin Renes notes with regard to Indigenous Australians: "The case . . . over the last two centuries . . . may speak back to European fears of displacement by the ethnic Other."[49] Black women were constructed as exotic sexual seductresses, "vessels and conduits for transporting pollution and contamination into the German national body,"[50] writes Campt, luring German male colonists into having mixed-race children. As noted, in contradistinction, the bodies of white German women were positioned as sexually available protectors of the German stock, and many white German women took up the position as a barrier to the pollution of the (white) German empire.[51] White women's roles, power, and value thus became positioned only in relation to their uteruses. After Germany's defeat in World War I and the signing of the Treaty of Versailles on June 28, 1919, Imperial Germany did not resolve the debates surrounding banning interracial marriage, mixed-race children, or who makes up the German national body.

The ripple effects of Germany's colonial rule continued. Long gone was the memory of the Moor's African history and the cultures, learning, languages, and military might that came with it. There was no collective oral or visual memory (in Germany or in the world) of the roles that people of African descent played in Europe prior to that of the enslaved, savage, inferior Other. Rather, there was a collective inditement against Black people. This means that in every sense, Black people in Germany were not part of German citizenry and culture. There was no citizenship for the perpetual foreignness that was registered on their bodies. The Herero and Nama peoples endured some of the same genocidal atrocities in the concentration camps of 1904–8 that the Nazi regime later perfected during World War II. The echoes of Germany's colonial past continued as Namibia, in claiming its own agency, took Germany to court again in 2018 for reparations (the first lawsuit in 2001 was unsuccessful). It has taken Germany more than a hundred years to apologize for and recognize the genocide the former colonial power wreaked on Namibia from

---

49. Renes, "Stolen Generations," 30.
50. Campt, "Converging Specters," 330.
51. See Wildenthal, *German Women for Empire*.

1904 to 1908, but now "descendants of the victims" will receive $1.3 billion "for reconstruction and development [of Namibia]," and Germany has "ask[ed] for forgiveness for the 'crimes of German colonial rule.'"[52] The German colonial government killed up to eighty thousand Herero and Nama people when they resisted colonial troops "over land seizures."[53] The settlement, however, was not acceptable to former attorney general and paramount chief of the Herero people, Vekuii Rukoro, who believes the settlement is a public relations stunt: "Is this the kind of reparation that we are supposed to be excited about? . . . This is a sellout job by the Namibian government. [The reparations] didn't need to go to individual people, but should be in the form of a collective payment to the descendants of those killed and pushed off their land during the genocide."[54] This critique is an Afrofuturistic indictment of the way reparations were handled. The issue is likely not the amount but that giving money to individual people promotes a Western cultural value rather than looking out for the collective whole of the community. By valuing the individual over the collective, Germany's reparative act continues the harm, hence why it is read by the chief as a performance.

GERMANY AFTER WORLD WAR I, 1918–1933: CONSOLIDATING ANTI-BLACK SENTIMENT

> You know, after [World War I] during the Occupation, we had a Negro down the street from us. I was afraid. Then my mother said, "A person is a person. Don't be frightened by his skin color. He is probably just as afraid of you as you are of him."
>
> —Greta, personal interview

The Weimar Republic (1919–33) was the government put into place after Germany's defeat in World War I, and it solidified anti-Black sentiment in Germany. The Weimar Constitution highlights that "all Germans are equal and have the same civil rights and responsibilities,"[55] but this right did not extend to Black people, who were considered outside the compact of "white" Germany. In distinction to colonial Germany, where the threat of "Black pollution" of the white German race was placed *outside* the German national body, the Rhineland occupation by approximately thirty to forty thousand

---

52. Schmidt et al., "Germany Will Pay Namibia."
53. Schmidt et al., "Germany Will Pay Namibia."
54. Schmidt et al., "Germany Will Pay Namibia."
55. See Constitution of the German Reich.

primarily African French colonial soldiers resulted in a threat from *within* the national body.[56] These African soldiers came equipped with training and guns and were the complete antithesis of the racist postcards showing brown eggs running away that Germany once sold to its white populace. The presence of these Black troops, as authority figures within Germany, upset the boundary between whiteness (cultural supremacy) and Blackness (cultural inferiority). The Western world used mediated propaganda campaigns to denounce the presence of these African French troops. The same countries that had just waged war against Germany were suddenly allies due to their collective condemnation when these Black troops, and any potential biracial children, were left on so-called white soil. As Campt states, an "ensuing propaganda campaign [was] waged in German, French, and British newspapers that denounced the presence of these African troops and their biracial offspring as the 'the black scourge of European culture and civilization.'"[57] The most popular propaganda campaign, referred to as *die schwarze Schmach* (the black shame),[58] produced stereotypical images of hypersexualized Black colonial soldiers as polluted genetic stock and threats to the white women of Germany, and as Campt finds, "the children were depicted as the carriers of the infectious diseases of their fathers, in particular sexually transmitted diseases."[59] These children became the visual signifier of military defeat for Germany. As a result, Black German children became the bodies upon which anti-Black discourses played out throughout Germany. The biracial Black Germans born after World War I are "remembered as the victims of Nazi Germany's first measure of mass sterilization."[60] Subjected to forced sterilization as early as 1919, biracial German children of African French Colonial soldiers and white German women were constructed as victims of their own circumstances and simultaneously unacceptable threats to the homogenous white German citizenry,[61] and thus they were castrated. With the biracial children castrated, Germany eliminated the fear of a mixed-race citizenry procreating and further challenging their myth of a "pure-white" Germany.

---

56. Knowing the anti-Black racism that ran through German society, the French government intentionally placed their African colonial soldiers there in order to not only police Germany and its government but also to antagonize Germany and its racist citizenry. See Oguntoye et al., *Showing Our Colors*. See also Koller, "Recruitment of Colonial Troops"; and Wigger, *Black Horror on the Rhine*.

57. Campt, "Pictures of 'US'?," 67.

58. See Wigger, "'Black Shame.'" See also Florvil, *Mobilizing Black Germany*.

59. Campt, "Converging Specters," 336–37.

60. Aitken and Rosenhaft, *Black Germany*, 3.

61. See Oguntoye et al., *Showing Our Colors*; Campt, "Converging Specters," 322–41.

The language and images circulating in the anti-Black propaganda of the Weimar Republic revealed a societal fear that white German women would fall victim to the imagined racist sexual threat of Black colonial troops. When white German colonial soldiers impregnated Black women (by consent or rape), this was seen as a colonial "fling" because these women and their biracial children were *not* German citizens and therefore were seen as outside the German polis.[62] The fear generated by the presence of such a small number of African colonial soldiers in juxtaposition to the overall white German population is difficult to fathom, unless the racist, white supremacist propaganda is considered. As El-Tayeb aptly notes, the fear of a "constant onslaught of 'inferior races' on its pure blood explains why the tiny group of an estimated 800 Afro-German children in the Rhineland was seen as a serious danger to a population of 80 million."[63] Germany lost World War I and with it, their African colonies. According to Aitken and Rosenhaft, "the loss of colonies became part of a national trauma that took political expression in the rise of Nazism, avenging itself on the bodies of black people with a violence proportional to the extent to which they had made themselves at home."[64] From the Moor as magi and saint to the later image of the *Neger*, what all of these visual representations do is place Africans in Germany as alien and outside of the citizenry.

These Black soldiers, through the white supremacist lens, were trespassers into what was believed as white masculinist terrain. Additionally, the presence of biracial children created during the "occupation" of Germany by these African soldiers upset white masculine power. If a Black African man can seduce, love, and impregnate a white German woman, then that places the white German man in a position of failure because he failed to keep blackness from creeping into the supposedly pure white German body—the pure body of the woman and the pure body of the nation. For Greta (my *oma*), as a youth, the presence of African occupying soldiers was frightening, and this fear was capitalized upon in media campaigns. As is shown in figure 1.3, the gorilla, a racist representation of a Black man, and in particular an African colonial soldier with his military issued hat and backpack, is taking possession of an iconic referent of white womanhood and white purity in order to defile

---

62. For mixed-race Black German children, the laws about German citizenship remained surprisingly consistent in terms of efforts to deny them citizenship and enfranchisement into the polis, whether in the colonial, post–World War I or post–World War II eras. Over this time, German citizenship laws changed from privileging the citizenship status of mother to that of the father, but in reality, bans on interracial marriage largely stood as a roadblock preventing Black Germans from being citizens.

63. El-Tayeb, "'If You Can't Pronounce My Name,'" 72.

64. Aitken and Rosenhaft, *Black Germany*, 21.

FIGURE 1.3. This propaganda image is from Berlin and was published in the satirical newspaper *Kladderadatsch* on May 30, 1920. The text reads, "Der Schwarze Terror in Deutschen Landen" (the black terror in German lands). The artist is unknown, but the African soldier is mocked as a gorilla carrying away a white woman. University of Heidelberg and Creative Commons, public domain image, https://digi.ub.uni-heidelberg.de/diglit/kla1920/0317.

her. Soldiers in possession of such whiteness were a visual signifier of German defeat both as a nation and for whiteness overall, as they walked across Germany uncontrolled.

THIRD REICH GERMANY, 1933–1945: INSTITUTIONALIZING ANTI-BLACKNESS

The first time I met my *oma*, Greta, I distinctly recall going into her house, sitting on her couch, and visiting. This would be the primary location in which all future conversations and interviews took place but not necessarily the place in which all interview information was collected or where I learned about my German family. As I sat on her couch, I noticed a built-in library shelf with hundreds of books, but what prominently stood out was Hitler's *Mein Kampf*. I was initially startled that she would have such a book, but then thought perhaps she, like me, is a voracious reader, wanting to know all sides of an issue the way any good scholar would. Perhaps she was, but when Lore, Greta's daughter and my mother, who sat beside me on the dated, light tan-colored couch said, "Oh, what a terrible time to be living under those conditions," Greta inferred that my mother was referencing Hitler and not the horror of the war and said, "No. He wasn't as bad as they say. He was a great man. Before him, we were starving, and he provided us with food and jobs." I was stunned into silence. My mother was equally shocked. This was the first time in fifty-two years Greta had seen her own daughter, whom she had so breezily left behind to go on with a new life and to make new memories, and this statement was made on the first day of our reunion. I wanted to debate Greta, tell her she was wrong, and tell her she was glorifying a white supremacist monster. But instead, I fell silent. I was afraid that if I pointed out her racism and anti-Semitism, she would kick me out of her house and never speak to me again, as I had only a tenuous grasp on my German family and did not want her to reject me in the same way she had rejected her own twin daughters. I visually represented all the anti-mixed-race media campaigns Greta was subjected to during the years of the Third Reich and World War II. While Greta and I have the same nose and face shape, phenotypically no one would immediately think we were family due to the differences in our accents, age, hair texture, height, and skin color. I would have to "out" myself to strangers for our familial connection to be known, in part because she never would. Silence became my inadvertent strategy with anything controversial with Greta because I wanted her to see me as kin, as part of *ein Volk*. I needed her to see that below the visible differences, we were one, *oma* and granddaughter.

I wanted her to see that we had culture, language, and most importantly, DNA in common. Much like in Octavia Butler's novel *Kindred*, I wanted to ensure my survival with Greta by engaging with and being seen by my biological family. If Greta saw me, and saw herself in me, I would have been included in *ein Volk* with relative strangers, my family. However, in my Afrocentric creative imaginings, I failed. Greta saw me only as belonging to *das Volk*, and because of that, in the end, as she had with her twin daughters, she and the rest of my German family rejected me anyway.

Das Volk and *ein Volk* were phrases originally used during the Nazi era to engage white German people to the exclusion of Black people. In English, *das Volk* means "the people," but there is a distinct and important rhetorical difference between *das Volk* and *ein Volk* (one people) as Hitler and the Third Reich used them. As Alexander Weheliye finds, *Das Volk* "signifies the people as an undifferentiated mass of humans, including the oppressed and *ein Volk* as a specific and supposedly homogenous ethnic, cultural, and/or linguistic group. . . . Nazism [transformed] *das Volk* into *ein* [one] ethnically pure Volk."[65] Understanding Nazi Germany as a fundamentally racialized state, in addition to a particularly anti-Semitic state, is important to understanding the power relationships during the era, particularly since, as Gellately and Stolzfus point out, "most of their targets were individuals and groups long regarded as outsiders, nuisances, or 'problem cases.' . . . For the Nazis this idealized community could never see the light of day unless it was based on racial purity."[66] This belief may explain, in part, why my desire to be familial *ein Volk* with my *oma* was unsuccessful. The other part was Greta's indoctrination into white supremacy.

In 1930 the League of German Girls was formed which, like the Hitler Youth group for boys, trained girls to become faithful to the Nazi Party. For example, in 1935 young white German women were encouraged to have as many Aryan children as possible as members of the Hitler Maidens, which was the only female division of the Hitler Youth and shorthand for the Bund Deutscher Mädel (BDM), in which all German women over the age of ten were mandated to participate. Greta was an active member of the Hitler Maidens, having been conscribed as all female youth were at this time and subjected to racial and racist indoctrination. The move to control German white women's bodies, as Campt reminds us, speaks to the "gendered and sexualized discourses" of the German body politic wherein the "German national body is

---

65. Weheliye, "My Volk to Come," 165.
66. Gellately and Stolzfus, "Social Outsider," 4.

a raced body made vulnerable through the female body" as a potential "conduit of racial pollution."[67]

The primary focus of this group was to teach girls how to be good German citizens as well as to learn the importance of motherhood. After the 1936 Nuremburg Rally, nine hundred young German women left pregnant.[68] According to Katharina Oguntoye, May Opitz, and Dagmar Schultz, "Aryan women who brought Aryan offspring into the world were glorified. Those who bore Afro-Germans, Sinti-Germans, or half-Jewish children were excluded from the cult of motherhood and were denounced as 'whores' in public and often by their closest relatives."[69] Thus, with the rise of Adolf Hitler in Germany and the establishment of the Nuremberg Laws, German women's choice of sexual partners were circumscribed to only those of pure Aryan heritage, and they faced severe prohibitions and sanctions for engaging in sexual conduct with foreign men including Black, Jewish, and Romani men.[70] The Nazi regime established a coercive pronatalist policy that called for a significant increase in births from white German Aryan women. Individual German women's rights of the womb did not factor into the decision calculus of the Nazi regime because the mothering body was understood to be a state interest and was operationalized to ensure the perpetuation of the Aryan race.[71] Aryan men, on the other hand, were not sanctioned for having sexual relationships with non-Aryan women as long as it was for nonreproductive purposes.[72] It is worth noting that women's roles and power of choice in Germany, particularly Western Germany, changed dramatically in 1972, when Western German women were allowed to retain their citizenship when marrying a non-German person, and when antiracist feminism was popularized in Germany by Audre Lorde in the 1980s.[73]

While Nazi racism was increasingly reduced to anti-Semitism and its consequence in public and official discourse, Aitken and Rosenhaft find "the racist tropes of a persistent but objectless colonial memory reappeared in the media to represent black subjects as ahistorical exotics."[74] In addition, during this time, with the establishment of the Nuremberg Laws, much of the anti-Black

---

67. Campt, "Converging Specters," 330.
68. See Skundrick, *Third Reich*.
69. Oguntoye et al., *Showing Our Colors*, 322–41.
70. See Fehrenbach, "Black Occupation Children."
71. See Patton, "I Want to Show You."
72. Fehrenbach, "Black Occupation Children," 34.
73. See Schultz, *Audre Lorde*.
74. Aitken and Rosenhaft, *Black Germany*, 21.

discourse that was exacerbated after World War I became enshrined in public law regarding interracial marriage and citizenship. According to Gellately and Stolzfus, "soon after Hitler was appointed chancellor on 30 January 1933, he made it clear that he would not retreat from the nationalist and racist elements of his vision of this 'community.'"[75] Simply being born within the confines of the state was not sufficient to garner the rights of the polis, and the Law for the Prevention of Hereditarily Diseased Offspring, or Gesetz zur Verhütung erbkranken Nachwuchses, called for forced sterilization of any person who was medically designated as posing a threat to the "health" of the social body.[76] While the hereditary health law did not mention race explicitly, the sterilization policy and medical surveillance were turned aggressively toward Black German bodies,[77] which resulted in hundreds of Black German children being sterilized and hundreds of other Black German youth being moved into concentration camps.[78]

For example, the scientific experimentation on their bodies and the racist epithets Black women Holocaust survivors described were part of the larger racist ideology that shaped Black German experiences in the Third Reich era in Germany.[79] The most recognizable image among Black men Holocaust victims and survivors was Jean (Johnny) Voste (see fig. 1.4). Sitting among the horror and rubble in an image labeled "Liberation Feast, Dachau," Voste was a visual signifier for being one of millions who endured the horrors of Holocaust, but he was also an unusual signifier for the Holocaust because he was the only Black German at Dachau and was not Jewish. Voste's inclusion in this photo contributes to the iconicity of it and is likely one reason this image was taken as the world and journalists grappled with the evil of the Holocaust and what was unveiled and revealed at the end of World War II.

The scientific justifications for the extermination of Black people and other people who did not meet the standard of a so-called superior being were vividly seen during German colonial discourses but also through the scientific foundation of genetics, which took off with the eugenics movement that was embraced throughout the Western world, including the United States and Germany. In the 1930s, Germany became the world leader in eugenics research, and Hitler had significant institutional support and wide approval from American eugenicists. Hitler's eugenics program, according to Edwin Black, included "brutal decrees, custom-designed IBM data processing

---

75. Gellately and Stolzfus, "Social Outsider," 3. See also Noakes, "Social Outcasts."
76. See Haas, "German Science and Black Racism."
77. See Haas, "German Science and Black Racism."
78. See Okuefuna, *Hitler's Forgotten Victims*.
79. See Lusane, *Hitler's Black Victims*.

FIGURE 1.4. Two survivors at Dachau preparing food after liberation. The survivor on the right is believed to be Jean (Johnny) Voste, who was originally born in the Democratic Republic of the Congo, formerly known as the Belgian Congo. Voste was the only Black person imprisoned in Dachau. Used with permission from the United States Holocaust Memorial Museum, Photo Archives #74095, courtesy of Colonel Alexander Zabin, MD, https://collections.ushmm.org/search/catalog/pa1034242.

machines, eugenical courts, mass sterilization mills, concentrations camps, and virulent biological anti-Semitism."[80] The father of the eugenics movement was a German professor of anthropology named Eugene Fisher, the first director of the Kaiser Wilhelm Institute (now the Max Plank Institute for Molecular Genetics) for Anthropology, Human Genetics, and Eugenics from 1927 to 1942. His research informed the 1935 Nuremburg laws that included antimiscegenation laws, paved the way for the passage of the Law for the Prevention of Hereditarily Diseased Offspring to be passed in Germany in 1933, and provided the foundation for the science behind Nazi racial policies.

In the US, intelligence tests were employed and, as Black states, "mandatory sterilization laws were enacted in some twenty-seven states to prevent

---

80. Black, *War against the Weak*, xviii.

targeted individuals from reproducing more of their kind. Marriage prohibition laws proliferated throughout the country to stop race mixing. Collusive litigation was taken to the US Supreme Court, which sanctified eugenics and its tactics."[81] Targets of US eugenics included "poor urban dwellers and rural 'white trash' from New England to California, immigrants from across Europe, Blacks, Jews, Mexicans, Native Americans, epileptics, alcoholics, petty criminals, the mentally ill and anyone else who did not resemble the blond and blue-eyed Nordic ideal the eugenics movement glorified," along with those who were blind, deaf, or suffered from mental health conditions like bipolar depression and schizophrenia.[82] American eugenicists' support finally subsided only when the horrors of the concentration camps came to light: "American eugenic institutions rushed to change their names from *eugenics* to *genetics*."[83] With this new identity via rebranding, the eugenics movement was able to reinvent itself and rhetorically divorce itself from the overt discrimination, racism, and genocide it once practiced and "establish the modern, enlightened human genetic revolution. . . . [But] the laws and mindsets were left in place. So for decades after Nuremberg labeled eugenic methods genocide and crimes against humanity, America continued to forcibly sterilize and prohibit eugenically undesirable marriages."[84] The Third Reich's eugenics program provided a state-sanctioned platform for people like Nazi physician Dr. Josef Mengele (a student of Fisher's) to wage medical experiments on people in the Auschwitz-Birkenau concentration camp, where 1.1 million people were murdered in an attempt to separate *das Volk* from *ein Volk* throughout the Nazi regime and the Third Reich's campaign of terror.

POSTWAR GERMANY, 1945–1955: DEMOCRATIZING ANTI-BLACKNESS

By 1949 the Republic of West Germany was constitutionally established and expressly prohibited racial discrimination, and in 1952 Konrad Adenauer, the first chancellor of the Federal Republic of Germany, West Germany, "committed to paying more and material indemnity for the unspeakable crimes committed in the name of the German people."[85] Jewish survivors of the Holocaust received (and continue to receive) reparations from the German government

---

81. Black, *War against the Weak*, xv.
82. Black, *War against the Weak*, xvi.
83. Black, *War against the Weak*, xvii.
84. Black, *War against the Weak*.
85. Timsit, "Blueprint."

for their imprisonment "in these forced labor camps," observes Jodi Kantor.[86] These reparations are sent monthly for amounts in "the high three-figures" along with a letter that says "für Schaden" (for harm).[87] While rightfully acknowledging the genocide of Jewish people, according to Fehrenbach, "by 1950 . . . West German federal and state Interior Ministry officials explicitly constructed the postwar problem of race around skin color and, even more narrowly, blackness."[88] Anti-Black racism was intricately linked to the process of democratization in postwar Germany, and much of it was transnationally learned and incorporated from the relationships developed between German citizens and segregated American forces. The United States military forces that occupied West Germany after World War II offered a point of contact between the German populace and the notion of democracy and made it apparent that democracy did not necessitate racial equality.

In the 1950s, the newly established West German Republic conducted its first census of the German population and, like the US, used skin color as a central characteristic, establishing a postwar preoccupation with color/blackness in German bureaucracy and the larger public discourse, as Maria Höhn notes, "regarding the reproductive consequences of defeat and occupation."[89] Recall the German archivist I mentioned in the introduction and her words on recordkeeping in the Jugendamt (the youth welfare office that most biracial children up for adoption after World War II were affiliated with), where related documents up to 1953 are supposed to be held. She also told me:

> All documents [in the post-Nazi era] should have been given to the archives. The point is civil servants are doing their work without considering the historical dimension, that's why a lot of documents never make their way to any archives at all. The files from the time between 1945 and 1953 should be kept and sent to the archives, but this [doesn't always happen]. (Personal interview, November 2018)

Clearly, much has been lost or revised in German postwar memories as they concern archives and biracial children and their voices and experiences. It is as if there is an intentionality in erasing their existence from any larger conversations about the effects of the war and the immediate postwar era on German society.

---

86. Kantor, "Story of Survival."
87. Kantor, "Story of Survival."
88. Fehrenbach, "Black Occupation Children," 38.
89. Höhn, *GIs and Fräuleins*, 38.

When I asked, "So what happens? Aren't the experiences of children during war and after war and specifically biracial children part of the historical remembering, particularly since unlike after World War I, there were an estimated five thousand biracial children born?," the archivist replied, "With regard to *afrodeutsche Nachkriegskinder,* archivists are not taught this history. They have no knowledge of what exists. If you don't know about it and don't study it in school, you can't tell patrons and can't catalogue the material, so in essence it doesn't exist." If the information does not exist, if the biracial children are treated as though they do not exist, and if the adults from the Black diaspora in Germany are not acknowledged, then they become inconvenient memories. How can Afrofuturism possibly bloom in this barren landscape? In their nonexistent status as Black, mixed-race bodies were largely written out of the historical narrative, which makes their current existence in Germany alien and precarious. In other words, mixed-race children in Germany were a reminder of how far Germany had fallen from their military might into yet another military defeat, and thus absence and erasure is needed in order to further marginalize Black Germans. Twins Lore and Lilli, born in 1948, were thrust into this liminal and precarious world.

CONCLUSION

The goal of this chapter was to show that through cultural erasure and obscuring the memory of Black people's presence in Europe, and Germany specifically, the diverse roles Black people have played over the millennia have been reduced to those of enslavement and Otherness, and this erasure has been critical in the formation of a mythical white identity. Yet, Black presence vibrates in mythic white Germany, with the foreshadowing of an Afrofuturistic reality that reappears as *ein Volk*, Black Germans whose experiences are seen and written into the hallowed halls of white German history as well as the German present and future. As Kendall Phillips states, "The cultural concern over remembrance is driven not so much by the fear that we will forget, but by the fear that we will remember differently."[90] The fear of remembering instances in which a Black person might leave an imprint on society outside the boundary of white supremacy can lead to what scholar Paul Connerton referred to as repressive erasure. Connerton says, "Repressive erasure need not always take malign forms, then; it can be encrypted covertly and without

---

90. Phillips, "Failure of Memory."

apparent violence."[91] Germany displayed its repressive erasure through language, visual culture, and violence, all of which communicate volumes about Black diasporic people and their place and space in Germany.

Germany is excellent at marketing its own public memory. Unlike the United States, which has never addressed its genocide and enslavement of two foundational and Indigenous cultures, Native and Black, Germany has embedded the Holocaust into its cultural memory in all aspects of its education and in its many public memory sites. Therefore, it would be a mistake to see Germany as evidence of a teleological and static certainty where anti-Blackness is essentially fundamental to the process of constructing Germanness, but in several hegemonic ways, the constitution of the German polis has been so established. Of concern is the complication or simplification of what it means to be German. At stake is the very possibility for recognition of Germanness that exceeds white hegemony and includes those who are disenfranchised due to their phenotype, and the potential for them to be Black Germans. Black Germans generally, and the children of white German women and often foreign Black occupying soldiers specifically, have been constructed as essentially and fundamentally exterior to the German social body, a contradiction in terms that has materialized through dangerous transgressions of the social restrictions on sexual relationships between white Germans and Black "aliens" of the state, resulting in the need for state sanction and surveillance.

Black people in Germany have inherited a liminal identity defined by verbal and visual marginalization. As El-Tayeb observes,

> Black Germans are probably the most completely assimilated ethnic minority, growing up in largely white neighbourhoods, often in white families. At the same time, their blackness codes them as completely "alien," they are hyper-visible, their mere presence a sore spot in Germany's perception of itself, constantly reduced to their colour and simultaneously made completely invisible, that is, non-German; under a constant demand to explain, justify, re-define their existence, expected to be something they are not and not allowed to be what they are, since what they are exceeds acceptable notions of Germanness.[92]

For example, Allison Blakely notes that "neo-Nazi groups are tolerated and Afro-Germans dare not go out on the street on Hitler's birthday for fear of physical assaults by skinhead bands" and relates what happened in the "savage

---

91. Connerton, "Seven Types of Forgetting," 60.
92. El-Tayeb, "'If You Can't Pronounce My Name,'" 83–84.

beating of an Ethiopian irrigation engineer"[93] in April 2006 in Potsdam. At a soccer match in 2006, midfielder Adebowale Ogungbure, who played for Nuremburg, endured monkey noises and racist epithets, to which he "responded angrily with a Hitler salute," yet initially he, and not the racist fans, was charged with "violating the German constitution, which prohibits this gesture. Later the charges were dropped."[94] In 2012 Berlin's Schlosspark Theater performed the play *Ich bin nicht Rappaport* (I am not Rappaport), which is about friendship between a Jewish man and a Black American; the Black American character was performed in blackface by a white actor.[95] In 2017 when I was in Kassel, I was standing at a bus stop, and an old German man walked up to me, stopped, looked me up and down and said, "Schade dass wir den Ersten Weltkrieg verloren haben" (Too bad we lost World War I), as if the only reason for my existence in Germany was the African French colonial troops who were among the forces that occupied the Rhineland. Yet, simultaneously existing in this space of Black German racism and exclusion is solidarity and support from Germany as well, such as in 2017 when the German soccer players of Hertha Berlin took a knee before their Bundesliga match, thus nonverbally taking a stand against racism and communicating solidarity with NFL players like Colin Kaepernick and social justice organizations like Black Lives Matter.[96] Various groups throughout Germany also participated in the Black Lives Matter 2020 protests with a focus on dismantling institutional and structuralized racism in Germany. This act of solidarity with Black diasporic lives is an intersectional and international identification with Black people.

Black diasporic people had and have a place within Europe generally, and Germany specifically. To recognize this fact is to rupture the false narrative of a white Europe and to rupture the myth of a white Germany. To recognize Black people within and as a part of European society from the Crusades forward is an act of engagement with Afrofuturism. It is through the recognition of a Black presence that Black people are rebirthed on the European continent. Knowing this history and amplifying their visibility has ripple effects today in terms of what we think we know about the foundations of Germany. The recognition highlights how, as Eshun states, "imperial racism has denied black subjects the right to belong to the enlightenment project, thus creating an urgent need to demonstrate a substantive historical presence."[97] Instead

---

93. Blakely, "Emergence of Afro-Europe," 16.
94. Blakely, "Emergence of Afro-Europe," 15.
95. See Breitenbach and Abbany, "Black or White."
96. See Associated Press, "German Soccer Team Kneels."
97. Eshun, "Further Considerations on Afrofuturism," 287.

of the image of a so-called Black German alien population, in transporting Black German bodies to the center, these images belie a forgotten and denied existence of Black people in Europe and their influence on the continent. This process echoes Eshun's statement on the importance of "recovering the histories of counter-futures created in a century hostile to Afrodiasporic projection."[98] As Janelle Monáe observes, "erasure is happening right underneath our noses, and its being done through lawmaking. Our memories define the quality of our lives. When you strip somebody's memory, you strip their identity. You strip them as human beings."[99] Reaffirming Black German presence highlights the cultures, stories, and experiences that have always been present and anticipates memories to come. When the veil of artifice is lifted, what is exposed is the frailty of memory, rootedness, and belonging in the imagined white supremacist world.

---

98. Eshun, "Further Considerations on Afrofuturism," 288.
99. Amanpour, "Janelle Monáe."

CHAPTER 2

Jim Crow in the European Theater

Institutionalizing Anti-Blackness in Germany

I live in the transnational world of war. Two of my family members, neither of whom I ever knew, fought on opposite sides of a world war: Albert (US grandfather) and Robert (German great-grandfather). Both men share the commonality of familial absence as well as military experience and patriotism, all of which are foregrounded in the composite narratives I have constructed for each of them. Composite narrative is an important methodological tool in this study, particularly when combined with postmemory and Afrofuturism, because it conjoins many different stories to shed deeper light on phenomena and experiences that are erased, forgotten, or missing. These two soldiers, with whom I share DNA, highlight war history as a cross-racial and international affair in one family. Using Afrofuturism, I problematize these war spaces to ultimately ask, "How do you reconcile the debt that manifests?" The debt here is what is owed to Black American soldiers. This Afrofuturistic view of what some may view as sacred, documented, memoried war history that should not be analyzed outside static recounting exposes how a global, systemic anti-Black racism persisted in the fight for democracy through two world wars, as Black American GIs could only imagine the freedom they fought for on behalf of Europe as such freedom did not exist for them in the United States. Further, these African American soldiers were forced to engage in creative imagining in Germany as they lived their lives in relative "freedom" in juxtaposition to the racist reality that existed on US military bases in Germany and the racist Jim Crow horror that awaited them upon their return. The Black American GIs who stayed in Germany after World War II engaged in what James Baldwin in 1948 would call "the distance one needs, for clarity."[1] The Black American GI experience, which is an extension of the larger Black European and Black German experience in Germany, shows what Davis calls "the ravages of racism; the penalties extracted by patriarchy; the hypocrisies of the elite; [and] the false promises of the American Dream."[2] Therefore, the central research questions of this chapter are the following: How did issues of race, racism, propaganda, and the importation of Jim Crow democracy in postwar Germany become a cross-cultural affair that ultimately reified anti-Blackness in the United States and Germany? How did the decisions made by political leaders and the military-industrial complex become lived experiences for Albert and Robert?

These research questions are particularly important because the foundational beliefs about race and racism shaped by white racist propaganda endemic to both Germany and the United States affected the decisions Greta would later make about her own family. Separating race and racism in Germany and in the United States becomes impossible. Centering Albert, in particular, is an engagement with Afrofuturism, because through composite narrative I am making visible the life of a man erased from mine. Afrofuturism provides me the opportunity to make space for imagined existences, a way of seeing through screens of invisibility and opaqueness, and after doing so, Albert emerges from erasure. Until I learned about the existence of Albert, I had no known relative involved in World War II on the US/Allied side. Instead, all of my World War II familial experiences were from the German side, and they fought for Hitler.

AN INCOMPLETE PORTRAIT OF A BLACK AMERICAN SOLDIER

The first time I learned about Albert Flowers in any kind of detail was near the end of my first visit to meet my *oma*, Greta. The first time I learned that this mysterious man even existed was earlier that same day, July 13, 2012. In just under an hour of conversation, I learned that the biological father of the twins was of the "Negro race." This was the first and only time Greta ever referred to Albert as a Black man. After that, Greta's racial description of him vacillated

---

1. Baldwin, "Autobiographical Notes," 8.
2. Davis, *Inessential Solidarity*, 6.

from "white" to "Native American." When I pushed Greta on Albert's ethnic origin, she continuously stressed he was Native American. In all likelihood, Albert had no Native American ancestry. In two DNA tests taken by Lore, the first listed her as having 16 percent West African ancestry and the second as 38 percent West African ancestry, but according to both tests, she has 0 percent Native American ancestry. Given her relatively low percentage of West African ancestry, it is safe to say that Albert, like many Black Americans, was biracial—part white and part Black—due to the legacy of enslavement. In all subsequent interviews, Greta blatantly erased Albert's potential Blackness and disavowed that she had ever described Albert in such a way, because as Greta said, "race never mattered to me, only the person." Yet every time I asked about Albert, I was met with Greta's oft-repeated phrase, "I don't want to talk about it." To mix it up a bit, she would claim that she "didn't understand the question" because her "English wasn't good," forgetting that I am fluent in both languages. Engaging in "forgetting as humiliated silence," Greta used this memoried strategy to evade and hold onto any power she had, as well as to save herself from the pain of remembering. Humiliated silence, as Connerton reflects, is a form of forgetting "because occasions of humiliation are so difficult to forget; it is often easier to forget physical pain than to forget humiliation."[3] My ability to language switch was a source of frustration for Greta, so often we would sit in stony silence, either on the phone or in person, until I steered the subject away from remembering the past.

I attempted to broach the subject of Albert with Greta on July 27, 2012, with no luck, but when I tried again on August 3, 2012, she said she was going to "reveal something" about Albert but then changed her mind and said, "Tracey, I have to be very honest. I am so tired from moving furniture, and I need to rest. We only talk about family issues one day, and then we have fun." I tried once more to learn about Albert on August 17, 2012, and irritated, Greta firmly said, "I will not answer any more serious questions on the phone. All will be revealed when you visit." I tried to imagine an Afrofuturistic space in which Albert lived, but I was unable to fill in any gaps, because I lacked the information Greta could have filled in but declined to. Line drawn and invitation accepted, my parents and I planned our first in-person visit with Greta for the next month. This would be the first time Lore had seen her mother in fifty-two years and the first time in my life I would meet my grandmother.

Over the course of our first visit, Lore and I found ourselves sitting face-to-face with Greta in her home in California. I was anxious to meet her and learn more about my German biological family, but Greta either refused to talk about Albert or dealt out just enough crumbs of information to keep Lore

---

3. Connerton, "Seven Types of Forgetting," 67.

and I sated: he was tall, he had dark curly hair, he had brown eyes. I had been there four days, Lore and my father nearly a week, and the day before we were supposed to leave, while sitting on a bench in front of Macy's at the Stanford Mall in Palo Alto, California, waiting for her husband to come around with the car, Greta abruptly stated, "I'm only going to say this once. His name is Albert Flowers. He was in the Army. He was a great dancer, tall. He was very light skinned with slightly curly hair. He was part African American, mostly Native American, and very proud of his heritage."

With just this general description of Albert, I was able to begin creating a composite narrative of Albert, a space where he existed in Jim Crow America, a place where he existed transnationally in Germany as a US soldier, and a space where he could begin to take shape in my imagination. His registration card said:

> Albert Flowers. Born October 1, 1917. Enlistment date: February 17, 1942. 4046th Quarter Master Truck Company where he was a "Technician Fourth Grade." Discharge Date: September 29, 1945.[4]

According to a newspaper article I was also able to locate, Albert was one of "two officers and 14 enlisted men of the 578th Field Artillery Battalion awarded the Bronze Star Medal for meritorious service in France and Belgium." Albert was a member "of a battalion which poured accurate and effective 8-inch howitzer fire on the enemy in support of the infantry. Due to the presence of these men in the battalion, constantly displaying professional skill, and a superb sense of initiative, they were instrumental in moulding the various sections of their batteries into teams capable of delivering artillery fire that has been commended by divisional and higher headquarters commanders."[5] Albert died July 11, 1953, at the age of thirty-five, shortly after returning to the southern United States.

When Albert met Greta, he was residing in Mannheim, Germany. I attempted to learn more about Albert's military record and his experiences in Germany, but I hit a wall. After petitioning the Military Personnel Records, at the National Personnel Records Center in St. Louis, Missouri, in March 2020, I received this response from their World War II Draft Registration Card Division:

> We are unable to locate a record with the information provided in your original inquiry OR the record needed to answer your inquiry was lost in

---

4. "WWII Draft Registration Cards."
5. "Sixteen Get Bronze Stars."

the July 1973 fire that destroyed millions of records at the National Personnel Records Center. The records stored in the area which suffered the most damage in the fire were those of Army veterans discharged or deceased between November 1, 1912, and December 31, 1959, AND Air Force veterans discharged, deceased, or retired before January 1, 1964, whose names come alphabetically after Hubbard James E. If the record were here on July 12, 1973, it would have been in the area that suffered the most damage in the fire on that date and may have been destroyed.[6]

Based on Albert's Bronze Star Medal, I know part of what Albert's life was like in the US Army. Apparently, some of his actions were officially recognized as heroic, but there are many gaps, spaces I try to fill by relying on stories from other Black American soldiers in war theaters in Germany. Albert's experiences were likely not much different from those of other soldiers of color in terms of race and racism and how they had to balance their liminal existences in and out of the war theater. Albert can be more fully understood through other documented histories of Black American soldiers, as his life experiences would have paralleled theirs in some respects, particularly their histories as Black men living in a white racist caste system and fighting for Black American civil rights. Many scholars have captured the voices of Black American soldiers through documenting the experiences of the Tuskegee Airmen (Black American fighter and bomber military pilots), the 761st Tank Battalion (a.k.a. The Black Panthers, who fought in Normandy, France, and took part in liberating thirty French towns before pushing into Germany), and the 92nd Infantry Division (a.k.a. the Buffalo Soldiers, who engaged in combat during the Italian Campaign). In order to better understand Albert's military experience, I must travel back in time and briefly recount Black American soldiers' military history prior to World War II.

PERSONAL GHOSTS: HAUNTED MEMORIES OF FAMILY AND WAR

World War I: Black American Military Experiences in War

Albert became one of millions of Black Americans who fought in wars for the US only to never be able to fully participate in the ideals promised to them in the Declaration of Independence. Albert volunteered to serve in a US military known for its history of overt racism and discrimination. For

---

6. "WWII Draft Registration Cards."

example, as early as the 1600s, Black men (enslaved and freemen) served in colonial militias alongside white men. Benjamin Franklin, as David Colley observes, "opposed the enlistment of blacks and Congress agreed to eliminate them from the military"[7] in 1775, but Black men, enslaved and free, had been deemed necessary in the American colonies' fight against the British during the Revolutionary War (1775–83). Black men served in George Washington's Continental Army, were present at the Boston Massacre in 1770, defended the lines during the Battle of Bunker Hill in 1775, and fought at the Battle of Monmouth, New Jersey, in 1778. Yet despite their valor as soldiers, these men were painted as ineffective warriors, and "the treatment of blacks following the Revolution established a government pattern in which blacks were called to serve in time of war but were ignored and excluded once hostilities ceased."[8] From the War of 1812, the Civil War (1861–65), the Spanish-American War (1898), World War I (1914–18), and through to the present day, every US war has included Black American soldiers. The US has not won a single war without their participation.

My family's military story, Albert's story, really begins in World War II, but the foundational messaging, persuasion, patriotism, and propaganda from World War I set up the historical and rhetorical context that affected Albert's military service in World War II. In World War I, as Nina Mjagkij recounts, "404,348 black men served in the US military," and the German military engaged in targeted propaganda campaigns wherein they used airplanes to drop "leaflets . . . behind American lines [to] capitalize on low troop morale among black soldiers."[9] One such pamphlet read,

> Hello boys, what are you doing over here? Fighting the Germans? Why? Have they ever done you any harm? . . . Do you enjoy the same rights as the white people do in America, the land of freedom and Democracy, or are you not rather treated over these as second class citizens? Can you get into a restaurant where white people dine? Can you get a seat in a theatre where white people sit? . . . And how about the law? Is lynching and the most horrible crimes connected therewith, a lawful proceeding in a Democratic country? Now, all this is entirely different in Germany, where they do like colored people; where they treat them as gentlemen and as white men, and quite a number of colored people have fine positions in business in Berlin and other German cities. . . . You have never seen Germany, so you are fools if you allow people to make you hate us. Come over to see for yourself. Let

---

7. Colley, *Blood for Dignity*, 13.
8. Colley, *Blood for Dignity*, 14.
9. Mjagkij, *Loyalty in Time of Trial*, 177.

those do the fighting who make the profit out of this war. Don't allow them to use you as cannon fodder."[10]

The German military circulated this propaganda, which argued that Black American soldiers were being used by the racist US system, in hopes of exposing racism and creating further divides between American soldiers. Similar to the experiences that colonial African troops had in Germany, racism was written upon the bodies of Black American soldiers in World War I, and in spite of it, they performed heroically. According to Carolyn Johnston, "General Pershing referred to the 92nd Division as 'one of the best of the American Expeditionary Force.'"[11] The Harlem Hell Fighters, the 369th Infantry Regiment, was "the first Allied unit to reach the Rhine River," and "the French awarded the unit with the *Croix de Guerre* in recognition of its heroism [and] many of the soldiers received medals for bravery."[12] Black American GIs strove to show through their military heroism, might, and patriotism that they were worthy of full enfranchisement in the United States. Through their military service, they tried to realize an Afrofuturistic imagining and create a place where their military efforts brought all Black Americans the civil and voting rights that were long overdue to them. This imagining was not to be. The international recognition of the heroism, bravery, and military skill these Black American soldiers demonstrated was lost on a United States that could see Black Americans and soldiers only through the guise of racism and white supremacy. When these Black American soldiers returned to the US, they returned to a country where Jim Crow was still in place, where jobs for these veterans and all other Black Americans were difficult to obtain, and where lynchings were common and even soldiers in uniform were not protected from such white terrorism. As Carter Woodson aptly observes in 1922, "the uniform on a Negro man was like a red flag thrown in the face of a bull."[13] These Black American soldiers were welcomed back home to a country where they had no civil rights or voting rights. Regardless of whether these men were in uniform, the terrorism of white racism marked their bodies and their daily lives.

The central question here is why any Black American soldier would volunteer to serve a nation that did not enfranchise him as a full citizen. Why would any Black American soldier during World War I and World War II agree to

---

10. Addie W. Hunton and Kathryn M. Johnson, *Two Colored Women with the American Expeditionary Forces* (Brooklyn: Brooklyn Eagle Press, 1920), 53–54, quoted in Mjagkij, *Loyalty in Time of Trial*, 177–78.
 11. Johnston, *My Father's War*, 20.
 12. Johnston, *My Father's War*, 20.
 13. Barbeau and Henri, *Unknown Soldiers*, 175.

serve an overtly racist nation that merely wanted their bodies, without rights, for a war that freed white people on another continent but did not free themselves? What Afrofuturistic imagining did these men, and later Albert, engage in whereby the same patriotic messages that were transmitted to white American men also moved them? Similar to Eshun's notion that because Black people have been "denied . . . the right to belong to the enlightenment project" there is "an urgent need to demonstrate a substantive historical presence,"[14] these Black American GIs needed to establish their presence, participation, patriotism, and inclusion in the world war in order to make themselves visible in a way that contradicted the white supremacist narratives that had been written about Black people generally since 1619. Making use of an Afrofuturistic sense of hope, these soldiers imagined a future, and an America, that could be, if only the racist US would participate in their futurity building. I imagine that a similar drive toward imaginative being fueled Robert when he served Germany in World War I.

World War I: Robert's Composite Narrative in Postmemory

I often wonder if my German great-grandfather, Robert, was also swept up in the formation of a new identity for Germany via his engagement with World War I and later World War II. World War I, even though it resulted in a loss, had afforded Germans an opportunity to solidify their national identity, as differences of politics, religion, and socioeconomics seemed to evaporate in the combined war effort. Engaging in prescriptive forgetting, forgetting the differences of the past, became a rhetorical success and a gain for the identity of Germany.

I know very little about Robert, and what little I do know was shared by Greta, who said that Robert was kicked out of their house around the start of World War II in 1939, when Greta was seventeen and her two younger sisters, my great aunts, were five and seven years old. My great-grandfather participated in both World War I and World War II for Germany. After World War I, he was an alcoholic, and his marriage became rocky, and after World War II, he disappeared. When I look at an image of him from World War I, he seems to be proud to wear his uniform (see fig. 2.1). During World War II, Robert was too old to be on the frontlines, but he was involved nonetheless.

In World War I, Robert, like many other young men of his day, was a frontline soldier. In my postmemory imaginings of Robert, I picture him, like

---

14. Eshun, "Further Considerations on Afrofuturism," 287.

FIGURE 2.1. The author's German great-grandfather, Robert, in his World War I German military uniform. He is first on the right. Family photo, author's private collection, supplied by Greta.

most infantrymen on the front lines for Germany, fighting with poor equipment, little rest, little food, and inadequate shelter and living under the constant threat of death. However, the photograph in figure 2.1 challenges this postmemory since he is in a nice restaurant, waiting for food, and not dealing with, for the moment, inadequate shelter and poor equipment. The image does not signal military struggle but perhaps strength and hope for a German victory rather than German military defeat. Robert is the archetype of a soldier, sitting proudly with his unit, and I find myself putting him into these fixed categories of war. This image shows Robert as a successful soldier who appeared to be of higher rank simply because he was sitting around a fancy dinner table with other soldiers and not in the trenches digging ditches. He appears to have food and shelter and carries himself with confidence. This image, however, shows one static point of being, and memory and postmemory tell of others.

I wonder how Robert felt after the war, after Germany lost, after Germany lost its colonies on the continent in Africa, and after Black colonial soldiers came to occupy Germany. Was Robert outraged by what most of the white Western world saw as Black foreign occupation in a "white" nation? Did Robert believe in and support white supremacy? Was Robert fueled by the racist proclamations made by Hitler and the Third Reich? Did Robert have any inkling about what it might be like to be Black, to be a Black German and be under Hitler? My guess is that Robert, like millions of other white people, bought into a so-called white superiority and never considered what it was like to be Black in Germany. The next section of this chapter examines what it was like to be Black and under Hitler and the Third Reich in order to better situate how Albert lived as a Black American GI, in Germany, fighting for the Allied side and the US military that imported Jim Crow to Germany.

BEING BLACK UNDER HITLER

Hitler was elected in 1932 with 37 percent of the German vote. To Greta and millions of other Germans, Hitler symbolized a memoried moment of redemption, a way to erase or forget the humiliation of defeat. For Austrian-born Hitler, who fought for Germany in World War I, Germany's World War I defeat and occupation by African French colonial troops evoked a fear, he said, that "every n—— might accidentally shoot me to bits."[15] Fear inflamed his hatred and radical patriotism, which likely jumpstarted his path toward prescriptive forgetting. This "prescriptive forgetting" of the World War I defeat allowed Germany, through the election of Hitler, to "discard memories that serve[d] no practicable purpose in the management of one's current identity and ongoing purposes."[16] For Germany, this allowed for a reinvigoration of patriotism to burst forth and, as Clarence Lusane finds, a "national redemption and reassertion of Aryan might—a manifest destiny of the worst kind"[17] The German defeat in World War I and the Treaty of Versailles, coupled with economic issues, joblessness, and the depression, were aspects of German society that were exploited and weaponized by the Nazis, as it was the common workers who, as Lewis argues, "had opposed the war in the first place."[18] Opposition to war did not mean that the common workers were not racist. On the contrary, fanning the flames of racism and blame was rather easy in a country that had white supremacy, anti-Semitism, and anti-Black racism as part of its memoried and historical foundation. Therefore, an assessment of the racial ideology of the Nazi regime is important to an examination of violence imposed on Black German bodies during the Nazi era, and any attempt, as Lusane aptly notes, "to dismiss the anti-Blackness character of Nazism and the subjugation

---

15. Lusane, *Hitler's Black Victims*, 79.
16. Connerton, "Seven Types of Forgetting," 63.
17. Lusane, *Hitler's Black Victims*, 3.
18. Lewis, *W. E. B. Du Bois*, 736.

of its black victims is a historical whitewashing."[19] Understanding Germany from 1933 to 1945 as a fundamentally racialized state is essential in evaluating the Nazi regime. Recognizing the anti-Black components of the Nazi regime helps explain how Black Germans living in Germany after the First World War were used to mobilize the Aryan project.

The Nazi regime had several options when figuring out what to do with the very small population of Black German people.[20] Black Germans were part of German society for hundreds of years (see chapter 1) and were allowed to attend schools and universities (in roles as students and instructors), whereas Jewish and Romani people were not afforded these opportunities. Similarly, Black Germans were allowed to work, whereas Jewish and Romani people were not, and Black Germans were integrated into general life in Germany. However, the integration into German life did not mean equality for Black Germans; rather, this so-called integration allowed for survival in particular sanctioned areas in the face of violent racism. For example, according to Lusane, on June 21, 1933, a Black German and "anti-Nazi labor organizer, performing artist, and communist,"[21] Hilarius "Lari" Gilges, was murdered. Similar to the murder of Emmett Till, whose body was found floating in the Tallahatchie River in Mississippi twenty-two years later in 1955, Gilges's body was found "in the luminous and buoyant blue waters of the Rhine . . . , brutalized and battered . . . under the Rhine bridge,"[22] floating as a visual signifier of *ein Volk* racial purity and power.

As viewed through Hitler and the Third Reich's propagandistic claims of racial purity, Black Germans were alien to the nation-state. Similar to Black Americans living in the United States, Black Germans were viewed as inferior to white Germans and treated as a monolith, but unlike in the US, there was "no black racial community formed during these early years." While Black German people may have seen themselves as a diverse community, "an Afro-German community failed to appear. . . . There was no social ground on which a racial community of Afro-Germans could be established—culturally, politically, socially, or economically."[23] Thus their segregated liminal existence

---

19. Lusane, *Hitler's Black Victims*, 3.
20. There are no official population numbers of Black Germans, but the best guess is that fewer than 1 percent of the population was Black given that there were only "several thousand Black Germans from the continent of Africa . . . Caribbean, South America and the United States . . . present in Germany" during its imperial/colonial era. In 2019 there were nearly "one million Black people living in Germany," which is only about 1.2 percent of the population. See Aitken, "Making Visible the Invisible."
21. Lusane, *Hitler's Black Victims*, 3.
22. Lusane, *Hitler's Black Victims*.
23. Lusane, *Hitler's Black Victims*, 32–33.

remained. Hitler joined the US Jim Crow laws with the Nuremberg Laws, most evidently by mirroring the US "one drop rule." Hitler's blood purity insistence and perversion was also embraced by Italy, Portugal, and Spain (which had blood purity precepts in place in the city of Toledo as early as 1449).[24] While these blood purity tests were overtly directed toward the Jewish community, covertly, the laws of blood purity, citizenship, and marriage (similar to US antimiscegenation laws) were also applied to Black Germans. Black Germans were like Black Americans in that they wanted to prove their loyalty and patriotism and to fight for their equality via military service. However, military service looked very different under Hitler. As Lusane reminds us, "Africans had a long history of participation in the German military," but the May 21, 1935, "Compulsory Service Act . . . technically limited military service to those of Aryan origin with certain exceptions allowed."[25]

Why would Hitler largely limit Black German men from fighting in World War II? Because military service involves sacrifice, commitment, patriotism, and seeing oneself as the protector of one's country. Military service is a way marginalized people can write themselves into the place, space, land, and memory of a nation, which was the antithesis of Hitler's desires for a nation he crafted as solely Aryan. Whether they volunteered or were conscripted, there were Black German men who fought for Germany in World War I—a fact German citizens conveniently forgot while they virulently complained about Black French African soldiers left in the country after World War I. Germany had Black veterans, but as a whole, it is fair to conclude that Black Germans were persecuted in the name of white supremacy, and even if fleeing Germany was one option, most Black Germans, according to Lusane, "had their passport seized and were declared stateless."[26]

The United States had little to no ability to claim a higher moral ground given the US history of enslavement, Black Codes, sharecropping, and Jim Crow.[27] In fact, Lusane points out, "Hitler would later send a delegation of

---

24. Lusane, *Hitler's Black Victims*, 107.

25. Helmut Krausnick and Martin Broszat, *Anatomy of the SS State*, cited in Lusane, *Hitler's Black Victims*, 113.

26. Lusane, *Hitler's Black Victims*, 99.

27. Black Codes and Jim Crow laws applied specifically to Black Americans and enormously limited their civil rights after the Emancipation Proclamation in 1863. Black Codes (1865–66) were in response to the Fourteenth Amendment, which ended legal slavery in the US. Jim Crow laws made Black Codes legal. Jim Crow laws legalized segregation between Black people and white people, and challenging Jim Crow resulted in a range of punishments, including death. Among other things, Jim Crow laws enforced separate entrances and segregated education, public events, places, sporting events, and voting rights, which Black Americans were not fully able to exercise until 1965, with the passage of the Voting Rights Act. See Blumberg, *Civil Rights*; and C. Vann Woodward, *Strange Career of Jim Crow*.

Nazis to the United States to study the policies of racial segregation against African Americans for the purpose of implementing them against German Jews."[28] Anti-Blackness was part of the Nazi regime that worked concurrently with its anti-Semitic, anti-LGBTQ, anti-disability, anti-Romani, anti-Slavic, and anti–Jehovah's Witnesses positions. All of which were on display in Hitler's 1925 *Mein Kampf.* For Black Germans, this meant that a thin veneer of tolerance was established rather than any attempt at wholesale genocide like that which was eventually enacted against Jewish people.

Black German boys and teens were forbidden to join groups like the Hitler Jugend Gruppe (Hitler Youth Group), barring local or isolated circumstances or forced enrollment, as Black German Hans Massaquoi documented, and this same proscription affected Black German girls and teens.[29] Black German women under Hitler and the Nazi regime suffered through the double bind of racism and sexism. Blackness was weaponized against Black German girls, teens, and women because they were seen as one of the greatest threats to the German idea of *ein Volk.*

The greatest asset a white German woman could bring to the nation-state was her ability to reproduce and bear children in the furtherance of the Aryan nation. There was no glorification of Black women's wombs, because they were mothers of a Black future Hitler could not allow. The fear of a Black Europe was prominent and central in the mind of Hitler and the Third Reich, and he used this as a strategy to engage in governmental policing of Black bodies, which functioned as another form of state-sponsored eugenics in which Black German women and their children had no value at all to the state's vision of society. Black German and mixed-race German children had to be removed from the national populace. Therefore, Black German girls and women were forbidden from joining groups like the Hitler Maidens and Bund Deutscher Mädel (Association of German Girls), which celebrated white womanhood and white motherhood, and, thus, Aryan heredity as the first and primary requirement (see fig. 2.2).

As noted, my *oma*, Greta, was a member of the Hitler Maidens. Racist stereotypes guided her formative thoughts about race and racism, and Greta came to understand Black people through public memory, static images, and symbol use and misuse. When speaking about symbols and architectural structures, David Jacobson's argument is apt: "Because such symbols and monuments arrange 'place,' locating and orienting peoples spatially and temporally, and

---

28. Lusane, *Hitler's Black Victims*, 95.
29. Hans Massaquoi was the former managing editor of *Ebony* magazine and originally from Hamburg, Germany. He documented his experience as a Black German who was also in the Hitler Jugend Gruppe in his book *Destined to Witness: Growing Up Black in Nazi Germany* (1999).

FIGURE 2.2. A parade featuring members of the Bund Deutscher Mädel followed by the Hitler Jugend Gruppe, ca. 1933–39, in what is believed to be Germany. Used with permission from the United States Holocaust Memorial Museum, Photo Archives #63939, courtesy of Mrs. John Titak III.

are critical in binding and mediating the body politic . . . they determine who 'belongs' to the nation and on what terms."[30] This visual orientation of Black Germans means that once objectified and removed from society, like statues and monuments, they can be razed from existence. Germany was haunted by these Black faces in German places. With her foundational education in race cemented by the Nazi regime's indoctrination, it is stunning that Greta would eventually fall in love with Albert, but it is less surprising that she would later view her twin daughters and her granddaughter, me, as "mistakes," because our existence challenged the cultural brainwashing she was subjected to. Greta would have been conditioned to feel shame and embarrassment for having a familial relationship with someone of color.

World War II: Albert's Composite Narrative in Postmemory

I wondered if Albert and Robert ever crossed paths in World War II since they were on opposite sides: Albert on the Allied side and Robert on the Axis side. Since Albert enlisted in the army two months after the bombing of Pearl

---

30. Jacobson, *Place and Belonging in America*, 128.

Harbor, it appears that he responded to the call for soldiers in the same way Robert most likely did, full of a sense of patriotic duty, though in Albert's case, the boot of white supremacy and terrorism was already standing on his neck. It must be noted that engaging in military service was one way of being part of the civil rights movement for African Americans. Other Black Americans who did not choose to enlist, who were not drafted, or who were women and not part of segregated medical units, fought for Black American civil rights at home. They actively put into practice the two-pronged approach of the Double Victory campaign, Victory Abroad and Victory at Home. In attempting to fill in the gaps of Albert's military life, I imagine him as a soldier ready to fight and actively engage in this campaign. As we know, he apparently fought with valor since he was a Bronze Star Medal recipient. This was likely Albert's way of engaging with the civil rights movement, and in particular the Double Victory campaign.

"Abroad" meant fighting for a Europe free from the Third Reich and Hitler, and "at home" meant fighting for a US free from Jim Crow. This social justice movement was a clever way to lobby for Black American support of and participation in the war while simultaneously protesting racism and white supremacy in their own backyard as well as an Afrofuturistic way to reimagine Black lives in overtly heroic terms. White America needed Black American involvement, and Franklin D. Roosevelt (FDR) helped fuel this Black reimagining when he issued Executive Order 8802 on June 25, 1941, which banned "discriminatory employment practices by Federal agencies and all unions and companies engaged in war-related work. The order also established the Fair Employment Practices Commission to enforce the new policy."[31] To Black Americans, Roosevelt's executive order added legitimacy to their Afrofuturistic vision. Internationally, England did not believe the US would involve and use Black American soldiers in the war, and when they did, British officials, as Hervieux notes, "asked the Americans to keep their black troops at home," as did Alaska (which was still a territory), Australia, Bermuda, Hawaii (also still a territory), Iceland, Liberia, Panama, and Venezuela."[32] England claimed that they were "worried about violent reactions from white southern soldiers if Negroes were welcomed with dignity."[33] The US War Department ignored all requests to *not* bring Black American men into the war except in one instance in the British colony of Trinidad, "where black troops were replaced with Puerto Ricans after the British complained that the black

---

31. "Executive Order 8802."
32. Hervieux, *Forgotten*, 164.
33. Hervieux, *Forgotten*, 164.

Americans' 'self-assurance' would influence the islanders."[34] It must be noted that the Puerto Rican replacements in this case were likely not Afro Latino but rather Puerto Rican men who were not considered Black. When the US War Department ignored the majority of these requests, despite the military being segregated, it allowed Black Americans to dream that through their participation in yet another war, this would finally be the demise of Jim Crow. To add further validity to their Afrofuturistic vision, many British citizens, even though their government asked the US to keep Black soldiers at home, found the US Jim Crow policy "alien" and discriminatory; they objected to the segregated, servile, and racist treatment of Black American soldiers and "took the side of the black GIs."[35]

However, Executive Order 8802 was no match for the institutionalized racist framework within the US and within the military itself. The US military commanders' white supremacist stance trickled down through all the ranks of the military, where Jim Crow festered and flourished. Jim Crow formed the place where two legally separated Americas existed in one country: one privileged world for white Americans and one oppressed world for Black Americans. Geographically, soldiers may have been in Europe and Germany, but in reality, they were situated between two white supremacist regimes, neither of which was fair or equitable to Black people. Despite the facade of US patriotism through which the US military tried to sell the war to Black Americans, often through the Black press, Black American bodies were still inscribed with the mark of dehumanization, and wearing a military uniform was no protection.

All this violence against Black American bodies was just what Germany had hoped for since Germany's propaganda campaign took advantage of Jim Crow and further weaponized US racism in an effort to bifurcate and implode the army from within. According to Colley, "Propaganda Minister Joseph Goebbels threatened to stir up trouble in the United States. 'Nothing will be easier than to produce a bloody revolution in America. No other country has as many social and racial tensions. We shall be able to play on many strings there.'"[36] In this aspect, Goebbels was correct. It is this US hypocrisy of saving Europe from Hitler and the Third Reich while at the same time oppressing Black Americans that Germany used to its needed advantage. The Third Reich mirrored US forms of terrorism against the Black American soldiers they captured, which included executions and lynching, as is most popularly recounted with the 333rd Field Artillery Battalion, whose slaughter during

---

34. Hervieux, *Forgotten*, 164.
35. Hervieux, *Forgotten*, 164.
36. Colley, *Blood for Dignity*, 128.

the Battle of the Bulge has been overshadowed by the Malmedy Massacre—in which eighty-four American POWs were gunned down—in the memoried retelling of one of the most famous battles of the war. The 333rd, an all-Black unit supporting the 106th Division, was overrun by the 1st SS Panzer Division. Eleven soldiers of the 333rd managed to escape and hid on a farm that the soldiers stumbled upon after hours of trudging through cold and deep snow in Wereth, Belgium. The soldiers were later found, and they surrendered the only two weapons between all eleven of them to the 1st SS Panzer Division. After surrendering, the soldiers in the 333rd were tortured, eventually told to run, and were gunned down while fleeing.[37] As Chávez notes regarding white hegemonic nation-states, "genocide, lynching, the plantation, the reservation, the ghetto, the [imprisonment] camp, the prison, the hospital, the quarantine, ban, or deportation[,] fundamentally, those with inalienable rights have the power to alienize; those without them do not."[38]

Wanting to exclude Black American men from war, but needing to use them in war theaters nonetheless, there are very few images of Black American soldiers going into German enemy territory because, as Maria Höhn and Martin Klimke find, "military officials . . . took pains to avoid circulating photos portraying black men poised to fire weapons or commanding tanks because such images presented a threat to the existing social order based on white supremacy."[39] Seeing Black American GIs with weapons might legitimize the Afrofuturistic view of Black masculinity and simultaneously, by default, challenge white supremacist Jim Crow.

Three exceptions to the missing images of Black American GIs with weapons include the famed Tuskegee Airmen, the 761st Tank Battalion, and the 92nd Infantry Division. On April 11, 1945, Black troops, specifically the 761st Tank Battalion and the 183rd Engineer Combat Battalion, liberated the Buchenwald concentration camp, and on April 29, 1945, the 761st Tank Battalion liberated the Dachau concentration camp. However, there are no US Army records noting this heroism, and thus their presence is under dispute. However, the voices of the survivors remain. Nobel laureate and Buchenwald survivor Elie Wiesel shares this: "The most moving movement of my life was the day the Americans arrived, a few hours after the SS had fled. It was the morning of April 11. I will always remember with love a big black soldier. He was crying like a child—all the pain in the world and all the rage. Everyone who was there that day will forever feel a sentiment of gratitude to the American

---

37. See Colley, *Blood for Dignity*, 128; see also Michaels, "Emerging from History."
38. Chávez, *Borders of AIDS*, 9.
39. Höhn and Klimke, *Breath of Freedom*, 29.

FIGURE 2.3. The US 92nd Infantry Division in battle near Massa, Italy, during World War II. Public domain image, ca. November 1944. US Army, National Archives, National Archives Identifier: 535546. Local Identifier: 208-AA-47U-6, https://catalog.archives.gov/id/535546.

soldiers who liberated us."[40] Gunter Jacobs, another Buchenwald survivor, said, "The first Black people I ever saw in my life were the black soldiers who liberated us on April 11, 1945."[41] Like the Black soldiers who came before them, whose labor and sacrifice went unseen and unacknowledged, forty-seven years later, these soldiers were finally recognized by the Anti-Defamation League in 1992 for their contributions to liberating these concentration camps.

On April 5 and 6, 1945, near Viareggio, Italy, the 92nd Infantry, as Johnston recounts, "destroyed several machine-gun emplacements" and machine-gun nests, navigated mine fields and enemy fire, killed or wounded enemy soldiers, and saved wounded 92nd Infantry GIs[42] (see fig. 2.3). These military engagements on the battlefield and visual documentation of them add to the narrative that Black American soldiers were engaging the enemy, even in light of

---

40. Milloy, "Liberators Worth Seeing," para. 16–17.
41. Lusane, *Hitler's Black Victims*, 176.
42. Johnston, *My Father's War*, 154.

the minimization of these contributions in the mainstream press and by the US military itself. The 92nd Infantry Division, according to Bultman, "earned more than 12,000 decorations and citations including two Medals of Honor."[43] The Tuskegee Airmen, the 761st Tank Battalion, and the 92nd Infantry Division are instrumental in driving forward the Afrofuturistic narrative of those Black American soldiers serving during the war. They breathed further life into the Double Victory campaign and other civil rights movements of the time. They created new images of action and bravery that were seen around the world, thereby overtly challenging white racist propaganda of so-called Black inferiority as these Black soldiers claimed their place not only in the war but also in courage and heroism. They commanded the gaze of white racists (military and otherwise) who then had to retreat into their false racist narratives to justify the continuance of Jim Crow. In other words, racists redoubled their efforts in the maintenance of Jim Crow and so-called white supremacy, and they ignored military successes gained by Black GIs.

Perhaps in remembering the feeling of being unwanted by white culture generally, and white US commanding officers specifically, Black American GIs often focused on building cross-cultural understanding with German children, and this included postwar Black German children. Many mediated campaigns about *afrodeutsche Nachkriegskinder,* run variously by the German government, the Catholic Children's Home, and US journalist Mabel Grammer, were directed at Black American veterans. The ads targeted toward Black Americans in some cases encouraged Black GIs to come back for their own children, and other wildly popular marketing campaigns focused on building Black families and providing homes for these unwanted Black German children. To get the word to as many potentially qualified adoptive families as possible, Grammer used the full force of the NAACP and Black American media outlets to help cover stories about these biracial children needing homes—coverage appeared in African American newspapers like the Baltimore *Afro-American,* where Grammer worked, and the covers of *Ebony* and *Jet* magazines. Such adoptions of *afrodeutsche Nachkriegskinder* took place beginning in 1945 and tapered off in 1955. Lilli and Lore were adopted in 1960 by a member of the 92nd Infantry Division, and I met him twice (once when I was six months old and once when I was fourteen years old). This World War II veteran would later be the person who emotionally and physically abused Lilli and Lore. I wonder if Albert and this soldier who adopted the twins ever crossed paths in Germany. If Albert could have somehow altered the course of his life, would he have made it so this abusive soldier would have

---

43. Bultman, "Remembering the Service," para 7.

never adopted Lilli and Lore? In my postmemory imagining of Albert, I would like to believe he would have somehow donned the superhero cape he wore during the war and protected the girls. If Albert could help liberate entire nations, why not his own daughters? If he had lived longer, if he had made other choices or even been in control of some of the options afforded to him, could he have manipulated the institutionalized system of white racism and, coupled with his own actions, as hooks suggests, "open[ed] up the possibility of agency"?[44]

Underneath the surface of public memory are Black soldiers like Albert who operate in postmemory spaces as Afrofuturistic ghosts, where they challenge their positionality and the fixed categories and limitations white supremacy placed on them. As I came to know Albert through the historical/memoried documentation of aspects of his military career, I knew one small aspect about him. My postmemory imaginations of him, on the other hand, as soldier, lover, and absent father, offer a fuller representation of a man I came to know only through Greta. On opposite ends of the spectrum sit two soldiers in liminality, two soldiers I am related to: Albert on one end and Robert on the other, both ghosts haunting what we think we know about the soldier's experience in war and the reality we can never quite know. This similar complication of personhood is found in Robert and in his German soldier's experience in World War II.

World War II: Robert's Composite Narrative in Postmemory

By the time Germany became involved in World War II, Robert was too old to be a combat soldier in Hitler's Third Reich. Instead, according to Greta, Robert was a train engineer. He was one of the men who drove Jewish, Romani, Black German, sexual minority, and disabled people and their Nazi jailers, torturers, and murderers to concentration camps. In German, there is a phrase, *Erinnerungskultur*, which means "culture of remembrance." *Erinnerungskultur* is a strictly confined societal code of conduct related to what aspects of history are to be remembered. Firmly situated in a memoried approach, *Erinnerungskultur* chooses what can be remembered from the past, in what ways, and how that affects the present. This makes the act of remembering an active response to history because remembrance means exactly that, looking back upon a situation and reflecting in a way the hegemonic hierarchy (those in power) allow. My engagement with *Erinnerungskultur* pushes the boundary

---

44. hooks, "Oppositional Gaze," 116.

FIGURE 2.4. The author's great-grandfather, Robert. Family photo, author's private collection, supplied by Greta.

of the term and German cultural memory since I am actively resisting erasure—what *Erinnerungskultur* left behind. My instances of engaging, exposing, and bringing to light an imagined space of being, a postmemory space, is the antithesis of *Erinnerungskultur* because I am trying to understand Robert beyond his role as a soldier. How do I begin to imagine Robert in this memoried and postmemoried space when there is little left of him to remember (see fig. 2.4)? Robert-as-a-person conflates with my imaginings about who he might have been in juxtaposition to the space he occupied in German military history. Beneath the surface of the World War I photographs I have of Robert, I learned from Greta, there is another Robert, and the image of Robert as a representation of a successful soldier fades as a more complicated image of him as husband, father, and alcoholic emerges.

Before and after World War II, Robert was an inconsistent presence who would slip in and out of his family's life. Robert and Hermine (my great-grandmother) eventually separated, but this too was an inconsistent marital arrangement. "He drank too much, [but] he came home periodically after binge drinking, in an attempt to win my mother and family back," said Greta. According to Greta, her youngest sister was the "reconciliation baby," but after a while, the drinking resumed. Therefore, Hermine made a very bold move and sought a divorce before the onset of World War II.

Hermine's filing for divorce was unique not only because my family were practicing Catholics but also because women during that time (regardless of religious status) rarely had the ability to exercise their right for one. According to Greta, Hermine cited American cultural influence related to gender norms as a reason why the divorce was justified. American cultural influences from both World War I and World War II allowed German women to see a different way of being in the world. American dating and marital relationships, compared to German dating and marital relationships, were more equalitarian. Gendered rules and norms are dynamic, yet Hitler's authoritarian grip over all propaganda attempted to control women and their own ideas about their identities. Hitler attempted to limit women's multifaceted gender identities to patriarchal notions of being a wife and mother for the nation-state above all else.

Hitler created financial incentives for German people to marry, including marriage loans, financial subsidies for large families, education of children, and "removal of tax burdens,"[45] as Clifford Kirkpatrick notes. In 1933 Hitler passed the Law for the Encouragement of Marriage, which gave newlyweds an interest-free loan of 1,000 Reichsmarks (which equaled US$305 in 1933), of which 250 Reichsmarks (US$16.22 in 1933) could be kept for each child born.[46] However, in 1938 Germany passed the Marriage Law of 1938, which made it easier for men to make claims of divorce. Women also found their voice in the law, even if that was not the original intent, and one of those women was my great-grandmother Hermine. The marriage law is written and geared toward white German men. For example, according to the BBC's "Life for Women and the Family in Nazi Germany," "if a man already had 4 children with a woman, he had the right to divorce her so he could remarry and have more children. Couples could also divorce if they were childless or after three years' separation."[47] While this portion of the law was clearly written for men, Hermine took advantage of it since she met some of the criteria: she had three (not four) white German children, she and Robert were separated, and their separation likely accumulated to three or more years. She had the toxic environment of alcoholism to bolster her argument, and the claim of desertion could have been leveled considering the on-again, off-again seesawing of the marital relationship.

In an effort to reimagine the forgotten details of my great-grandparent's marital relationship, I wonder what their marriage was like as a couple before

---

45. Kirkpatrick, "Recent Changes," 654.
46. "Life for Women," para. 2.
47. "Life for Women," para. 6.

the impact of war. Was Robert an alcoholic before or after the war? If Robert's drinking was a result of war, then perhaps his alcoholism was due to post-traumatic stress syndrome (PTSS, more commonly referred to as PTSD). If so, his traumatic war experiences are yet another thread of my postmemory inheritance, another trauma passed down through generations while largely erased from the official record.

I imagine Robert engaging in and confronting unspeakable and unimaginable horrors during the war. As an echo of a memory, I tried to imagine Robert's ghostly presence hobbling around with visual and physical signs of war wounds like many other mutilated survivors, but his war wounds were psychological and invisible and were likely expressed through depression and alcoholism.

Because Robert was divorced and removed from the family, Greta said, "I don't know what happened to him." Greta had no knowledge of where he lived, how he lived after the expulsion from the family, how he died, or where he was buried. The opaqueness of his presence haunted Greta, who told me, "I loved my father. I was much closer to him than my mother." Learning of Robert's existence, and in particular his role in World War II, haunts me but for very different reasons from Greta. Greta felt the absence of a beloved parent. I, on the other hand, often wonder if he would have accepted and embraced the twins knowing their father was a US soldier of color. Would he have rejected them? What I do know is that in my postmemory imagining of Robert, his body is the visual signifier of national defeat.

SOLDIER OUTSIDER: WAR AND RACISM

One aspect of war, any war, is marketing, and I often wonder if the outcomes for Albert and Robert—loss of family, racism, and war trauma—were worth it for each of them. Like the Black French colonial soldiers stationed in Germany after World War I, Black American soldiers became the visual signifier of German defeat and a challenge to the German conception of *Heimat* (homeland), once cast as the land of *ein Volk*, a place for white racial purity and power. In shifting the signifier of defeat onto the backs of Black people, West Germany was pushed to deny its Nazi past and move toward Americanized, Jim Crow democracy.

In light of the Nazi defeat, was Robert no longer proud? Was he ashamed? Was he a racist? Was he anti-Semitic? Would he have driven people to concentration camps were it not his assigned military position? Or did organizations like Gesellschaft für Christlich-Jüdische Zusammenarbeit (Society for Christian-Jewish cooperation) that sprung up to fight anti-Semitism, racism, and white supremacy resonate with him as Germany moved toward a US model of democracy and citizens imagined a new future for Germany without Hitler and the Third Reich?

Based on my interviews with Greta, Albert was a patriotic man, yet he saw how racism and Jim Crow became even more entrenched as he fought to liberate Europe from Nazi Germany. For example, in 1946 "military governor General Joseph McNarney declared that it would take 100 years for Negroes to attain the developmental level of whites."[48] Also in 1946, in Auerbach, Germany, Black GIs according to Heide Fehrenbach "were quartered in barracks that recently housed German prisoners of war. Surrounded by barbed wire fences, the barracks had been neither cleaned nor upgraded after the German POWs were vacated. The black troops entered a filthy, garbage-filled, louse-ridden compound with overflowing, noxious latrines, and no electricity or bathing facilities. . . . African American troops were assigned to live literally amidst German shit."[49] And in 1947, "Ernest Harmon, commander of the Constabulary, informed his cheering audience of all-white soldiers . . . that sending 'colored soldiers' to Europe had been 'America's stupidest mistake' and . . . warned the government not to send any 'N——s' because they had now become 'a much bigger problem than the Germans.'"[50] Even the KKK crossed the Atlantic Ocean and filled the gap by putting down roots where Nazism had once existed. However, after twelve years under the stench of Nazi rule, and then witnessing the US racist segregation and Jim Crow policies, Germany had willing participants who promoted the exotic otherness of Black American soldiers, similar to that of the Black Magi from long ago.

As they watched their Afrofuturistic visions fade, Black American GIs were often referred to as "chocolate soldiers" by Germans, and not just because they shared food rations, including the rare treat of chocolate, with starving Germans. *Schokoladensoldaten* was also a deprecating racist reference to their brown phenotypic hue. I wonder if Albert was called a "chocolate soldier." I wonder if Albert would have equated "chocolate soldier" with the dehumanizing "boy," which he, like many other Black American men, would have been called during Jim Crow at some point in time in the US. The playful-sounding "chocolate" still signaled a second-class existence, and it echoed the memoried reality of those who could be consumed by violence in the continuation and advancement of white supremacy. Greta, on the other hand, saw chocolate as a fact of survival, saying, "We were starving. Albert gave me things like chocolate and stockings and was nicer than the German soldiers."

---

48. Höhn and Klimke, *Breath of Freedom*, 41.
49. Fehrenbach, *Race after Hitler*, 28.
50. Höhn and Klimke, *Breath of Freedom*, 41.

The US continued its segregationist policies through the celebration of V-E (Victory in Europe) Day on May 8, 1945, and V-J (Victory over Japan) Day on August 14, 1945, marked by the iconic image of a white American soldier kissing a white American nurse in New York City. In a postwar interview with Black GIs in 1945, even with all of the racism and other challenges they faced in Germany, an Army Service Forces Technical Intelligence Report found that "40 percent of those interviewed, expressed a desire to remain overseas"[51] since they already knew what racial caste system awaited them back home. Trezzant Anderson further found that "37 percent of the men in the famed 761st Tank Battalion decided to extend their tour of duty."[52] For future Black army enlistees, their place of choice to be stationed was Europe, where "a whopping 85 percent of black enlistees in 1946 requested a posting,"[53] as Höhn and Klimke note. This phenomenon suggests that Black GIs sought to redefine themselves and their future through an existence, place, and space of their choosing. This Black agency provoked a sense of panic in both Germany and the United States as soldiers challenged their positionality in these international places and spaces. There was no question that Black American soldiers occupied two planes of liminal existence. On one plane, they had to consider how they saw themselves in Germany and how they existed in Germany, where racial segregation was made illegal in 1949. On another plane, they had to deal with the liminal existence of their potential or perhaps inevitable return to the US. These Black American GIs were forced to engage with the constant push and pull of negotiating how they had existed in the US, how they existed in Germany, and how they would exist again upon return to the United States. No wonder Albert stayed in Germany for three years after the war: even though Germany did not outlaw segregation until after he left, he was still in a better position as a Black man in Germany than in the US, and thus he, like many other Black American GIs, delayed being thrust back into the Jim Crow USA and the racist regressions that country offered.

President Truman tried to address segregation in the US military on July 26, 1948, with Executive Order 9981, which "abolish[ed] segregation in the armed forces and order[ed] full integration of all the services: 'there shall be equality of treatment and opportunity for all persons in the armed forces without regard to race, color, religion, or national origin.'"[54] However, US military bases ordered to desegregate adopted the slow-go pace of integration

---

51. Army Service Forces Technical Intelligence Report quoted in Höhn and Klimke, *Breath of Freedom*, 33.

52. Trezzant W. Anderson, "Germans Gradually Accepting Colored Occupational Troops" (*Pittsburgh Courier*, February 2, 1946, 13), quoted in Höhn and Klimke, *Breath of Freedom*, 53.

53. Höhn & Klimke, *Breath of Freedom*, 53.

54. "Executive Order 9981."

mandates happening elsewhere on American shores. Even after Soviet propaganda turned American racial hypocrisy into a consistent embarrassment, forcing the Department of the Army to more actively push integration of US troops in Europe, white GIs used anti-Black tactics to maintain a functionally segregated German experience for Black and white troops.[55] Cultivating Jim Crow like a prized plant that needs tending in a garden, the US military, despite Truman's order, took from 1948 to 1954 to complete the mandated desegregation orders. According to Fehrenbach, this "meant that for the entire period of military occupation (1945–49), and throughout most of the High Commission in Germany (1949–55), postfascist German society was democratized by a country whose institutions, social relations, and dominant cultural values were organized around the category of race and a commitment to white supremacy."[56] Under these conditions, Albert met my grandmother, Greta.

After World War II, Albert did not return to the US until 1948. Greta said that Albert was "a very proud man." I wonder if he still felt this pride when he left Germany after getting his girlfriend, Greta, pregnant. I wonder if Albert's story was among the many anonymous accounts I read while researching this project in which a Black American soldier came back to a nation that took no pride in their heroism but rather assaulted them with the reminder that they were back in Jim Crow USA. Albert got on a plane bound for the United States and found himself back home with his family in the Deep South. Was he as proud as Greta indicated? Did he walk taller and with his head held high when he returned? Did he now look white people in the eye? Did he now refuse to cross the street when a white person commanded the public sidewalk? Did he drink out of the water fountain or go through the door that was labeled "For Whites Only"? Did he wear his uniform around his town to the ire of white racists?

Almost all World War II soldiers ended up back in the US at some point. Albert was initially one of 1.6 million American troops in Germany, and even though he stayed in Germany for a time after the war, Albert made no documented attempt to see his twin daughters and no documented attempt to adopt his twin daughters. Albert's involvement in Lilli and Lore's lives is only one of absence. Lore said she remembers "being around two or three years old, at Mom's [Greta's] job, the Heidelberg Post Exchange, when I was held by a man in a military uniform. I was not passed around to anyone else, and this man held me for a long time. I think he was African American." Is her recollection accurate, or is it a postmemory creation willed into being by a child to fill in an absence? There were ninety-five thousand children born

---

55. See Höhn, *GIs and Fräuleins*.
56. Fehrenbach, *Race after Hitler*, 19.

in the postwar era in Germany, and many had no fathers. If their father was an American GI, the odds were even higher that children would never know or meet their biological fathers. This was not unusual. When soldiers are sojourners in a foreign land, sent there to do a temporary mission, they are expected to return home. Albert, a Bronze Star Medal recipient and a vibrant thirty-five-year-old, disappeared from Greta's life sometime in 1948, and five years later, in the United States, he died.

CONCLUSION: CLINGING TO THE RACIAL CASTE SYSTEM

Historical narratives tend to favor reductionist good-versus-evil narratives of the "greatest generation," as iconic US reporter Tom Brokaw dubbed it, but Albert and other soldiers of color in World War II effectively highlight the transnational history of the diplomatic and political relations that established legal structures of race and racism in the wake of World War II. This chapter has highlighted the inherent contradiction in war experiences between Albert and Robert but also showed the commonalities between their lived experiences, such as patriotism and familial absence. Both the US and German militaries shamelessly exploited a white supremacist system that reified racist power structures. In fact, Höhn argues that "twelve years after the end of the war German attitudes toward black GIs were far less uniformly friendly than they had been in 1945, when black soldiers had handed out Hershey bars and Lucky Strikes."[57] The entrenchment of the US racial caste system does not forget the historical, memoried, and sanctioned second-class position of Black Americans simply because of Black heroism and a German defeat in war, nor did Germany. Black American GIs quickly realized that they liberated Europe from Hitler and the Third Reich yet were unable to free themselves from the unrelenting US racial caste system.

Even when the US transferred Jim Crow to Germany, World War II allowed Black Americans a sense of imagined freedom they had never before experienced. The time Black American GIs spent in Germany, as Höhn reflects, enraged white "Southern segregationists [who] were appalled at what was happening in Germany [and] threatened that African Americans would have to be reined in upon their return to the United States. . . . Numerous returning GIs were in fact lynched as white southerners tried to reverse the empowerment African American men had gained abroad."[58] Black people may

---

57. Höhn, *GIs and Fräuleins*, 222.
58. Höhn, "Love across the Color Line," 109.

not have been free from the inhibiting transnational white gaze, but as civil rights movements in the US against Jim Crow gained more support nationally and internationally, Black GIs in Germany kept up their Afrofuturistic vision through vehemently protesting Jim Crow on US military bases and in the German towns that surrounded them, staging lunch counter sit-ins in parallel with those that were happening in the southern US and coordinating "with German students who had spent time in the United States and with African American students studying at German universities to propagate the goals [of the US civil rights] movement,"[59] as Höhn and Klimke relate. In challenging the currency of race and the absoluteness of white supremacy, Black GIs put into practice an Afrofuturistic challenge to the fixed "racialization of space,"[60] as Pile terms it, since they attempted to dismantle the white supremacist performance that white culture is rooted in. Globally, the US fixation with Jim Crow was broadly seen as out-of-step for a nation founded on democracy and freedom. It meant the whole world was watching, and the youth of a country once strangled by Hitler and the Third Reich were reengaging with the Western world in this social justice cause.

By the time World War II ended, Greta was twenty-three years old, and her notions of race and Blackness would have been shaped by another round of foreign occupation and another shift in the discourse of race, gender, sexuality, and citizenship. Was Greta moved by some of these social justice actions aimed at dismantling the importation of Jim Crow in Germany? After her membership with the Hitler Maidens, what was the cognitively dissonant moment that allowed her to fall in love with the enemy, a Black American GI? Through my postmemory lens, I have difficulty imagining that she saw Albert as simply "a person," based on her indoctrination in white racism. While I wish I could write that my *oma* was swept up in love and saw her relationship with Albert as one she could throw back in the face of racist ideologies in both Germany and the US, in reality, as I came to know, Greta was a very practical woman. She was not a civil rights protester. Her love of Albert likely bloomed on account of pragmatism—a pragmatism she expressed when she said he was "nicer than the German soldiers" and was able to fulfill exigent and luxury needs like "food, chocolate, and stockings." As I will show later in this book, particularly as it relates to interracial marriage, there were limits to Black American "freedoms" in Germany as well as limits to what an Afrofuturistic vision could accomplish in the face of white supremacist agency and power, whether enacted by the nation-state or my own grandmother.

---

59. Höhn and Klimke, *Breath of Freedom*, 3.
60. Pile, "Skin, Race, and Space."

CHAPTER 3

Womb Wars

*Interracial Relationships and the
Historical Construction of White German Identity*

Gebärmutterkrieg (womb wars). This notion is reminiscent of "Motherland Blitzkrieg." In times of war, women's identities are constructed against those of men, as their wartime labor takes center stage. Women's work, during and after war on the other hand, is reduced, erased, or invisible. In the history of German women (and here I am including the racist construction of Black German women), two types of forgetting are in effect: (1) structural amnesia (only remembering those aspects of a person that are deemed important) and (2) constitutive forgetting in the formation of a new identity (forgetting as a positive gain).[1] In both aspects of forgetting, an erasure occurs in that white German women's power, roles, and value become positioned only as in relation to their uterus, and Black German women were simply erased.

In haunted visions of the past, the identity of women during the war was related to the conservative whims of the nation-state (whether Imperial Germany, the Weimar Republic, or Hitler and the Third Reich), and in post–World War II democratic Germany, the US continued the white racist foundation and relied on Jim Crow and antimiscegenation laws they imported. White women's bodies were used as a defensive strategy to reify and firmly cement white men's power in the construction of womanhood and white women as the vessels of a white imagined Aryan future. Even when Germany lost World

---

1. Connerton, "Seven Types of Forgetting," 67.

War II, white supremacist transnationalism became mapped onto the bodies of white German women, since aspects of white supremacy flowed onto the women of this era, defying traditional concepts of borders and boundaries. Because of the transnationalism of white supremacy, the action of white racism and white hegemonic masculinity lives and breathes as an overt and dynamic expression cloaking and affecting all. Situated in a cost/loss or win/gain system that privileges some and oppresses most, the example in this chapter shows how racism, under the thin veil of neo-Victorianism in the protection of white womanhood, can live in a new way when given transnational oxygen. During and after World War II, German women had to face the cold, hard facts that white men would define what womanhood is and what being a woman means, regardless of any personal identity formation these women had prior to male decrees. This marking of white women's bodies made them nation-state property. In an ironic twist, Black presence in Germany, whether African colonial soldiers or Black American GIs, stoked and exposed German and white American soldiers' fears about Black male access to freedoms, white womanhood, and interracial coupling.

It is here where postmemory and Afrofuturism overlap as they relate to white women, because white women also needed to engage in creative imagining to survive, particularly when interracial coupling was involved. Since their bodies were also surveilled, German women's bodies showed the impact of the state in curtailing their choices and how the historical, societal, and transnational aspects of racism negatively affected all interracial couples, including Greta and Albert. Women involved in interracial relationships had to ponder how gendered agency is imagined outside of conservative forces committed to their oppression.

Problematized throughout this chapter are the relationships between race, gender, and the rights of the womb in Germany after both world wars. How have racism, sex, sexism, and notions of citizenship been intertwined throughout German history, generally, and during World War I and World War II in particular? During World War II, how were German women's bodies, specifically the maternal body, subjugated to the interests of the state? Did white German women during World War II have any rights over their wombs, or did governmental policing of interracial coupling function as another form of state-sponsored eugenics in the postwar era? German history did not develop in an isolated national arena but rather developed through international and local contradictions and pressures that gave specific meanings to notions of Germanness across different social positions and locations. Critical discourse analysis of German history from the colonial period through the foundation of the Western German Republic suggests that there is a complicated and often contradictory theory of the notion of Germanness that is intimately tied to notions of race, gender, sexuality, and citizenship and that has been rooted in a fundamentally anti-Black characteristic. There appears to be an unflinching continuity in the discursive positioning of white German women as the symbol of the German national body and the fact that the individual rights and interests of German women have regularly been placed beneath the interests of the state in consolidating a homogenous whiteness in the German citizenry. The statutory restrictions on German women's rights to their wombs in the Third Reich and during the processes of constructing a post-Nazi democratic Germany are analyzed to understand the continuities and breaks in constructing the German polis as essentially white. Ultimately, it is argued that different tactics of constituting Germanness as homogenously white come at the expense of German women's rights over their bodies.

POST-WORLD WAR I GERMANY, 1918–1933: JUSTIFYING ANTI-BLACKNESS IN GERMANY

Lora Wildenthal (1997) maintains that the bans on the rights of White German men to marry in the colonies first brought forward the notion that race is a relevant factor in defining the German political subject.[2] Colonial debates over interracial marriages linked notions of citizenship with race (whiteness) and utilized gender, sexuality, and colonialist discourses to establish the mixed-race child as an eminent threat to the purity of the German national body, which was understood to be essentially and wholly white. Even as some paternalistic gendered discourses proposed the ban on interracial marriage as a means to protect African women from white male colonial exploitation and to maintain the appropriate cultural barrier between "civilized" white Germans and the "uncivilized" Indigenous subject, other gendered and sexualized discourse drew from racialized notions of Indigenous female sexuality to construct Indigenous womanhood as a danger to the German national body.[3] While Imperial Germany did not resolve the debates in favor of banning interracial marriage, the debates legitimized anti-Blackness and were meant to stop any reimagining Black people had about themselves and within the German compact. According to Aitken, between "1897 and 1933 there is archival evidence of well over four dozen mixed marriages taking place. A new generation of Black Germans developed out of these as well as other, non-marital

---

2. Wildenthal, "Race, Gender, and Citizenship."
3. Campt "Converging Specters," 322–41.

relationships."⁴ These new postcolonial and post–World War I Black Germans were not accepted as German, and issues of who made up the polis continued, as "under the terms of German citizenship law both the wives and children of these men inherited their liminal status."⁵

After World War I, the presence of Black colonizing troops in Germany embodied a challenge to the idea of power and who had it, because the inversion of the hegemonic hierarchy, in the eyes of Germany, placed German troops on the bottom and African colonial troops at the top. As Campt argues, "the use of Black troops as a force of occupation in Germany in this way both reversed this relation and transgressed this sacred [whiteness] boundary."⁶ Rather than admit white German patriarchal defeat, propaganda campaigns about the imagined assault against white womanhood resounded across the country, attempting to clip any idea of Afrofuturistic envisioning before it even had a chance to fly. Germany weaponized racism into a propaganda rallying cry to deflect defeat and stoked white supremacist fear of the Black Other from all across Europe as well as the United States. In Germany military figures, social and political leaders, intellectual figures, and the press responded swiftly, and with vitriol, against the Black occupying forces and pushed a campaign, with near universal support, for a parliamentary petition that demanded the Allied occupied forces withdraw their Black troops from the Rhineland.⁷

To incite domestic and international panic over the use of Black occupying forces on German lands, Germany relied on propaganda and accused other European nations of threatening the so-called superior white race by erring toward racial parity. Under the white supremacist panopticon, the visual propaganda campaigns against Black troop occupation drew on another set of gendered, racialized, and sexual threat discourses to pose the specter of the mixing of races. In one news report, cooperation with Black troops was situated as a threat to larger European culture:

> What offends European sensibility in the use of black troops, is not their blackness, but rather the fact that savages are being used to oversee a cultured people. Whether these savages are totally black or dark brown or yellow makes no difference. The prestige of the European culture is in danger. That is what is at stake. And precisely those peoples, those such as England and France who are dependent upon the dominance they exercise over col-

---

4. Aitken, "Making Visible the Invisible."
5. Aitken, "Making Visible the Invisible."
6. Campt, "Converging Specters," 331–32.
7. Oguntoye et al., *Showing Our Colors*.

ored peoples, should consider that with the degradation of Germany in the eyes of the colored, they degrade the white race and with this, endanger their own prestige.[8]

German media campaigns against Black occupying troops initiated a shift in the discourse of race, from a focus on ethnic differences between Europeans toward a black/white binary that assumed an inherent white European cultural supremacy. White German men, stripped of the security of military prowess to protect their masculinity, attempted to invert their status through presenting the Allied cooperation with Black troops as the true loss of the First World War. While the above news report attempts to deny that skin color itself is relevant, it merely obscures it under the essentialist moniker of "culture." Culture, specifically civilization, is assumed to be an intrinsically white European asset that is only undermined through approximating social racial parity. Germans consolidated support, domestically and internationally, by positioning, as Campt notes, "Black troops as a common 'enemy' of all white nations, against whom they should unite and overcome their differences."[9] With the call to whiteness issued to the rest of Europe and the United States, Germany attempted to assert its authority through its construction of the German citizenry as fundamentally anti-Black in the preservation of an assumed white-dominated world, and it rested this argument upon the shoulders of white womanhood.

The transnational appeal of protecting white womanhood flowed easily between Germany and the United States due to their various antimiscegenation policies and practices. In both countries, white women were rhetorically constructed as being weak and in need of white male protection from corruption. In this sexist, neo-Victorian transnational cultural commonality, white women were restricted by the tenets of both possessive patriarchy and racism, and this was on display in both German and US propaganda. Through their whiteness and wombs, white women became property in the white hypermasculine rhetorical and literal construction of womanhood. In Germany, white women were frequently depicted as the vessels and the saviors of the Aryan people. In the US, white women, and the protection of ideal white womanhood, was rhetorically embodied in the Statue of Liberty, who was shown to be in need of protection from both Germans and Black men.

Before the end of World War I, the US circulated a racist visual signifier of its own, so the fear of Black men during and after the war, and the call to protect white womanhood, would have resonated with or at least been familiar

---

8. Quoted in Campt, "Converging Specters," 331.
9. Campt, "Converging Specters," 335.

FIGURE 3.1. "Destroy This Mad Brute, Enlist," US Army propaganda poster from ca. 1918. Harry R. Hopps, 1869–1937, artist. Library of Congress, public domain image, https://lccn.loc.gov/2010652057.

to white American culture. The "Destroy This Mad Brute" image shown in figure 3.1 is an example of US propaganda encouraging enlistment to fight against the Germans.

This recruitment poster conjures the image of Germany coming onto the shores of the United States and kidnapping the Statue of Liberty. However, this image bears no resemblance to the average-looking white German man, and the image certainly does not bear any resemblance to a Black man. However, the propaganda poster signals that the gorilla represents a German man through the spiked helmet resembling what World War I German soldiers wore, which is emblazoned across the top with the word "militarism." The moustache is reminiscent of Kaiser Wilhelm II's, and the partially destroyed and bloodied club says "kultur" (culture). Visually, this propaganda poster is suggestive of the racist and white supremacist imaginings of Black men, particularly after the US Civil War, which eventually led to Black Codes and Jim Crow. Long gone were racist images of the so-called docile slave (e.g., the Mammie figure, Sambo, Uncle Tom), and instead the propaganda depicting Black men as violent, dark, animalistic, and the antithesis of white culture emerged.

Like the imaginary destructive force of Blackness, the poster stokes fear of Germany crossing the border and destroying the US and does so by aligning Germany, which viewed itself as the pinnacle of white purity and might, with racist images of Black people. The image in this poster is strikingly similar to the racist propaganda images Germany used to fend off perceived threats to white womanhood, and here, apparently, Lady Liberty is another white woman in need of protection. This is not a neutral recruitment image, because both Germany and the United States constructed Black men as apes and gorillas who were supposedly set on raping white women (see, for US examples, Reconstruction-era stereotypes, the 1915 film *The Birth of a Nation,* and various KKK propaganda). Visually, the persuasive enthymeme is that white culture and womanhood need protection. Germany used the visual rhetoric of white womanhood to argue for white protection and purity, and the US used racist imagery about Black people to argue its case about needing protection from Germany and to promote the fear of what could happen if these now-blackened "savage" German soldiers found their way across the US border. In other words, this poster needed to depict Germany as a threat to the US and to whiteness, and the most powerful way to communicate that impending peril was to make Germany "Black."

The German public campaign to eliminate the presence of Black occupying troops in the Rhineland, and the construction of white German women as the victims of the hypersexualized Black male sexual lust this entailed, in many ways parallels the white supremacist campaigns in the United States sanctioning neo-Victorian white American womanhood during Reconstruction. A prominent cultural discourse of fear linked the female body with racialized notions of citizenship, purity, and pollution.[10] Campt's textual analysis of the 1919–23 "Rhineland Bastard" newspaper campaign suggests that scientific discourses of race and colonialism converged with "the deployment of gender . . . the deployment of race and sexuality . . . [and] the deployment of the figure of the Rhineland Bastard as a threat to the purity of the 'German race.'"[11] White German women's bodies simultaneously became the visual signifier for hope, the future, and betrayal, depending upon how women used their bodies, in favor of the nation-state or against the nation-state, and this rhetorical device was also weaponized during and after World War II.

Regarding Black soldiers and white German women, Campt notes:

> In several articles the white German woman was presented as the channel of this threat, portrayed as both a whore and a victim and, as such, as both

---

10. Pascoe, *What Comes Naturally.*
11. Campt, "Converging Specters," 337.

an active and passive conduit of Black male sexuality. The latter, in turn, was demonized as, among other things, infectious, instinctual, uncivilized and most notably, insatiable and uncontrollable. At the same time, Black men were also seen as irresistible seducers of white women, who were supposedly unable to resist their exotic colonial desire for Black male sexuality.[12]

Black soldiers were defined as hypersexual threats, riddled with sexually transmitted diseases and possessing a polluted genetic stock, so their access to white women was a primary discursive concern for German men and their masculinity. Yet, at the same time, passivity was central to this discourse. In the eyes of Germans, as well as US Americans, Black men needed to be controlled in order to protect white women, who were passively intoxicated by the perceived sexual prowess of the exotic Black man. Posing the threat of the Black soldier encouraged white women to become, as Oguntoye et al., argues, "more inclined to place themselves under the 'protection' of white men,"[13] consolidating the whiteness of Germany across gendered lines. Constructing Black men as a sexual threat also yielded a complicated positionality for German women, who became both passive victims to the irresistible seduction of the Black soldiers and whores who had forgone the civilizing influence that is inherent to the German essence. German propaganda campaigns against Black troops highlighted this fear of the Black sexualized Other, particularly for white German women and children, the "true" victims of the threat to the German race.

Indeed, according to Höhn, the "image of the black rapist defiling German womanhood and thus German honor . . . had been a staple of Weimar election propaganda."[14] A notable absence in the discourses surrounding sexual contact between Black soldiers and white German woman after World War I is the possibility that a mutual and reasonable desire could occur between the two groups. Voluntary and mutual desire in an interracial relationship was seen as improbable according to white supremacist propaganda. German discourses of race and gender were intertwined with conceptions of the responsibility of sexuality to work toward the purity of the citizenry and ultimately situated the potential sexual relationship between white German women and Black soldiers as the downfall of the Aryan race. The colonial period and the years following World War I cemented a memoried pattern of structural defeat after which the role of women's bodies was proscribed and any transgression of sanctioned white womanhood signaled a larger violation of the nation-state in terms of racial and gender expectations.

---

12. Campt, "Converging Specters," 334.
13. Oguntoye et al., *Showing Our Colors*, 47.
14. Höhn, *GIs and Fräuleins*, 90.

POST–WORLD WAR II GERMANY, 1945–1955: DEMOCRATIZING ANTI-BLACKNESS IN GERMANY

The notion of race, in addition to anti-Semitism, undergirded much of the behavior in the Third Reich era and is critical to understanding the complex and contradictory operations of power during this time period.[15] As discussed in chapter 1, the use of eugenics justified Nazi violence against Black bodies. According to Campt, because eugenics linked "scientific and colonial discourses of racial purity" and "gendered and sexualized discourses," the German national body became "a raced body made vulnerable through the female body as the conduit of racial pollution."[16] In other words, the idea of a white Germany was vulnerable if white German women betrayed Aryan fantasies and engaged in interracial sex and birthed mixed-race babies. In order to address such potential "disloyalty" by white women, Hitler developed the sterilization and incarceration programs targeting Black Germans discussed earlier. There is a moment for intersectional feminism that is historically missed here in recognizing the shared constraints of Black and white German women under strict definitions of womanhood within the white nation-state. Neither woman could fulfill the goal of the nation if a biracial child was born, and even a white German woman who birthed an Aryan child fulfilled a male-defined duty.

Nazi Germany relied on a gendered coercive pronatalism to enable the biological propagation of a homogenous white German race. Adolf Hitler and the National Socialist German Workers' Party seized control of the German political apparatus in 1933 and immediately implemented a series of laws that were meant to, as Oguntoye et al. finds, "bring female reproduction under greater control, thereby ensuring the existence of the racist system" at the heart of the Aryan project.[17] This meant that during the Third Reich, any German woman who engaged in sexual relations with non-Aryan men were subjected to countless abuses, including public humiliation (see fig. 3.2), forced sterilizations, forced abortions, and prohibition of interracial marriage.[18] Hitler, the Third Reich, and the Geheime Staatspolizei (more commonly known as the Gestapo) relied not only on official oppressive structures to police women and potential interracial couplings but also on ordinary citizens, informants, and neighbors to report on women engaged in interracial sex and interracial relationships as well. This policy no longer came solely from the Nazi nation-state

---

15. Burleigh and Wippermann, *Racial State*.
16. Campt, "Converging Specters," 330. See also Gellately and Stolzfus, "Social Outsider," 4.
17. Oguntoye et al., *Showing Our Colors*, 50.
18. Oguntoye et al., *Showing Our Colors*, 49.

FIGURE 3.2. A German woman is publicly humiliated in 1942. The sign states, "I am expelled from the national community" (translation mine). Information online suggests she was being punished for having an affair with a Polish man. In addition to such shaming, arrest, imprisonment, and even the death penalty could be levied against those who engaged in interracial coupling. Rare Historical Photos, public domain image, https://rarehistoricalphotos.com/german-woman-public-humiliation-1942/.

down; instead, people actively engaged in this reporting on their own, lobbying accusations of *Rassenschande* (racial defilement or shame) against members of their own neighborhoods in order to insulate themselves from the Nazi regime and the Gestapo.

As World War II came to a close, Germany was divided into Soviet-controlled East Germany and Allied-controlled West Germany, and with these changes came a reworking of the ideological foundations that had given much of the German polis a sense of meaning during the Third Reich.[19] In

---

19. See Fehrenbach, *Race after Hitler*.

opposition to the "zero hour thesis," the notion that the end of the Nazi era brought about an immediate change in racial discourse throughout Germany, the historical reality within Germany continued to reflect changing notions of race, particularly since the US imported Jim Crow to its military bases and the immediately surrounding areas just as Black American soldiers began developing relationships with white German women. Further, legal protections against discrimination did not end racism in Germany; rather, the taboo on race talk enabled a "new racism" to develop, in which the language of cultural difference was used to make racist assumptions about essential difference seem reasonable and respectable and continued to offer a way to perpetuate racial hierarchy throughout the German community.[20]

The concept of "new racism," the idea that people of color are no longer primarily reduced through explicitly biological notions of inferiority but rather are conceptualized as having an essentially deficient or pathological culture in need of correction, has been explored by several scholars of American race relations.[21] As racial difference becomes coded in cultural narration in ever more subtle and inferential ways, it becomes increasingly difficult to combat. Thus, new racism can be understood as uniquely insidious, dangerous, and naturalized, particularly as it is something that is carried out by individuals and not the nation-state.[22] As in the United States, German white men established a social compact that allowed for a continuing divide between insiders and outsiders of the law *without* the participation of Black Germans, mixed-race Germans, or white Germans in interracial relationships in developing the compact itself.[23] As the notion of "ethnicity" displaced "race," it enabled a variety of minoritized people that the Nazi regime sought to exterminate (Jews, Slavs, etc.) to be incorporated into the white German polis, while at the same time leaving intact a white/black binary that left Black Germans fundamentally outside the reconstituted, yet culturally homogenous, German nation.[24] The taboo on race discourse did nothing to challenge the everyday racism that Black Germans experienced, while preventing public discussion about working with the differences that people in Germany faced.

The significant efforts by US white soldiers to ostracize their Black counterparts speaks to the entrenched anti-Black sentiment felt by many in the armed forces and to the limits that declarations of equality had in ensuring meaningful integration. Intimidation, slurs, and violence were also part of the

---

20. Chin and Fehrenbach, "Introduction: What's Race?," 13.
21. See Collins, *Black Sexual Politics*; Fiske, *Media Matters*; and Van Dijk, "New(s) Racism."
22. Van Dijk, "New(s) Racism."
23. See Condit and Lucaites, *Crafting Equality*.
24. See Chin and Fehrenbach, "Introduction: What's Race Got to Do with It?"

tense race relations that structured the American military in the 1940s and 1950s, a system of violence that was structurally enforced by white American military police.[25] Segregation of social venues was also part of the constructed competition between white and Black soldiers over access to German women and a point of cooperation between German men and the white occupying American GIs.[26] The antifraternization movement throughout US occupation areas in Germany after World War II highlighted the serious opposition that many German citizens felt toward the mingling of what they saw as their new oppressors.[27]

Women as independent breadwinners in postwar Germany fought against conservative desires that, in turn, bristled against gender equality. Because of the rise of neo-Victorian stereotypes of white womanhood, wherein single women needed white men to protect their bodies and of their virginity, Boehling further argues, "unmarried women were treated as outcasts in public, both at work and in social situations."[28] The presence of Black American soldiers was weaponized in juxtaposition with sexist and racist stereotypes of white womanhood and met with a mixed response that the German press inflamed. Much of the German press condoned and supported the violence visited upon Black GIs by white soldiers, and US military police (MP) enabled a bond to be built between German and US men who, as Fehrenbach learns, "both agreed upon the necessity to 'defend' white womanhood and police white women."[29] Violence used to maintain racial segregation throughout the US military provided one example for the German democratic path forward and reasserted that democracy was still only for whites.

While white Germans' treatment of the Black occupying GIs was mixed, and often more sensitive than the that of white Americans, anti-Black sentiment was still linked to gender, sexuality, and citizenship discourses, and interracial coupling was met with fierce opposition by white German men and white American troops.[30] Reports from southwest Germany, where Greta (my *oma*) and her twins are from, revealed that the presence of Black American soldiers was increasingly met with "expressions of racism" that became "prevalent as popular attention shifted from the soldiers' interactions with children [where kindness, food, and sweets were given] to their relationships with

---

25. Höhn, *GIs and Fräuleins*.
26. Höhn, *GIs and Fräuleins*.
27. Biddiscombe, "Dangerous Liaisons."
28. Boehling, "Gender Roles in Ruins," 64.
29. Fehrenbach, "Black Occupation Children," 34.
30. See Goedde, *GIs and Germans*.

women."³¹ Despite the early indoctrination from organizations like the Hitler Maidens that white German women have only Aryan men as sexual partners, many German women were not opposed to interracial sexual relationships. Greta was one such woman, and her experiences became intersectional (as they related to gendered and racist oppression) when she learned she was pregnant. Both while Greta was pregnant with the twins and after she gave birth to them, she said she was frequently called "Negerhure" (n—— or Negro whore), an experience shared by Black German women who were taunted for polluting the genetic pool with their biracial children from the colonies. For Greta, the assumption was made she must have been impregnated by a Black American soldier because there were military bases in and around her home city, she frequented integrated bars and clubs like most twenty-somethings, and she also had two jobs, the important one being with the Heidelberg Post Exchange, where she was employed on the military base and met many Americans. The intersectional understanding that Greta could have had with Black German women and other women in Mannheim who were pregnant with biracial children ended, because she did not want to see herself in them. She felt betrayed by Blackness as she clung to her white identification.

Greta embraced the postwar period as one in which she could throw off the confines of her Hitler Maiden proscriptions, explore beyond the confines of white womanhood, and challenge notions of nation and race. Many German women sought such freedom, and initial accounts highlighted fraternization with both Jewish and Black American soldiers as ironic racial transgressions: "The Negro troops are doing particularly well with the Fräuleins.... It is also true that Jewish boys are having a field-day."³² Black American GIs too leveraged their Afrofuturistic imagining to engage in a freedom outside the US that was buoyed by joy, faith, and optimism—kryptonite to white racism.

INTERRACIAL COUPLING—DESIRE AND DENIAL

Debates over miscegenation did not suddenly come to an end after Hitler was no longer in power in Germany. Rather, race discourse after World War II was nearly always linked to discussions of interracial sex and reproduction between German women and Black Allied soldiers. In particular, local newspapers positioned single Black American GIs as the primary instigators of problems, always highlighting the race of the alleged perpetrator, even when

---

31. Goedde, *GIs and Germans*, 65.
32. Grossman, ""Big Rape,"" 43.

there was no evidence. According to Höhn, the press painted Black GIs as "a danger not only to women and girls but also to young men and boys": "Young boys were in danger of homosexual seduction because it was not always easy for the 'Negroes . . . to establish relationships with women . . . but because of their flashy cars, German boys were judged easy targets."[33] In weaponizing both racism and homophobia, local newspapers turned the Black GIs' generous treatment of German children into a sexual threat, suggesting that the occupying troops were using rations as a quid pro quo to procure women or even to coerce children into sexual relationships.[34] As with previous discourses of interracial sexual desire, the idea that love or a reasonable desiring was the affective bond between German women and Black men was not seriously considered, because it would subvert the memoried/historical and visual understanding of Germany as "white" nation. Vocal opposition to miscegenation in surveys and reports (often targeting blame toward women participants) belied the notion that anti-Black prejudice had disappeared from the German community, despite German communities' attempts to distance themselves from their racist Nazi past.[35] Black soldiers' sexuality continued to be construed as to a threat to the German citizenry due to past constructions of Black men, but now it was proposed under the guise of democratization and as a taboo on discussing race openly.

German women who developed sexual relationships with Black men continued to face serious constraints in their rights to their own wombs and were discursively constructed as either passive victims or shameful dirty whores in need of state sanction. Fehrenbach's analysis of a 1950 survey on mixed-race relationships shows that German women who had developed sexual relationships with Black GIs were seen as "materialistic and morally deficient."[36] Many white German women who engaged in interracial or interethnic coupling were accused of being greedy, opportunistic, and oversexed. German women who had sex with Black soldiers were characterized as sex workers and sometimes forcibly sent to VD clinics, jail, or workhouses where they were held against their will.[37]

Women's reproductive health care was left in the hands of local- and state-level German authorities and was not guided by any specific Allied occupation imperative. The resulting effect was that abortion requests were disproportionately denied to women who had been raped by white GIs or white Russian

---

33. Höhn, *GIs and Fräuleins*, 94–95.
34. Höhn, *GIs and Fräuleins*.
35. Goedde, *GIs and Germans*.
36. Fehrenbach, "Black Occupation Children," 38.
37. See Fehrenbach, "Black Occupation Children"; and Goedde, *GIs and Germans*.

soldiers (see chapter 4). If a white German woman survived the rape, these pregnant rape survivors were forced into motherhood because their rapist was white, and they were carrying white fetuses. Juxtaposed against this mandatory motherhood, German authorities subtly encouraged white German women who conceived children with Black soldiers to have abortions.[38] While the government coercion of abortion of Black German fetuses occurred at the local level, the Catholic Church offered space for the care of Black German children out of public sight in Church-organized orphanages.[39] In fact, following the Allied occupation of West Germany, abortion laws were relaxed, but as Fehrenbach notes, "while compulsory abortions and sterilization ceased in May 1945 due to nullification of Nazi laws, the elective abortion of fetuses continued apace from the first months of 1945 and over the course of the year became a mass phenomenon."[40] While the rationale of the German medical board that granted or denied abortion requests had shifted from a discourse of racial purity, approval was still influenced by anti-Black conceptions of emotional health. Focus shifted from the purity of the offspring to a concern for the emotional state of the mother, or "from an emphasis on biology of race to the psychology of racial difference."[41] German women who desired to have an abortion, even in the instance of white GI rape, could be denied because the gynecologists that staffed the medical boards could find no reason for concern for the woman's physical or mental health because the white offspring would easily be integrated into the white German social body.[42] By contrast, a mixed-race fetus was something that the medical board could not imagine and would not make space for since they were guided by an anti-Black ideology that disproportionately punished relationships between German women and Black men.

German men and the white occupying American GIs cooperated in their opposition to interracial coupling. White German women and Black American GIs who dated and desired to marry met stiff opposition in both Germany and the United States, and the US most often denied Black GIs' marriage applications, leaving hundreds of German women and children without their partners and fathers.[43] In some cases, the application for marriage licenses were not only denied, but the soldiers were immediately transferred

---

38. Fehrenbach, "Black Occupation Children."
39. Fehrenbach, *Race after Hitler.*
40. Fehrenbach, "Black Occupation Children," 35.
41. Fehrenbach, "Black Occupation Children," 36.
42. Fehrenbach, "Black Occupation Children."
43. See Fehrenbach, "Black Occupation Children"; and Goedde, *GIs and Germans.*

to other military bases and barred from having contact with their partners.[44] US military officials justified this behavior by claiming that Black servicemen's relationships with white women in Germany would be unacceptable in the United States and thus undermine social cohesion domestically when the troops returned.[45] Despite the US War Brides Act (1945), German mothers of Black German children were not offered much opportunity to immigrate to the United States because American visas for Germans from 1945 to 1951 were capped and often quickly filled by many of the acknowledged victims of the Nazi holocaust, primarily Jews.[46] Institutional and ideological constraints on the long-term coupling of German women and Black GIs inhibited the opportunities for family building in Germany and in the US, and in this way embodied racist memoried/historical constructions of unsullied Western whiteness and absent Blackness.

POINT OF ORIGIN: AN ILLICIT INCEPTION

Twenty-three-year-old Greta met Albert in 1945 in Southwest Germany, where Albert was stationed after the war. Mannheim, Germany, became a hub of interracial dating, but that does not mean it was widely condoned or that the children born were accepted; rather, many of these children ended up in orphanages. When I imagine this relationship, I see Greta sitting at a club, socializing, out with her girlfriends drinking and smoking when she meets Albert (see fig. 3.3).

I imagine there are smiles exchanged and that the strains of popular jazz music like Charlie Parker's "Billie's Bounce," Dizzy Gillespie's "Groovin' High," Louis Jordan and the Tympany Five's "Is You or Is You Ain't My Baby," or Thelonious Monk's "Round Midnight" are popping in the background as Albert navigates around the dancers and makes the long trek across the dance floor to ask Greta to dance. In the time I knew Greta, she did not seem to be a risk-taker, but as a twenty-something German woman, she may have been more willing to take chances by venturing out to clubs that allowed interracial dancing. Interracial nightclubs in Germany were a flashpoint for white American GIs holding steadfastly to imported Jim Crow laws. According to Höhn, "off base, white soldiers introduced Jim Crow laws into German communities, just as they had done in Great Britain during the war. By using economic pressure . . . the soldiers threatened the owners by telling them that all white members

---

44. Oguntoye et al, *Showing Our Colors*, 89–90.
45. Oguntoye et al, *Showing Our Colors*, 89–90.
46. See Fehrenbach, "Black Occupation Children."

FIGURE 3.3. Greta (*center*) at a club/bar with her girlfriends after World War II. Family photo, author's private collection, supplied by Greta.

of the unit would boycott their businesses if they served blacks."[47] However, on the US side, there would have been no question: going to mixed-race clubs would have been banned due to Jim Crow restrictions in the US and by the Jim Crow laws the military imported. Höhn explains that "all establishments in close proximity to military bases that catered *exclusively* to American GIs were segregated by race. . . . On base, white soldiers succeeded in keeping black soldiers out of their clubs by playing only country and western music instead of jazz and boogie-woogie."[48]

The integrated clubs located off military bases likely had an element of "cool" and "danger" that did not exist in the restrictive clubs on the military bases, which would have monitored and prevented interracial dancing under the guise of protecting white womanhood. Black American GIs found these off-base clubs allowed for a way to exhale from the oppression and racism the US imported as well as a way to get to know the locals and have a modicum of freedom they could only dream about when in the US. These GIs were

---

47. Höhn, *GIs and Fräuleins*, 96–97.
48. Höhn, *GIs and Fräuleins*, 96–97.

FIGURE 3.4. Stollenwörthweiher See, Mannheim, Germany. Image taken by Prof. Dr. Hans-Peter Schwoebel, September 2018.

temporarily out from under the surveillance of the racist US and could simply live. The social opinion of women like Greta who patronized these mixed-race clubs likely varied depending on whether the establishment owner succumbed to white soldiers' boycotts.

In exercising a bit of joy and freedom, two people on opposite ends of the oppression continuum—Greta as related to gender and Albert as related to race—found one another. As Greta wistfully reminisced, "Albert was the love of my life. He swept me off my feet, literally. He danced like an angel. He twirled me around. I never knew I could dance like that. He was very nice, we were friends." I can imagine the dancing Greta and Albert enjoyed. I swayed to the imaginary music as she spoke, and a faint, distant smile broke out on Greta's face as she described the pleasant memory. In their courtship, Greta said Albert gave her things like "chocolate and stockings" and she said he was "nicer than the German soldiers."

In the Mannheim-Neckarau region, for example, interracial couples often met by Stollenwörthweiher See (see fig. 3.4), which was frequented by white German women and Black American and Puerto Rican soldiers. "Sex Lake," as it was nicknamed according to Susanna, a Puerto Rican German woman I interviewed, was "more of a pond from the Rhein [Rhine River, where] people met." One side is heavily wooded, and I speculate that this was the place Greta and Albert met occasionally, before they lived together.

In visiting and viewing "Sex Lake" myself, I was initially in disbelief that cross-cultural, interracial sexual coupling had once regularly occurred here because the location is so exposed, open, and visible. However, when gazing across the lake and considering the dense shrubbery and trees on the opposite shore, it became clear how sexual coupling could transpire right underneath the panopticon of the US military and the German community. Driving around on the other side of the lake in an attempt to access it from the military side, where the US soldiers would have lived and been housed, I encountered a dead-end street. At the end of this street is where the lake is located, and it is quite concealed. As I attempted to walk to the lake from this former military side, I had difficulty getting back in view of the lake. From this wooded side, I would have never even known there was a lake because of all the foliage concealing it. I would have never believed that a large lake could be both visible and invisible, seen and concealed, containing everything and nothing at all. The only time evidence of the secret dalliances came to light, and "the tea spilled," was when a white German woman from this region ended up pregnant.

Greta and Albert continued to date, and eventually she moved in with the man who swept her off her feet. Greta said her mother, Hermine, "never met Albert," but her World War II American soldier provided her with the most desirable thing of all . . . housing. An apartment for the two of them to live in was crucial, because she previously lived in a two-bedroom apartment with her mother and two sisters that was crowded due to the postwar housing shortage. For Greta, being in a relationship with a mixed-race American GI was quite a departure for a woman who was once an active member of the Hitler Maidens. Traditionally, when people engage in such a dynamic and cognitively dissonant change from one view to another, something drastic has transpired. In this case, the American Jim Crow democracy and social structure would not have been such a drastic change, as it related to the white racist society in which she was raised. Could her radical change in race relations have been out of rebellion? Perhaps, but since the default cultural ideal is white hegemony and middle-class status, why interact romantically with someone who was seemingly the antithesis of that, particularly in a racist society with the power to take away white privilege from anyone who challenges white supremacist norms and expectations? Could her change have been rooted in love, practicality, and resilience? Did she simply see Albert as a person, someone with whom she could recognize commonality and humanity? There need not be an absolute answer to these rhetorical and critical ponderings, because whatever aided her in navigating the cognitive dissonance she must have encountered was likely rooted in memory and rebellion. Saidiya Hartman's critical fabulations[49] become apt here, because in this postwar era, Greta (and other women) engaged in free love, cohabitation, and for some, single motherhood, all which signified a feminist challenge to the neo-Victorian ideals that Hitler mandated. This social upheaval gave Greta permission to walk a different path.

The roots and routes Greta traveled to reinvention and forgetting first allowed her to reevaluate a racist conviction, and by disavowing any Nazi ideologies she may have held in the past, she moved forward with a positive gain in terms of food, shelter, and love. She was able to, as Connerton describes, "discard memories that serve[d] no practicable purpose in the management of [her] current identity and ongoing purposes, [because to] not forget might . . . provoke too much cognitive dissonance: better to cosign some things to a shadow world."[50] In Greta's act of prescribed forgetting, in her new memoried identity and existence as someone who said, "Race never mattered to me. It was always the person, never the color," she was able to move forward into a liminal space, even if that space created room for societal disapproval and racism to fall onto her. In forgetting, she made "living space for present projects,"[51] in this case her survival. This is also likely why, later, when I suggested that Albert might have also been part African American (and not only Native American as she said he proudly proclaimed), Greta resisted. Greta was very quick to correct me; it was safer, more acceptable, for Albert to be anything but Black, because to position Albert as Black challenged her postmemoried recrafting of who he was in juxtaposition to how she saw herself now and the memories she chose to emphasize and forget. Greta's remote proximity to Blackness and her disclosure of it decades after her relationship with Albert challenged and threatened her composite narrative of herself as white immigrant woman. As Blair et al. explain, "public memory is understood . . . as activated by concerns, issues, or anxieties of the present. That is, groups tell their pasts to themselves and others as ways of understanding, valorizing, justifying, excusing, or subverting conditions or beliefs of their current moment."[52] Her postmemory practices were predicated on how white

---

49. "Critical fabulations" refer to the gaps that are found in archives and historical records. Hartman's term combines archival and historical research with critical theory and fiction to help fill in the spaces that the archival and historical record leave. See Hartman, *Wayward Lives*.
50. Connerton, "Seven Types of Forgetting," 63.
51. Connerton, "Seven Types of Forgetting," 63.
52. Blair et al., "Introduction: Rhetoric/Memory/Place," 6.

racist societies (Germany and the US) would view her and her actions, and how she saw herself and her decisions reflected in the pool of white racist cultural environments.

How complicated is race and so ingrained is racism that Greta, even in 2012, was unable to admit that she was attracted to and loved a man who happened to be a biracial Black man? The legacy of Albert being potentially Black, coupled with German and US racism, haunted Greta. Through her reconstruction of herself and her identity, she knew she was not a violent racist like the Nazis or the staunch pro–Jim Crow racists of the US, because in her mind she constructed a narrative of personal healing and liberalism. This is why she could ask me, upon our first meeting in 2012, if I was a Democrat and say, "I hope you aren't a Republican." This is also how she was able keep an image of US Olympic gymnastics champion Gabby Douglas on her refrigerator yet throw the photographs of me that I sent to her in the trash. In such seemingly contradictory actions, Greta can show publicly that she is not a racist and at the same time erase her mixed-raced granddaughter from existence without any internal dissonance, keeping her memories, her imagined life, and her self-narrative in balance. The contact with her twin daughters, and then later an introduction to her only granddaughter, was a visual and material reminder of the past she tried to bury. "A person is a person," as Greta liked to say, until those people upset the delicate balance of the life she had created in the fifty-two years without their memoried presence. Lilli's, Lore's, and my existence haunted her and threatened to destroy the postmemoried identity she had crafted. The past, in her view, must stay entombed. For Greta to move forward with her own imagined beginnings starting in 1948, something had to launch her forward, and in her case, it was Albert's betrayal.

I'M PREGNANT

"I'm pregnant," said Greta. Greta expected a marriage proposal from her American GI, and instead Albert said, "I have a wife back in the US." "And he broke up with me," Greta told me, "choosing the other woman. I never heard from him again." He left. Greta never forgave him for his silence or his disappearance. Unbeknown to Greta, the entire time Albert flirted with her, wooed her, and loved her, he was indeed married. Apparently, his marriage, to an older friend of the family who was a widow with one child of her own from her first marriage, was not a love match. If indeed Albert's 1942 marriage was something more akin to a practical product of war, then he ensured his family friend would be able to benefit from his war pension. It is difficult to tread through the memories of Greta, who felt the sting of the betrayal in 1948, which still wore on her and sat at the surface of her life experience. Even if Albert was not married, he would not have been able to marry Greta since interracial marriage was illegal in the US until 1967 and difficult to obtain in Germany. As Greta reminisced about Albert, I was no longer listening to and looking at a woman in her nineties, but rather a twenty-six-year-old woman whose lover's betrayal was palpable. Abandoned, Greta never forgave Albert and said she "never spoke to him again."

What I was witnessing as Greta provided glimpses and bits of her life with Albert was structural amnesia. Connerton notes that structural amnesia occurs when "a person tends to remember only those links in his or her pedigree that are socially important."[53] It was socially important, as Greta sat next to me on her couch for the first time, that she talk about her story of betrayal and abandonment. It was important for her to make sure that I understood that she was the victim, not Albert. Was Albert's marriage *only* a marriage of convenience for a family friend (his self-sacrifice), one in which his altruistic act prohibited Greta from grasping at her own bit of happiness, or was his marriage something more, something deeper, something based on love? Based on the timing of his marriage to the other woman, there is a strong suggestion that the marriage was for her to receive his pension when he died. Albert stayed in Germany for three years until Greta revealed her pregnancy. Would Albert have eventually returned to his wife? Would Albert have stayed longer in Germany (never revealing he was married) if Greta had never become pregnant? What happened to the apartment Albert and Greta shared since they had their lives together as a couple to untangle? Did Albert attempt to talk with Greta later, only she refused to see and speak to him again? Did Albert promise to somehow take care of her and the unborn twins? All these questions remain unanswered because Greta did not address these queries when I asked her. She simply ignored them.

Greta's lack of detail fits not only with Paul Connerton's research on memory but also with Cheryl Glenn's scholarship on the power of silence. Silence as Greta used it was a tool of power that allowed her to control what memories, experiences, and truths she chose to share. Rather than being a rhetorical act of passiveness, silence has the ability to control what is learned, by whom, and when. Glenn notes that "employed as a tactical strategy or inhabited in deference to authority, silence resonates loudly along the corridors of purposeful language use. Whether choice or im/position, silence can reveal positive or negative abilities, fulfilling or withholding traits, harmony

---

53. Connerton, "Seven Types of Forgetting," 64.

or disharmony, success or failure. Silence can deploy power; it can defer to power. It all depends."[54] Greta could have used silence to subtly let me know that she was not going to answer certain questions, and it could have also been a strategy of power in terms of our age differences, her white privilege, and our identity roles (grandmother versus granddaughter, interviewee versus interviewer).

Greta's intentional silence speaks back to Albert and the racial risks of their relationship, as it took place transnationally and illegally when antimiscegenation laws and Jim Crow thrived in both Germany and the US. Greta's silence surrounding deeper details of her relationship with Albert are in keeping with the forced silence and shame she felt after engaging in interracial coupling and the public acknowledgment of interracial sex and loss of white womanhood due to the twins' birth. By speaking through silence, Greta did not have to risk the white womanhood she was only able to regain through immigration to another country.

Because of her pregnancy and Albert leaving, Greta tried, but she could not afford the rent for their apartment. She was forced to move back to the overcrowded apartment where her mother and her sisters lived. Albert was not the man she imagined him to be. He was no longer her military superhero, and any freedom she felt with him ended. The door to their forbidden love firmly closed once she was pregnant, as there were no other avenues to keep this couple together, not only because of US antimiscegenation laws and the reluctance of the German government to allow interracial marriages but also, above all else, because Albert was married. Greta attempted to hide the pregnancy from her family, but eventually her mother asked if she was pregnant. Greta responded, "How should I know?" At a loss, abandoned, and overwhelmed, Greta sought advice from her local Catholic priest in Mannheim, but he condemned her for premarital sex and for sex with an American GI: "The priest told me he could not and would not help me and then kicked me out of the religion and the church. He told me I was no longer part of the Catholic Church and to leave. People called me *Negerhure*. After that, I was in denial about the whole pregnancy." As a twenty-six-year-old single woman working two jobs in the post-Hitler era, Greta chose silence as the option to deal with her unplanned pregnancy. Greta continued with the pregnancy, and Albert never had any other known biological children apart from the twins.

Who is German? What does a German look like? From colonial German debates on interracial marriage through resistance to integrating Black

---

54. Glenn, *Unspoken*, xi.

German children into post–World War II democratic Germany, a German was understood through a racial lens that positioned Blackness as separated, excluded, and antithetical to the notion of the white German political body. Constructing the homogenous citizenry was a state interest that justified the discipline of German women's bodies, including through restrictions on the right to marry, on the choice to reproduce, and on social support for raising Black German children, as will be further discussed in the next chapter.

CHAPTER 4

Aborted out of Germany

Born, Kept, and Abandoned

> Lore: "Why do I look so different from everyone else?"
> Sister Melissa: "We are part of nature. Look around. There are no two trees or two flowers that look alike. Everything in nature is different."

Aborted and *abortion*: these are politicized trigger words, and they are associated with a woman's right to choose. Synonyms for *abort* include *discontinue, end, halt, stop,* and *suspend*. Greta chose not to engage in the physical act of abortion, though that was an option afforded to her. *Abort,* as I use the term here, is meant to evoke the idea of erasure, from both an individual standpoint and a nation-state perspective. An act of memory, remembering, and forgetting, Greta's act of aborting her children involved memory strategies, such as trying to forget and deny the pregnancy. By removing Lilli and Lore from her home, by making them invisible, Greta reclaimed a life before the twins and an imagined present and future without them. Greta's creative/postmemory present and her postmemory future allowed her to carry on a life without her twin daughters for fifty-two years. Greta's newly crafted story about herself went like this: "I am an immigrant from Germany. I came to the US after the war. I became an American citizen. I have no children." Even her youngest sister participated in this creative reimagining, admitting, "I told people Greta was never able to have children." Thus, denied and erased, Lilli and Lore were aborted. The West German nation-state also attempted to abort biracial Black German children out of the national narrative and out of visibility when constructing a Western democracy modeled after the US, a country that was committed to Jim Crow and overt racial discrimination against Black Americans.

You notice how noticeable you are. The twins noticed their hypervisibility as biracial German children and the racism against their mother. The postwar era asked Germany to envision a new path, a new beginning, but not everyone was given the same opportunity. Rather than being granted an Afrofuturistic possibility of inclusion in a new West German democracy, *afrodeutsche Nachkriegskinder* were treated as trespassers in a white-imagined democracy through the importation of Jim Crow. Many of these mixed-race German children needed permission from the nation-state to exist, and they did not have it, some not even from their families and local communities. The right to exist within the West German borders was challenged for this small population of mixed-race German children.

By constructing paternal lineage in terms of both a national and racial perspective, the organizational structure of the census set the precedent for consolidating the whiteness of the German citizenry, de-otherizing Soviet children, rendering Jewish offspring invisible, and placing Black German children in a precariously distinct and visible place in relation to the German national body. As the Nazi racial state devolved after 1945, a focus on children emerged, and, as Fehrenbach observes, "children . . . remained a central social category for the postwar production of national ideology."[1] Regarding the prospects of Black German children in Germany in the wake of the Holocaust, three perspectives were prevalent.[2] First, some German citizens, and many mothers of Black German children, saw little reason to hope for a successful transition to democracy in German society, or at least one that would do away with a Black/white binary. Second, some German citizens held out belief that the de-Nazification process would take place throughout Germany and Black German children would be meaningfully incorporated into society. Finally, a very small group of Germans believed that Black German children should remain in Germany but in a segregated space apart from white communities. Because of the racist stigma white German mothers of biracial children faced, such as being called "Negerhoren," many of these women, as Werner Sollors shares, decided to "birth secretly[,] . . . letting German state welfare and adoption agencies, with their network of orphanages and foster parents, take care of the child. [This] became a relatively frequent outcome, generating political worries about public costs,"[3] but at least the stigma was no longer focused on the mother but rather on the living child. The mere

---

1. Fehrenbach, "Black Occupation Children," 31.
2. Lemke Muniz de Faria, "Germany's 'Brown Babies.'"
3. Sollors, *Temptation of Despair*, 222.

existence of these children posed a problem: the myth of a "white" German heritage was again under threat.

The placement of white supremacist cultural ideologies and stigma onto Black Germans, including through the continued presence of scientific racism throughout Germany during the post-Nazi era, is the focus of this chapter. Specifically, I ask the following: In what ways, and for what reasons, have Black German children been incorporated or excluded from the German polis? Did governmental and societal policing of Black German children function as a way for basic systems of white supremacy to sustain themselves? Of primary concern is what place Black German children and their mothers were allowed to occupy in the German national imagination and to what extent their individual rights and interests were superseded by the assertion of state interests in managing the German citizenry. The children could not dare to dream, because the nation-state refused to imagine them into being in equitable and inclusive ways. This chapter not only explores the limitations of Afrofuturism but also how well-meaning Black American people and agencies (like Mabel Grammer, Ethel Butler, the NAACP, and Black newspapers) attempted to help the *afrodeutsche Nachkriegskinder*, often with outcomes detrimental to the children due to the culture shock and the racism they experienced in the US.

FORCED MOTHERHOOD: FAMILY STAYS WITH FAMILY

In one of my interviews with Greta, she related some of the events of the twins' birth: "When I went to the hospital, I asked, 'What did I have, a boy or a girl?' I was absolutely shocked when the nurse told me, 'Twins! Twin girls!'" (see fig. 4.1).

Greta had no knowledge that she was pregnant with twins, because, as she said, "I never sought medical care for the entire pregnancy." Despite Greta's evasive answer when her mother asked her if she were pregnant ("How should I know?"), Hermine (Greta's mother) did not hesitate when she heard that Greta was rushed to the hospital from work, in labor, since Greta worked every day, including the day she gave birth. When I asked Greta about Hermine's reaction, Greta said, "She said nothing. She was so happy to have the babies." Greta explained that she was then asked to name the twins, which she did with a flippant wave of her hand: "I didn't care and just said, Li and Lo, but then the German government came in and denied the names, saying they were too short. The German government named them." Li, the firstborn, became Lilli, and Lo, born seven minutes later, became Lore. Greta is listed as the mother on both birth certificates, but only on Lilli's birth certificate (presumably, because she was the firstborn twin) can the father's name, Albert

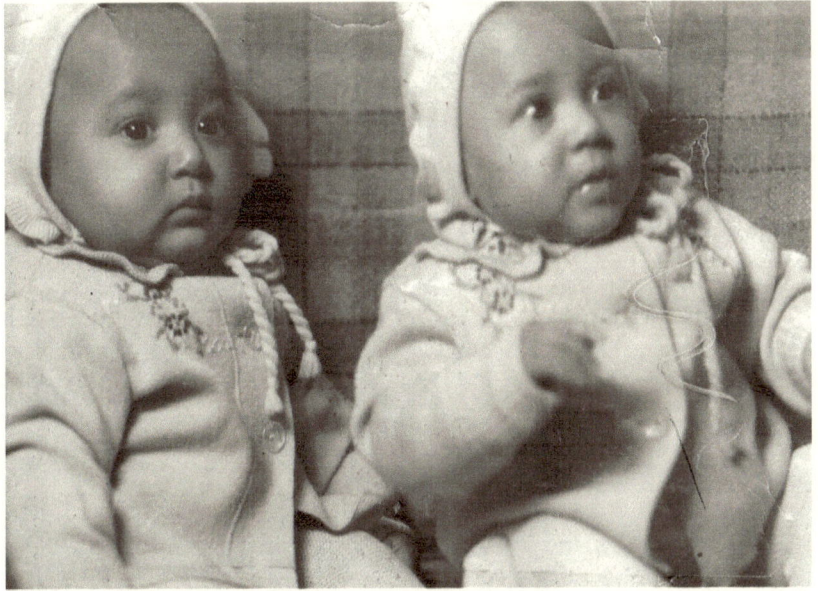

FIGURE 4.1. Lore (*left*) and Lilli (*right*) as infants, 1948. Family photo, author's private collection, supplied by Lilli.

Flowers, be found. Greta told me she "never wanted children": "I tried to give the girls up for adoption immediately after they were born, but [my mother] said no. 'They're family. Family stays with family.'" Greta, who said she had several white German families interested in the twins, was forced to decline their offers of adoption. When I asked her about this experience, she said, "Having children was awful, the worst day of my life."

It became painfully obvious learning about Lilli's and Lore's entry into the world that Greta never had any plans to be a mother, and her pregnancy with the twins derailed and negatively affected her imagined future. With motherhood thrust upon her, Greta's only form of power was pushing back against forced motherhood, only this time, instead of originating with Hitler and the Third Reich, the motherhood propaganda came from Hermine.

Greta had a positive relationship with Hermine and said, "I loved being an only child, and my mother once lavished attention on me" (see fig. 4.2). However, once Greta's two siblings were born a decade or so later, Greta was resentful of the attention she now had to share with her sisters. As a preteen, Greta witnessed the demise of her parents' marital relationship and blamed Hermine while valorizing her father. Greta adored her largely absent father (Robert), who was often away during the formative years of her life due to his duties as a soldier in World War I, his involvement in World War II, and

FIGURE 4.2. Greta (*left*) and Hermine (*right*), mother and daughter playing a board game. Family photo, author's private collection, supplied by Greta.

his bouts with alcoholism. The once-positive but now-strained relationship between Greta and Hermine suffered its final break when Greta was forced to keep the twin daughters she never wanted, whom at times she referred to as "mistakes." After that, according to Greta, she referred to Hermine as "horrible." There was no intersectional and intergenerational feminist understanding between Greta and Hermine. While Hermine did the progressive thing through divorcing Robert, she applied antiquated notions of motherhood to Greta, who rejected them. Hermine also leveraged her own power as mother over Greta as she, not Greta, had the final word. Greta's only recourse was to be an absent parent, much in the same way Robert had been absent from her own life. When I asked Lilli and Lore about their childhood memories with their grandmother, Lilli said, "I don't remember any." Lore, on the other hand, loved her grandmother unconditionally and said, "I remember being very close with my grandmother. I remember feeling loved." Hermine was the only person who wanted the twins to remain with the family. Ironically, after Hermine died (when the twins were ten years old), Greta scapegoated her and used her mother as justification for placing the twins in the foster care system in California.

Greta was like most women of working age in the postwar era, who, in their effort to help rebuild Germany, immediately went back to work once their children were born. Their mothers were then the primary caretakers for their respective grandchildren. Work was a necessity to sustain Greta's multigenerational family, but work was also a way of detaching from her undesirable situation. Work allowed Greta to seize control of an identity she cherished and one that she could temporally imagine: that of a woman without children. When I asked Greta about how she bonded with her twin daughters, she said, "I really didn't raise them. [My youngest sister] and my mother raised [Lilli and Lore]. I was always at work between [the Heidelberg Post Exchange] and a night job." Lost in the postmemory of war and its aftermath are stories about women such as this: mothers who had to go back to work immediately after giving birth as postwar exigencies unseated stereotypes around motherhood. Hitler and the Third Reich had imposed strict, conservative restrictions on the role of women in society, holding that motherhood largely defined womanhood, yet many of the mothers in the postwar era had no ability to access the "luxury" of being a stay-at-home mother. Nation-building in the postwar era was framed through a chiefly patriarchal vision, and this master narrative largely erased the efforts of women. Many of these invisible women had to help rebuild Germany and provide for their families through employment and, at the same time, many of these women were also mothers. In this postmemoried account of motherhood, women had many rights taken away from them by the nation-state, and Greta was no different, as the West German government moved forward and the capitalist machine of the new democracy consumed them and their children. Motherhood was now a secondary priority in the postwar era as many mothers, like Greta, were expected to go back to work immediately after giving birth in favor of building a new democratic nation. Rebuilding Germany became a masculinist mantra that was partly forged on the backs of German women.[4] Elevated now to mythic proportion was nation-building, and the silent fallout from the war was the shift from the past womanhood ideal (motherhood) to the collective memory of a new nation coming out of the ashes of defeat.

When I asked Greta who fed her infant daughters or if she was able to breastfeed them, she scoffed and said, "I didn't feed them. I don't know, maybe they had cow's milk." When Lore recounted serious childhood illnesses and asked Greta, "Did I ever have chicken pox? Measles? The mumps? I remember being very sick in the orphanage, but I can't remember with what," Greta glossed right over the question and never responded. Perhaps since

---

4. Boehling, "Gender Roles in Ruins," 52.

motherhood had never been an identity Greta wanted to wear, she simply did not worry about who fed her daughters or how they were fed. During the pregnancy and after the birth of the twins, she suffered personal loss and humiliation and was left not knowing where she could retain any power. As Greta tried to abort the twins' identities and existence in her life, perhaps she found power in her ignorance about their care. Armada notes that "the clash of competing memories can produce additional memorial effects characterized by ambiguity and unresolved tensions"[5] and silence. Greta bore no cultural affinity with the idea of motherhood she had inherited, because she did not meet the Hitler Maiden ideal and produce two "pure" Aryan children. If she is not a mother, then she does not need to address questions of the sort asked by Lore about her childhood. A humiliated silence can involve some reclamation of power, or at least face-saving. Indeed, Connerton argues that "few things are more eloquent than a massive silence. And in the collusive silence brought on by a particular kind of collective shame there is detectable both a desire to forget and sometimes the actual effect of forgetting."[6] Through Greta's humiliated memoried silence, lost are the details of quiet smiles she may have had with the twins. Lost is the laughter, the tantrums, and the tears. Lost is bath time and the general chaos that descends upon a house when not one, but two babies are born. Lost is the romantic partner, Albert. Greta had no significant other with whom to communicate her life stresses that surrounded her workday and her daughters. Who took the girls to the physician when they were sick? Who treated their bumps and bruises? Did Greta ever pass along stories, family narratives, and wisdom to the girls? Did Greta know about childhood questions, such as, "Why is the sky red?," posed by Lore to her grandmother? "That is the angels baking cookies," said Hermine, most like referring to the sunset. These familial gaps were filled by Hermine and Greta's sisters; ironically, Greta's early absence allowed Lore to feel and be safe and connected her to a family who are now strangers.

White supremacy afforded Greta the ability and power to not be implicated in her role as mother and in her memory of how she mothered. The lack of knowledge about her daughters' basic nutrition and healthcare signaled a detachment from her daughters, but there were also times when she verbally cared for them. For example, when Lore was lost in Mannheim, Greta did what any other parent would do and panicked. As Greta shared, "One day, at a café in Mannheim, Lore was running around from table to table charming people, but then she was gone. She just disappeared! I had all the people in

---

5. Armada, "Memory's Execution," 233.
6. Connerton, "Seven Types of Forgetting," 67.

FIGURE 4.3. Lore (*left*) and Lilli (*right*) at around eighteen months old. Family photo, author's private collection, supplied by Greta. As Greta noted, "I knitted these clothes and made clothes for Lilli and Lore."

the restaurant looking for her and told people in town too. Lore was gone for a while, and no one found her. I was a wreck, and then suddenly she reappeared, on her own, in the restaurant." Since Greta said she was "a wreck" when Lore was lost, I imagine she must have felt relief when Lore was found, because she still had to wear the mantle of motherhood on the weekends, and losing her child, even if that child was unwanted, would have reflected poorly on Greta. Greta needed to engage in the public performance of care.

Greta also nonverbally signaled care for her daughters by providing for basic needs like clothing, which all children need and outgrow quickly. Greta said she and Hermine "made all of the clothes for the twins" and Greta in particular, loved "knitting clothes for them," which sparked Greta's lifelong love of stitchery, for which she later would win awards (see figs. 4.3 and 6.3). In addition, Greta and Hermine dressed the twins in matching outfits. In all images of the twins shared with me, they are in matching outfits, right down to their socks/tights, shoes, and hairdos, which is something proud parents of twins often do to convey their love for their children. Lilli and Lore come to occupy what Lisa Flores describes as "discursive space": they "find themselves with a foot in [two] worlds [with] the sense of being in neither,"[7] and this magnifies a need to justify and push back against any real or imagined sense of unbelonging. The twins were included when their exigent needs were met with handmade, identical clothing, yet they were simultaneously unwanted and inconvenient for Greta when her needs and self-preservation were more important.

This kind of familial memory and postmemory tug-of-war allowed Lore to move forward toward a space of forgiveness and to an eventual reunion with her family fifty-two years later. This same process allowed Lilli to remain divorced from the past and say, "I don't want to talk about it. They didn't remember me. They didn't want me; I don't need them." Lilli as an adult, in juxtaposition to Lore, ironically mirrored Greta's perspective on the past with her desire to largely erase all familial connections. Lilli's desire to remain untethered to a past of unbelonging created a void in my life, but it allowed her to engage in a kind of Afrofuturistic re-envisioning wherein she could imagine and create a different life, a life on her terms including and excluding anyone she chose to, and often that meant excluding Lore and me because we were visual reminders of a memoried past she no longer wanted a connection to. This was an act of agency I did not understand (as I had an idyllic childhood in comparison) until I engaged in the research for this book.

While I rarely missed a grandmother I didn't even know existed until 2012, I missed the imagined relationship I could have had with my *Tante* (aunt) and felt her absence from our lives deeply. Lilli imprinted on me when I was just six months old, when she met me for the first time. Our inconsistent relationship was built through cards, letters, phone calls, presents, and rare visits. Given that Lilli and Lore are twins, I imagine that my mother felt confused and bereft with the on-again off-again nature of their adult relationship, on top of the impermanence of their lives with Greta. In the times when Lilli's life intertwined with ours, she was often guarded even with those who knew her intimately. I still cherish the few items she gave to me as a child, because they are all I have of her: a stuffed Snoopy, two watches, and a necklace. A life remembered in material goods more than in memories created by being consistently in one another's life.

---

7. Flores, "Creative Discursive Space," 142.

LIMINAL SPACES: KEPT AND ABANDONED

Even as Black German children were integrated into the German citizenry, the relationships that begot those children were saturated in dismissive anti-Black discourses. Biracial German children, after the founding of the West German Federal Republic (1949), were afforded German citizenship as part of the democratization effort, as it was argued that the children should not have to pay for the sins of their mothers, but children who were put up for adoption in orphanages were stripped of theirs.[8] As Petra Goedde recounts, in a *Survey* magazine article reporting on six hundred interviews with mothers of Black German children, a positive portrait of the mother's care for the children was presented and hopes of marriage were commonly reported.[9] Mothers of biracial German children faced unique challenges during the postwar era, including social stigma, insults, slurs, and restrictions on access to social services for their children.[10] For the first time in her life, Greta was the target of such racism. In Germany and around US Army bases, she was called an "Ami-hussy" (Army hussy) and a "wigger" (a US term that refers to a white person who likes or loves a black person),[11] while in the US, she was called a "n— lover" because of her twin daughters. Being the target of racism and racial epithets put Greta out of step with the collective memory of "white" Germany, out of step with the American Jim Crow democracy that had been exported to West Germany in the postwar era, and outside the collective social body.

"Family stays with family," Hermine stated, but that did not mean everyone was able to live with family full-time. The cramped apartment eventually became too crowded with four adults and two babies, so once the twins were old enough, they were carted off to a dormitory-style Catholic housing facility created specifically for white children and *afrodeutsche Nachkriegskinder*. It was not uncommon for children of young, unmarried German mothers to be placed in such dormitories whether or not they were put up for adoption. Many German children after World War II, regardless of ethnicity or "race," were placed in these Catholic facilities due to a housing crisis and for economic reasons.

The social worker documents varied drastically in their timelines, but sometime between the ages of eighteen months to three years old, Lilli and

---

8. See Fehrenbach, "Black Occupation Children."
9. See Goedde, *GIs and Germans*.
10. Lemke Muniz de Faria, "Germany's 'Brown Babies.'"
11. According to Phillip Herbst, a wigger is "a white person who befriends black people or adopts aspects of their culture or both. . . . Its derivation from white n— leaves little doubt of its pejorative origins." Herbst, *Color of Words*, 233.

Lore were moved out of the apartment and placed in a German Catholic orphanage.[12] The quarters Lilli and Lore resided in operated much like a boarding school, where parents visited their children during the week, and some of the children stayed in the family home on the weekends. According to the social worker documents, the twins lived in an orphanage with "70 other children (which had) [sic] dormitory-type living and on-site schooling." Lore was "particularly fond of two nuns" when she lived at the German Catholic home, and her "birth mother and maternal aunts visited frequently."[13] Some of these children were adopted out of these organizations and others were not—it depended on the desires of the mother. Since Hermine forbade adoption, the twins remained part of the German citizenry.

This move not only created breathing space for the family but also allowed for the distance that Greta craved from her daughters. The visual absence of the twins helped Greta alleviate her shame; as visual signifiers, the twins represented the mistake of premarital sex, the shame of not being married to the father of the children, and the shame of the twins not being "pure" German. The physical distance from her children allowed her to not only exhale and distance herself from racism; it also allowed her the ability to reclaim her whiteness, because the intersection of her imagined white life with Blackness was temporarily lifted during the weekdays. By allowing herself temporary access into the collective memory of what it meant to be white (the absence of biracial children), Greta temporarily became the visual signifier and representative of what it means to be white and could begin to move forward with a new memoried version of herself (a white women without mixed-race children), even if her postmemory reality belied that existence.

THE PUSH FOR INTERNATIONAL ADOPTION THROUGH MEDIATED PERSUASION

News stories and films in the early 1950s began to be produced in Germany as visually persuasive ways to show that something was being done to address the issue of orphaned postwar children, with particular attention paid to *afrodeutsche Nachkriegskinder*. Making the work of the Jugendamt (Youth Welfare Office) visible was one goal, as was making the orphanages seem like loving places in which to house thousands of unwanted children. The positive depiction of leaving the children at dormitories/orphanages (either temporarily or

---

12. Social Worker, Children's Home Society of California, accessed 2012.
13. Social Worker, Children's Home Society of California, accessed 2012.

permanently) made it socially acceptable for white German mothers to separate from their children not only for the advancement of the nation-state as it was rebuilt for a new democratic era but also as a means for saving face. The mothers were visually reassured that they were doing the best for their children. The 1952 blockbuster film *Toxi* was the precursor to all the films and newsreels that followed, allowing the question "What are we going to do about all of these Black German children?" to come to the forefront of mediated discussion in Germany and in the US.

Toxi brought issues of Black American GIs, biracial German children after World War II, and orphanages to the big screen.[14] In real life, Elfie Fiegert, the actor who played Toxi, was an *afrodeutsche Nachkriegskind*, which the advertising for the film capitalized on. Likely considered a progressive film for its time, *Toxi* follows the story of a Black German girl's interactions with a middle-class white German family as they try to figure out what to do with her after she arrives on their doorstep. As the film progresses, viewers see that some members of the Rose family immediately accept her, while others, like the elder Uncle Theodor, want to, and do, drop her off at an orphanage. An even older house guest refers to Toxi as a "child of shame." In facing his own racism head-on, Uncle Theodor, who visually represents antiquated, Nazi-era thinking as related to race and racism, comes around and joins the other members of the family who decide to keep Toxi, and he is the one to reclaim her from the orphanage. But just in the nick of time, the doorbell rings and the absent Black American GI father miraculously shows up on the Rose's doorstep to claim Toxi. Toxi, who was putting on a Christmas play with the other white children in the house, had put herself in whiteface (literally put on white makeup), and she wipes off the white powder makeup to show her Black father that she too is Black and not white. However, it is the conclusion that drives home the ultimate message about biracial postwar children: despite being born to German mothers, children whose fathers were Black American GIs were seen as American, not German, and as Black, not biracial. This line of thinking maps onto the US "one-drop rule," where one drop of black blood makes one Black, thus erasing any white parentage. Toxi, who speaks German—her native language—suddenly and out of nowhere tells her Black GI father that she "speaks English" and in this way is placed outside the compact of white German society.

The film performatively uses both whiteface and blackface to create one more layer of separation between Black German children and white German society. When Toxi wears whiteface makeup, she looks ridiculous and

---

14. For more on *Toxi*, see Stemmle, *Toxi*; see also Fenner, *Race under Reconstruction*.

unnatural, the visual message being that whiteness does not look good on a Black child. This awkwardness is meant to convey the belief that Black German children can no more naturally and seamlessly work themselves into a largely white German population. Similar arguments were used against the prospect of cross-racial adoption of Black children by non-Black parents both in Germany and the US. Toxi, even though adored by the young "progressives" in the film—Herta and her soon-to-be fiancée, Robert—is also used and otherized by them. Robert works in marketing and advertising and produces what he thinks is a cutting edge, liberal advertising campaign in which he makes Toxi the face of a chocolate candy bar. Saying, "They will just have to adapt their product line," Robert doesn't understand that he has turned Toxi into a blackface minstrel in order to the sell a product. Similar to her whiteface representation, Toxi's appearance in the ad campaign is exaggerated and exploited, with coal-black skin, large white round eyes, and large grotesque fleshy lips that take up nearly half of her face (see fig. 4.4). While Robert sees Toxi as a little girl, he also sees her as a commodity he can use to sell chocolates to white Germans. In much the same way that Black American GIs were referred to as "chocolate soldiers" and separated from the larger German population, so too were children like Toxi seen as the outsiders within[15] and the insiders without,[16] and attempts were made to remove them from the white German population.

Toxi sat at the intersections of liminality, collective memory, and currency because she was a terministic screen, an element that comes to symbolize how we view and understand parts of the world. As Kenneth Burke notes, "even if any given terminology is a reflection of reality, by its very nature as a terminology it must be a selection of reality; and to this extent it must function also as a deflection of reality."[17] While Burke in this quote is referring to language, images (visual rhetoric) are also a form of symbolic use and communication; images reflect a form of reality. Therefore, *Toxi* the film, and Toxi the main character, are visual representations of both the past and the postwar imagined future of Germany. Toxi is both the memoried desire that produced biracial children and the postmemory fear of Blackness in white spaces. The film and the subsequent newsreels, like the "Neue Deutsche Wochenschau newsreel [New German Newsreel] clip from 1954 in Imst, Austria," according to Sollors, "showed an idyllic children's village . . . full of orphans and children, making the institutionalization of the children with orphans and abandoned children

---

15. Collins, "Learning from the Outsider Within," 14–32.
16. See Small, *Rhetoric of Becoming*, 149.
17. Burke, *Language as Symbolic Action*, 45.

FIGURE 4.4. Scene from Robert Stemmle's 1952 film, *Toxi*, where Robert turns Toxi into a corporate advertisement.

look attractive."[18] The visual argument and mediated campaign centered the parental identification of Black German children solely with the longed-for absent parent (in this case, the Black American GI father). In the mediated persuasive appeal, *Toxi* sends the overt message that the Black German child *only* recognizes herself phenotypically in the African American parent and *never* in the white German mother who birthed her. This reduction of biracial acknowledgment erases any connection Germany may have to Black diasporic places of belonging outside of their control (e.g., Germany's defunct colonial empire, which it lost after World War I).

The *Toxi* film and newsreels served to create a memoried desire (a past desire of imagining) and created a visual argument for the return of whiteness, which found resonance in the United States. The film and other televisual images at this time longed to put the postmemoried present, in which more biracial children had been born than in any other postwar period in German history, in the past.[19] To put this into perspective, in West Germany in 1950,

---

18. Sollors, *Temptation of Despair*, 223.
19. See Chin et al., *After the Nazi Racial State*; Campt, *Other Germans*; Fehrenbach, *Race after Hitler*; and Höhn, *GIs and Fräuleins*.

FIGURE 4.5. Lilli (*left*) and Lore (*right*) with their mother, Greta, in Mannheim, Germany, on the day they graduated from kindergarten. Family photo, author's private collection, supplied by Greta.

the German population was sixty-one million people,[20] and among that number were three to four thousand Black biracial German children born in the postwar era. This means that the mixed-race threat from within West German borders constituted only 0.00655 percent of the population. This small population was continuously questioned because they violated the imagined and memoried racial existence of who white Germans thought they were and their notions of how Black Germans fit within the boundaries of that definition.

Lilli and Lore came into the world in a liminal state; they were born but not wanted, kept yet marginalized, and, once they were moved into the dormitory, erased during the weekdays. However, during the weekends, Lilli and Lore were integrated into their family, knew their biological relatives, and

---

20. "Population in the Former Territories."

stayed with family in the apartment. Greta said, "I picked [the twins] up in the morning [on Friday or Saturday] and returned [them back to the dormitory] on Sunday night" (see fig. 4.5).

Seeing Greta and other members of their family only on the weekends became routine for the twins, and usually the visits started at the end of Greta's workday on Friday. Speaking to Lore, Greta once said, "One day I picked you up after work, and it was just you. We really liked that." Lore asked, "Where was Lilli?" Greta said, "Lilli was being punished. She cut a little girl's hair in the orphanage. Cut her braids right off! Lilli was punished by not being able to go out with us and no Christmas gifts. So, I picked you up in the morning and returned you on Sunday night." Lilli, in the absence of Christmas gifts, essentially received a lump of coal. Even though Lore ultimately returned, how heartbroken Lilli must have been to know that Lore was picked up by and spent time with Greta and received gifts from Santa Klaus (Santa Claus). Lilli, in light of her punishment, not only received no Christmas gifts—not even from the nuns at the orphanage—but she was deprived of precious time with her mother. The experience of being picked up and returned furthered the liminality of the twins' lives. They were loved by family but put out of home. Visited by family who could leave and go on with life without them. This liminal existence eviscerated any Afrofuturistic identity that could be creatively imagined for the twins because having lived outside of the family home was used later as justification for leaving the children within the California foster care system.

LIMINAL EXISTENCE AND DIFFERENCE: SCIENTIFIC EXPERIMENTS

Unlike Lilli and Lore, who had weekend visits and stays with family, and therefore Greta and other family members as advocates, the most vulnerable Black German children were those who were up for adoption, with no parent protecting them. These biracial children were a scientific curiosity to anthropologists like Walter Kirchner, who in 1952, with the support of the Berlin Youth Welfare Office and State Health Office, studied the children to, according to Angelica Fenner, "assess whether different character traits and developmental patterns could be detected among Afro-Germans."[21] While Lilli and Lore were not subject to scientific experiments, Lore said she "remembers seeing physicians at the orphanage all the time." What she likely thought of as

---

21. Fenner, *Race under Reconstruction*, 93–94.

another child getting sick or sees now through her postmemory lens as good medical care for children in the dormitory/orphanage were likely medical and anthropological experiments on some of the children living there.

Whereas many of the earlier anthropological studies of mixed-raced children in Germany took Jewish German offspring as their object, postwar German anthropological studies reoriented their gaze onto the children of white German women and Black men. *Afrodeutsche Nachkriegskinder* became eugenic curiosities. Anthropologists like Kirchner and Rudolf Sieg relied on the post–World War I studies conducted on Black German children and set out to establish a theory to explain Black German children's deviation from the "white norm" and build upon the Nazi's scientific methods of analysis while reworking the paradigm toward a more "moral" postwar alternative.[22] The anthropologists used eugenic tactics and measured the children's skull size, recorded the size and width of their noses, eyes, and ears, and noted eye color, hair color and texture, and the lightness or darkness of phenotypic hue on a chart.[23] Kirchner's postwar research came to the same conclusions as that of his predecessors—the supposed superiority of white children and the inferiority of Black Germans.[24] This perpetual racist scientific gaze on Black German children not only expanded the coercive surveillance over Black bodies in Germany but also consolidated anti-Black notions not within biologically deterministic rhetoric but rather as owing to imagined cultural deficiencies that were perpetuated through blood lineage. Once again, being Black and German was essentially crafted as deficient in ways that made the incorporation of Black biracial children into the German polis a fundamentally dangerous prospect.

The potential trauma of such observations on the *afrodeutsche Nachkriegskinder* was profound, and Kirchner laments that "the great majority of the colored [sic] children live with the mother or the mother's relatives, that is for the most part with the grandparents."[25] His own research showed that between 1951 and 1953, 12 percent of these children were in orphanages and these were the children most at risk, because they had no advocate preventing them being treated like lab specimens. Martin Renes's research into the mistreatment of Indigenous Australians is apt here in comparison: "It is these children that became the main focus of assimilative government action; it is in their defencelessness that the breach of basic human rights is salient."[26] German

---

22. Fehrenbach, "Black Occupation Children," 44.
23. For more detail, see Fenner, *Race under Reconstruction*, 94.
24. See Oguntoye et al., *Showing Our Colors*.
25. Kirchner, "Academic Success of *Negermischlinge*," 2.
26. Renes, "Stolen Generations," 31.

anthropologists limited their study to those children who had Black American paternal lineage and falsely asserted that their findings broke with the overtly eugenicist determination of Nazi doctors because of their integrationist discourse. The anthropologists asserted that while Black German children were naturally disorganized and impetuous, the proper care from their mothers could ensure that the German community could deal with the problems of race.[27] These anthropologists particularly believed that the lighter-hued children (those who could pass for white) had a greater chance of assimilating into white German society, which again parallels what Renes notes about Indigenous Australian children: "Their part-white offspring was deemed intelligent enough to allow for their biological 'absorption' into the mainstream through basic training, child fostering, adoption."[28] This argument was particularly persuasive because the children of Black American World War II soldiers and German women were seen as benefitting from their already diluted Black blood through the legacy of rape that enslaved Black women in the United States endured from white men. Whereas, the French colonial fathers of World War I, being from Africa, were thought to have thoroughly disadvantaged their offspring through their so-called pure Blackness.[29]

This marginalizing visual construct in which a Black American descendant is preferred over an African descendant due to absurd notions of blood purity or impurity is similar to Karma Chávez's rhetorical concept of alienizing logic, which "refers to a structure of thinking that insist that some are necessarily members of a community and some are recognized as not belonging, even if they physically reside there."[30] Through the zeal to recraft postwar Germany as an imagined white nation, anthropologists like Sieg and Kirchner became complicitous with repressive erasure as they cast out mixed-race Germans and centered and retained white Germans. As Connerton defines it, "forgetting as repressive erasure appears in its most brutal form, of course, in the history of totalitarian regimes" with images of rulers, for example, being destroyed.[31] But, Connerton continues, "repressive erasure need not always take malign forms [and] can be encrypted covertly and without apparent violence,"[32] which is what happened to some Black German children. This means that the German facade of whiteness must reduce, marginalize, dehumanize, and erase biracial Black German children from the polis, creating "a historical rupture as well as

---

27. Fehrenbach, "Black Occupation Children," 41.
28. Renes, "Stolen Generations," 33.
29. Fehrenbach, "Black Occupation Children," 40.
30. Chávez, *Borders of AIDS*, 5.
31. Connerton, "Seven Types of Forgetting," 60.
32. Connerton, "Seven Types of Forgetting," 60.

bring[ing] about a historical break"[33] with a Germany that also included space for Black Germans. Similar to how the children of the Black French colonial soldiers and German women were represented to the greater German society, post–World War II biracial Black German children were seen as those who must be removed.

INTERNATIONAL ADOPTION: RECLAIMING IMAGINED WHITE COMMUNITY

In West Germany, the mixed-race children who were up for adoption were, according to Fehrenbach, "typically imagined as *Heimkinder,* or unwanted institutionalized children, [and] . . . most West German authorities viewed the children as a social problem and advocated international adoption as the preferred solution."[34] German-US adoption coordination reflected a strategy of the government to consolidate the white character of the developing democracy. After the war, the German government relaxed adoption laws for German children, but later, Fehrenbach continues, "white German children were . . . eagerly sought for adoption by white Americans, [and therefore], German federal officials began to demand more stringent regulation of international adoptions in order to keep such 'desirable' progeny at home in the Federal Republic."[35] The German government pushed for adoption of children of Black GIs, not by other white German families but rather by Black American families in the US, where the children would find that they "fit" into the community, thus formalizing denial of their German belonging and citizenship.[36] As Benedict Anderson observes, "Nation, nationality [and] nationalism—all have proved notoriously difficult to define, let alone analyze,"[37] but visually it becomes clear who are the insiders and who are the outsiders in the burgeoning German postwar democracy. "Communities are to be distinguished, not by their falsity/genuineness, but by the style in which they are imagined,"[38] says Anderson. In 1951, when it came to the potential international adoption of Black German children to the US, in several instances, Fehrenbach finds, "German officials expressed interest in including in their plan children who had *not* been surrendered by their mothers for adoption, even if they were

---

33. Connerton, "Seven Types of Forgetting," 60.
34. Fehrenbach, "Black Occupation Children," 45.
35. Fehrenbach, "Black Occupation Children," 47.
36. Fehrenbach, "Black Occupation Children," 45–48.
37. Anderson, *Imagined Communities,* 3.
38. Anderson, *Imagined Communities,* 6.

currently living in German families and would end up in orphanages in the United States."[39] The German interest in removing Black German children was an important part of integration/democratization efforts in West Germany.

Black German children were first given F visas, traditionally reserved for displaced orphans under the Displaced Person Act of 1948.[40] When that source of visas ran out, in 1951, the German government negotiated a deal with the United States to push adoptions of Black German children through nonquota visas for war orphans to circumvent the filled visa quota for Germans into the United States.[41] Here, the goals of Germany, the US, and adoption advocate Mabel Grammer aligned, because all three entities imagined a space where Black German children belonged, and this imagined space was Jim Crow USA. The imagined community, comradeship, and fraternity created simply because of the phenotypic hue and other visual traits of these biracial children made them candidates for removal from Germany.

Black American journalist-turned-adoption-advocate Mabel Grammer found herself involved in the international adoption of Black German children to the United States throughout the 1960s. Once a journalist for the *Washington Afro-American* newspaper (in the 1940s) and the *Baltimore Afro-American* newspaper (1951–54), Grammer lived in Mannheim, Germany, while her husband was stationed there as a navy warrant officer. Thrust into the nation's discussion of the liminal space of Black German children, from 1951 to 1953 Grammer, who "could not bear children,"[42] assisted in the adoption of up to seven hundred biracial German children out of Germany and into the United States and adopted twelve children herself.[43] Grammer viewed the adoptions as a form of social justice advocacy because of the poor treatment the biracial children received from the larger German community; "she personally witnessed discrimination against Afro-German children and their mothers on the streets of Mannheim,"[44] as Yara-Colette Lemke Muniz de Faria shares. The mothers also pleaded with her to help them. Lemke Muniz de Faria explains that these mothers had experienced "poverty, illness, [and] the stigma of being known as an 'Ami-hussy' or labeled a 'N——-whore.'"[45] Many of them found themselves in altered circumstances: their husbands had returned from POW

---

39. Fehrenbach, "Black Occupation Children," 46.
40. Lemke Muniz de Faria, "Germany's 'Brown Babies.'"
41. Fehrenbach, "Black Occupation Children," 45–48.
42. Fehrenbach, "Black Occupation Children," 47.
43. Peña, "Stories Matter," 251.
44. See Lemke Muniz de Faria, "Germany's 'Brown Babies,'" 355, for a detailed analysis of international adoptions under Mabel Grammer.
45. See Lemke Muniz de Faria, "Germany's 'Brown Babies,'" 355.

camps, or they were in new marriages in which the Afro-German child was no longer wanted. Newspaper articles like this one from 1951 in Bamberg, Germany, likely motivated Grammer as well:

> Three little Negroes—there they sit, on the bench in the kindergarten. They are called Karl-Heinz or Gisela or Monika, and when they open their little mouths, they babble in the purest Bamberg dialect. They have no inkling yet of the difficulties and the suffering they are unlikely to escape.[46]

This same article noted the difference between Black German children who were wanted and loved and living with their mother versus those up for adoption in children's homes:

> Most [of the children] live at home with their mothers, who—according to the experiences of the city's youth welfare office and social workers—are attached to their children with the same love as any other mother, and who would never give them up. The home children, however, are for the most part little human beings who have been abandoned by mother and father, and who have no one to look after them.'... "Hannele is three-and-a-half," [a] sister told us, "[and] the other day she stood in front of a mirror and looked at her hands and her face. Afterwards, she was sad." In another case, ... a melancholy little fellow tried to color his face on the white wall. Soon he will discover that that is useless.[47]

The nuns who largely ran these homes looked after the children but were unequipped to address the self-esteem issues related to race.

What was overlooked or misunderstood was that *afrodeutsche Nachkriegskinder* belonged in Germany. Unlike immigrants or settlers, these children had no other place to go, as any meaningful paternal connection to the US was not a factor in most cases. The notion of being from elsewhere—which is central to many immigrant stories and experiences around the world, did not readily apply. As Campt argues, "[postwar] Black Germans have no originary collective migration or displacement (either voluntary or forced) with which they can identify or trace their existence."[48] However, at the same time, Black German children in postwar Germany experienced a precarious mixture of liminality, erasure, and hypervisibility, their mere existence challenging notions of Germanness, which made the US, with its significantly larger Black

---

46. "Three Little Young Negroes," 5.
47. "Three Little Young Negroes," 5.
48. Campt, "Reading the Black German Experience," 289–90.

population, a viable option for transnational relocation. However, many Black German adoptees continued to experience identity dislocation. For example, Daniel Cardwell's adoption by a Black American couple was facilitated by Grammer when he was four years old. As Stephanie Siek relates, Cardwell's

> mother was a half-German refugee from Poland, and his father was native Hawaiian who was classified as "colored" by the military because of his skin color. "I've been run out of white people's houses: 'Who's this black person you're bringing here?' I've been run out of black people's houses: 'Who's this white person you're bringing here?'" Cardwell said of his adolescence and early adulthood. "There is no belonging, which is what brown babies sought most."[49]

Grammer was fully aware that the US was an enforcer of Black oppression, but in the space of imagined belonging, Grammer essentialized Black diasporic experiences to a visible place of belonging where, because of their one-drop of Black blood, these children would find a home in the US. In her Afrofuturistic imagining, she thought one drop of white blood might not matter to some Black American communities, and she already knew that one drop of Black blood would mean everything to many white American communities and Jim Crow laws. Further, Grammer had the support of the African American parents who wanted the children. African American communities in the United States also aggressively pursued adoption of Black German children after World War II, utilizing a pessimistic discourse about how most of the mothers of Black German children were institutionally segregated from their male partners, which meant most Black German children grew up in primarily white female community spaces,[50] disassociated from understanding their Black American paternal cultural heritage. Further, African American families sought out adoption of Black German children for a wide variety of reasons, including a sense of a kinship connection, as a palliative to the shame that some felt about the behavior of African American GIs who did not take responsibility for their children, and in hopes of improving the reputation of the Black soldiers who occupied Germany.[51] Promoting adoption of these *afrodeutsche Nachkriegskinder* resisted a white racist view of "absent fathers" and an uncaring Black American community. In addition, through the Afrofuturistic veil, these World War II Black GIs were reimagined as more

---

49. Siek, "Germany's 'Brown Babies,'" para. 24–25.
50. See Lemke Muniz de Faria, "Germany's 'Brown Babies.'"
51. See Lemke Muniz de Faria, "Germany's 'Brown Babies.'"

likely to be responsible caregivers were it not for laws in place preventing them from doing so.

Black American schoolteacher Ethel Butler's "Brown Baby Plan" resulted in several hundred adoptions of Black German children by African American families. Butler was interested in showing the positive effects growing up in Black communities had on Black German children.[52] Butler's plan cited the need for a racial fit in order to avoid discrimination, while ignoring the reality that the Black German children growing up in the Jim Crow South would also likely face vicious anti-Black assaults.[53] It should be noted that whether through the processes advocated by Grammer or Butler, adopting a Black German child was not easy. Rather, as Peña shares, "the restrictive and invasive application process often discourage[d] Black families who might have adopted children. Parents had to be less than 40 years of age, be financially stable, and undergo a medical examination to prove that they were infertile."[54]

Lemke Muniz de Faria's 2003 analysis of the circumstances of the hundreds of adoptions of Black German children by African Americans found that the Black press, and specifically the work of Ethel Butler, was critical in establishing the notion that post-Nazi Germany would never be able to adequately assimilate its Black children into society. A negative discourse regarding Black German integration into the European citizenry, as reported by the Black press touring Germany for their Black American readers, suggested that Black German children would continue to face severe discrimination as long as they stayed with their white German families.[55]

Beyond the racial fit justification of adoption, another argument for the displacement of Black German children was economic. After the war, the German government enacted a series of policy adjustments to attempt to reestablish economic security, and not needing to pay assistance to the families of Black German children was seen as a small but valuable means of ensuring that government assets were being received by the citizens perceived to be most productive for the state.[56] Never mind that biracial German children were German: they had grown up in Germany, and the only language and culture they knew was German. The pressure to establish a clean racial fit and avoid problems of integrating Black German children into German society was so severe that maternal rights and the interests of children were second to the state interest in reconstructing and projecting an image of a successful

---

52. See Lemke Muniz de Faria, "Germany's 'Brown Babies.'"
53. See Fehrenbach, "Black Occupation Children."
54. Peña, "Stories Matter," 251.
55. See Lemke Muniz de Faria, "Germany's 'Brown Babies.'"
56. Fehrenbach, "Black Occupation Children."

democratization effort. But, what about the biracial German children who were not adopted into foreign locales?

The children who were not adopted remained in Germany and were integrated into their community, like any other child. Fehrenbach finds that "all occupation children, including those of color, were grudgingly extended German citizenship—but only after Allied Military Government officials made it clear that they would not entertain paternity suits or grant citizenship to their troops' out-of-wedlock offspring born abroad."[57] One article in the *Overseas Weekly* in 1955, "Unwed Moms Can't Get GIs," reported that "Unwed German mothers of GI babies who thought sovereignty meant that they could sue the father for support of the child are most likely out of luck."[58] However, Dr. Friedrich Roth, spokesperson for the "Ministry of the Interior said . . . that the right of German mothers to sue was restored with the return of Germany to the Germans. But, he pointed out that the right extends only to those whose children were born after May 5th [1949], the day sovereignty took [effect]."[59] Roth then positioned his argument for the need for payment as one of exigence for the children, not the mothers. "We will be interested in seeing what happens if a soldier evades payment by asking for a transfer to another area. . . . We are not concerned with the claims of mothers, but with the claims of children against fathers."[60]

Munich lawyer Luis Jedelhauser claimed the Bonn government was denying the mothers their constitutional rights[61] and that he "would force a test suit on the question of the some 100,000 occupation babies," which would include back payments of child support by US GIs. The Ministry of Justice said Jedelhauser was "talking through his topper."[62] Many German women felt abandoned by both the German and US governments. As one woman who married a Black American soldier stationed in Munich, Germany, shared, regarding "[Black] American soldiers who fathered children with German women, . . . even if some of the African American soldiers were interested in adopting 'mixed' children, there were stipulations [like the couple] had to be married" (anonymous, personal interview). German women had no ability to marry their lover based on US anti-miscegenation laws, and the men had no ability to adopt their own biracial children, because of adoption rules, where marriage was a requirement.

---

57. Fehrenbach, "Black Occupation Children," 37.
58. "German Unwed Mothers," 5.
59. "German Unwed Mothers," 5.
60. "German Unwed Mothers," 5.
61. "German Unwed Mothers," 5.
62. "German Unwed Mothers," 5.

FIGURE 4.6. Lore (*left*) and Lilli (*right*) in school, in Mannheim, Germany. Family photo, author's private collection, supplied by Lilli.

The *Overseas Weekly* highlighted the back-and-forth conversation on where children of the postwar era belonged. One theme of this debate was a desire to hold the American GIs financially responsible for the drain these postwar children had on the struggling West German economy, an aim which was unsuccessful. In addition, the debate revealed a desire to "abort" these biracial Black German children out of Germany and make them a US responsibility. According to Ika Hügel-Marshall, "the US Army refused to [provide] any information. The fathers of 'occupation children' were to be protected from alimony suits."[63] As legal and social arguments raged on, these children continued to be integrated into German society. This integration into everyday German life caught the attention of the NAACP in 1952, particularly as it pertained to integrated schools and classrooms. The NAACP issued press releases praising Germany's progress on integrating classrooms, in juxtaposition to the US, which was still woefully behind (see fig. 4.6).

---

63. Hügel-Marshall, "Crossing Borders, Overcoming Boundaries," 172.

The press release read: "West Germany's decision to integrate schools without regard to race... surpassed the democratic United States in racial tolerance and equality."[64] In fact, because of the 1950s and 1960s US civil rights movements and the worldwide mediated coverage of the terrorism inflicted onto Black Americans by white Americans in favor of maintaining Jim Crow as a rule of law, the US eventually fell out of favor with Germany and was no longer considered a country where Black German children would be able to thrive.

Peña finds that "in contrast to [East] Asians who were most often adopted by middle- and upper-class whites, the Black Germans were placed in African American families, where it was expected that they would easily assimilate."[65] However, after the documented experiences of Black German children suggested otherwise—in reality, the children endured the culture shock of living in their new all-Black American segregated communities, the terrorizing racism of Jim Crow segregation policies, dizzying linguistic barriers and challenges, and the disorienting experience of being cast as "Negro" instead of German—sending Black German children to the United States largely halted,[66] and West German officials started looking for other countries they considered more compatible for Black German children. By the early 1960s, as Fehrenbach explains, "German psychologists [were] concerned with the children's emotional development in the segregated United States [and] described Danish mothers as more culturally compatible and less overbearing than the 'black mammies' who a decade before, had been seen as 'natural' nurturers to the children."[67] Thus West Germany centered on Denmark, and soon adoptions of Black German children there "outpaced those to the United States.... Denmark was portrayed in terms of cultural similarity; it was like Germany, only better since prospective Danish parents seemed 'more broad-minded about the children's origins.'"[68]

If people like Mabel Grammer represented possibility for reluctant white German mothers, Greta likely never attempted to engage Grammer's services. Instead, Greta told me she worked two jobs; in addition to her job at the Heidelberg Post Exchange, she worked a mysterious second job, about which she refused to talk beyond saying it was "a job in the evening." Nor was this mysterious second job disclosed to the social worker at the Children's Home Society of California when the twins became wards of the state and Greta severed her

---

64. Quoted in Fehrenbach, "Black Occupation Children," 47.
65. Peña, "Stories Matter," 245.
66. Fehrenbach, "Black Occupation Children," 48.
67. Fehrenbach, "Black Occupation Children," 48.
68. Fehrenbach, "Black Occupation Children," 48.

parental rights.[69] The silence surrounding the second job made me wonder if Greta secretly kept that money for herself rather than include it as money for the household. Or, instead of coming from a second job, I wonder if this money possibly came from falsely claiming that her phenotypically white twin daughters were Russian and born from rape. The German government gave a monthly stipend to women who bore German-Russian children from rape, and many women who had phenotypically light *afrodeutsche Nachkriegskinder* claimed this money. It is possible Greta did as well. When the German governmental payments ran out in 1955, Greta, who supported her family, surprisingly had enough money to purchase a one-way ticket via ship to the US—a purchase not one member of her family in their cramped apartment knew about. Greta simply vanished from Germany in the middle of the night and immigrated to the United States, leaving her twin daughters behind.

RAPE AND ABANDONMENT

Women's bodies are a site of struggle in war and are often used as a military strategy as well as a tool of propaganda. During wartimes, there is opportunistic rape and there is rape as part of the so-called spoils of war. Even though rape as a war tactic was banned by the Soviet Military Administration, rape was used to display the power of the conqueror. Russian soldiers emasculated the defeated white German men through the rape and control of white German women, whose bodies were once considered the carriers of the Aryan future and a visual sign of Aryan dominance. Through rape, the Russian soldiers who engaged in such physical violence and terrorism were able to exert social control as well as pollute the Aryan narrative of purity and power. Atina Grossman reveals that "in keeping with the images provided by Nazi propaganda, [Russian men] appeared as the drunken primitive 'Mongol' who descended on Germany like a vengeful 'hungry locust' in an 'orgy of revenge.'"[70] If German women gave birth to half-Russian children, these children would be seen as Russian and not German and, therefore, as not "pure" based on twelve years of firmly entrenched laws enacted by Hitler and the Third Reich. While there are many consequences of rape, including disease and emotional, physical, and psychological trauma, there is also damage done to the future of the community and society.

---

69. Social Worker, Children's Home Society of California, accessed 2012.
70. Grossman, "'Big Rape,'" 35.

Germany is known for keeping excellent records, and some of those records include women's reports of rape in the postwar years. When I went to archives in Berlin, Cologne, Frankfurt, Hamburg, Koblenz, Mannheim, and Wiesbaden, however, all but the Institut für Stadtgeschichte in Frankfurt denied me access to this haunted, horrible history, which was redacted in order to protect the survivors, the women and children. In the postmemory of rape, white male rape of white women is largely absent from the narrative. There was no mass media coverage of Russian soldiers or white US soldiers raping white German women that aimed to engender support for rape survivors.[71] Rather, in the instances when the rape of German was acknowledged, mediated policy used the bodies of rape victims as propaganda to reignite patriotism. In 1944 Goebbels "rushed camera teams forward to film the corpses of women and girls who had been raped and murdered by drunken Red Army soldiers. The images on the Nazi newsreels had been so appalling that many women presumed they were part of a gross exaggeration by the 'Promi,' the propaganda ministry."[72] And after the war, the policy of erasure and forgetting continued, such that in 1945 "Stalin was merely amused by the idea of Red Army soldiers having 'some fun' after a hard war" and "no document from the Soviet archives indicates" rape being used as a tactic of war.[73]

Rebuilding Germany and not engaging in a potential war with the Soviet Union was the focus, and so Germany's approach to this period of intense sexual violence involved prescriptive forgetting, an "act of state [that] differs from [repressive] erasure because it is believed to be in the interests of all parties," per Connerton's definition.[74] If nothing else, Germany had no moral high ground to stand on as related to rape. Karen Hagemann and Sonya Michel found that "both in wartime and afterward, sexual violation was rampant on all sides. During the war the German Wehrmacht ravaged in Eastern Europe, while American GIs preyed on French women."[75] In addition, sexist and sexual stereotypes about white German women worked to cast doubt on their claims of rape, as Grossman reveals: "If there was any rape," the prevailing story went, "it certainly wasn't necessary,"[76] the implication being that German women were sexually available, either as a matter of survival or sexual desire. Of the eighteen narratives I was granted access to, where there were births

---

71. For more information about German women who were raped, see Teo, "Continuum of Sexual Violence."
72. Beevor, introduction to *Woman in Berlin*, xiv.
73. Beevor, introduction to *Woman in Berlin*, xix.
74. Connerton, "Seven Types of Forgetting," 61.
75. Hagemann and Michel, "Introduction," 5.
76. Grossman, "'Big Rape,'" 43.

of Russian and Polish children born to white German women, none overtly mentioned rape—rape was only mentioned with regard to mixed-race Black children born to white German women. For women survivors, there was no support, sans a small payment that ended in 1955.

As noted above, women who were raped by Russian soldiers and became pregnant with a child were allotted a small stipend from the German government. After World War II, many German citizens had a difficult time meeting their basic needs, such as having enough food to eat. According to one woman who was married to a Black American soldier stationed in postwar Mannheim, "At one point, the caloric count for a day's ration was less than 1000 calories per day." Even Greta recalled, "We were hungry." Once it became known that the German state financially helped those women who said they were raising children born from rape by Russian men, German women whose biracial children could pass for white suddenly claimed their children were Russian too.

Greta needed money and refused to disclose any information about her second job, and coincidentally the monthly checks from her "second job" ceased at the same time the German government suspended the stipend program for Russian rape survivors in 1955. Claiming Lilli and Lore were Russian would have been another way for Greta to receive money, even if the amount was meager. Greta, like the other women, did not need to name the man, just show her twin daughters who passed for white. There was no money offered by the German government if a woman claimed that the father of her child was a Black American GI—even if there was an accusation of rape.

In the US Army, accusations of rape led to disproportionate suspicion of Black soldiers. As World War II soldier Frank Penick recounts:

> Once my unit was mustered out to be looked over by an Italian woman for a rape charge. I give our commanding officer credit for one thing: he made sure she understood she had better know what she was talking about if she selected one of his men. She didn't. I understand being mustered out only once for such a thing was something of a record. The practice was as soon as the word "rape" was mentioned anywhere[,] the first guys hauled out to be looked over were Negroes, and you know during war rape is a hanging offense.[77]

As was long established by both German and US racist propaganda, Black men were seen as oversexed beasts in need of control.

---

77. Motley, *Invisible Soldier*, 53.

However, it has been estimated that Russian soldiers raped two million German women and that approximately one in ten of these women died after the rape, whether from the rape itself or by suicide.[78] In the archive I was allowed to view, rape was mentioned in only two cases, and the alleged rapists were Black American soldiers. The focus of the accounts was not on the women but rather on what to do about the children.

For example, in searching File 1251 at the Institut für Stadtgeschichte, in Frankfurt, Germany, I discovered one document that told the story of Annelie who was put up for adoption because she was a child of rape by an African American man, and it was her part-Black heritage (her darker phenotypic hue) that prevented her from being adopted. As written in the file:

> According to the Youth Welfare Office, Adoption Office, Dusseldorf negotiations are pending at the youth welfare office there about adoptions of black occupation children by American families. The child Annelie, born '46, is in the local Augustinian pen. The child comes from a rape and is an unmistakable negro type. The mother is ready to put the child up for adoption. Despite the best efforts, however, it is not possible to find an adoptive family for the child. I asked the Dusseldorf youth welfare agency to find out whether similar cases exist there and whether the child might be placed in America. The mother is a reliable person who lives in orderly circumstances. I will provide further details when the child can be placed through the local office.[79]

Unlike the Russian and Polish white children in orphanages who may also have been children of rape but whose appearance went unremarked upon, Annelie is racially and stereotypically marked as "the unmistakable negro type," though the markers of such a "type" remain implied. The possibility of Annelie being sent to the United States is raised, presumably because her Black American status is hypervisible and centered while the white and Germans aspect of the child are erased. Therefore, Annelie-as-alien should go where there are more Black Americans: the Jim Crow US. Here, the document suggests, Annelie will feel at home because of the higher Black population and having a Black American father. Thus, the racist liminal space the child occupied in Germany would be eliminated.

In this same 1251 file, I came across one document that detailed an alleged rape that was under investigation:

---

78. Skundrick, *Third Reich*.
79. Courtesy of the Institut für Stadtgeschichte, Frankfurt, Germany, File 1251. Translation mine.

In reality, however, it is a question of a child who cannot have come from the husband because he is absent. The wife stated that she was receiving two Americans. Soldiers attacked. The child was initially in a home and is now sheltered in a place because the mother did not care about the child's placement. It was found that the child had the typical look of a Moroccan. Whether or not [the father is Black] has not yet been established.[80]

The absent husband, we assume, is white, given the omission of any reference to color or mention of any other nationality. The wife is under suspicion because she "received" two American soldiers and was attacked. While the language "soldiers attacked" could imply anyone, the description of the child as having "the typical look of a Moroccan" is racist, coded language for not white, and thus the accusation sits at the feet of an unnamed Black man. The child, based on phenotypic hue, is marked as Other through color and rape and is therefore unwanted.

When the German payments to Russian rape survivors ran out in 1955, so did Greta. According to Greta, her middle sister said something horrible, something racist that Greta refused to give voice to ("There are some things that you don't speak about [that] just hang over you"), and it severed their relationship forever. With her money saved, Greta purchased a single one-way ticket and booked passage on a ship leaving Bremen, Germany. Greta prearranged international sponsorship and passage to the United States in 1955, becoming one of many immigrants to go through Ellis Island on her way to California. Like a fugitive, she left her seven-year-old twin daughters behind in Germany, to be raised by their grandmother, their aunts, and the orphanage, and told no one she was leaving or where she was going. She simply left. Later, she contacted her youngest sister to tell her that she had safely arrived in the US. Without her biological children, she embraced the freedom she had once lost.

FLEEING TO FREEDOM: A CONCLUSION

Greta, like her father, Robert, became an apparition. While her youngest sister eventually learned Greta had immigrated to the US, her mother, middle sister, and the twins initially had no idea what had happened. She simply vanished. In reconstructing the past, I imagine what life might have been like for

---

80. Courtesy of the Institut für Stadtgeschichte, Frankfurt, Germany, File 1251. Translation mine.

the twins, who once saw their biological mother weekly, to then experience her absence. When I asked the twins what it was like to go from seeing their mother weekly to not seeing her at all, Greta's first departure appears to be, on the surface, less traumatic than when the twins became wards of the state of California and were placed in the foster care system. Perhaps this is because even though Greta left her children behind and immigrated to another country, the twins still received weekly visits from Hermine and Greta's sisters, they were still in German school, and they still had their same friends. While a grandmother and aunts are not able to fill the presence of a mother, no matter how absent she was from their lives, Greta's physical absence reads like silences that hold places and fill rooms. Though Greta's absence was still felt, Hermine and the sisters were able to partially fill the space of longing, and Lore and Lilli had little idea of the extent to which they were in the realm of unbelonging, or in the words of Chávez, "aliens that have been quarantined."[81]

In leaving Germany and her children behind, Greta participated in the erasure of memory, but instead of erasing the object of the undesired (the twins), she erased herself. She left her memoried past (as a single woman and mother) behind to begin anew. In order to have the freedom to create new memories in a culture and society that would not judge her, Greta, who could not hide her German accent, visually signaled that she had no past. Greta embraced structural amnesia and only remembered those things that she deemed socially important, those things that would add to, not take away from her creative imagining.[82] Greta's postmemory future was built on the common tropes of US immigrant narratives, but lost and forgotten in the story were her twins, who had no ability to create an Afrofuturistic imagining, because they had no idea they were forgotten and erased in the first place.

The twins, on the other hand, were bodies at the mercy of a system, in this case the vast orphanage system that sprung up across Germany after World War II. Lilli and Lore found themselves at the intersection of racism and the reproduction of a system that never made space for their bodies. The twins were the intersectional embodiment of illicit sex, race, racism, and shame, thus, for Greta, this meant that either they go, or she goes. The twins, even before they were born, were undesired and unwelcome, born into a space built on a foundation of anti-Blackness and Jim Crow. Framed through the lens of regret and shame, the memoried white racist pasts of Germany and the US meant that the twins would have difficulty birthing an Afrofuturistic vision, as

---

81. Chávez, *Borders of AIDS*.

82. Connerton borrows from John Barnes in laying out his ideas on structural amnesia, a process by which "a person tends to remember only those links in his or her pedigree that are socially important." Connerton, "Seven Types of Forgetting," 64.

their mere existence "was a mistake." Already pushed to the brink of liminal survival when they were removed from their home, after Greta temporarily vanished, Lilli and Lore were adrift.

Greta was far from being the only postwar single mother in Germany, but she only focused on how she felt in being hypervisible, and the uprising growing in her body. Being a mother to unwanted mixed-race twin daughters was exhausting. Greta was intently focused on the children's phenotypic hue and wondered if her twin daughter's skin would darken. Greta feared everyone could see the one drop of Black blood that flowed through her twin daughters and how that "defect" would be reflected in judgments about her and her sexual "promiscuity." Having children out of wedlock violated gendered stereotypes for woman during this time in history and announced her non-virginity. Greta, however, bought into the white supremacist system because it gave her motivation and permission to leave. She could leave her past for her imagined white-only future. Greta wanted to be welcomed back into the fold of white supremacy and white privilege and be in a place where no one knew her name or her past. Greta could make new memories through divorcing herself from the visual markers of race, racism, sex, and shame—her twin daughters Initially, fleeing to the US allowed Greta to regain freedom and white privilege instead of surviving in an unequal marginal existence with two mixed-race daughters in Germany. In the chapter that follows, the adoption experience of Black German families, and specifically Lilli and Lore, are examined along with their identity formation and the power of visual images and communicative rejection.

CHAPTER 5

The Transatlantic Appeal of Jim Crow

Reclaimed, Abandoned, and Adopted

Content warning: This chapter contains depictions of sexual assault and rape.

> Lilli and I were adopted into an Army family.... They may have
> had good intentions initially, but our upbringing was not ideal.
> —Lore's reintroduction letter to Greta, 2012

A place of possibility. This was the appeal of the United States for Greta, and this where she began to create a new identity in a new country. Once there, Lilli and Lore, on the other hand, had to contend with an imposed Black identity, specifically a Black American identity, that ran counter to how they saw themselves and understood their lives as German children. The twins arrived in the United States and were immediately in the stranglehold of Jim Crow, written upon with the racist language and symbols marking their new identity. The national violence and racial terrorism enacted against Black Americans long predated their arrival, and despite their knowing nothing about it, this racial and racist script became part of their ascribed identity, one that ran counter to their own constructions of self. Lilli and Lore, once constructed as dross that needed to be removed from Germany, now became a problem that needed to be removed from Greta's new life in the US.

Within this chapter, postmemory is centered, particularly in relation to Greta's life because she challenges static constructs of white womanhood, showing instead how womanhood is something that can be lost and regained depending upon what one is willing to sacrifice in exchange. In this case, Greta lost the albatross of motherhood and the twins but regained white womanhood, white privilege, and freedom. The reclamation of white womanhood, and with it, power, shows the resiliency of whiteness as a fantasy construction and also reveals its gatekeeping function, with only so many people allowed in. Because Greta was willing to forget her memoried self, she was rewarded with the chance to remake her life. Greta thrived, while Lilli and Lore's future with Greta crumbled. The twins are examples of the limits of an Afrofuturist creative imagining. Afrofuturism is not a one-way journey from bad to imagined good but rather a dynamic process and should be thought of as a circle. There were times when Lilli and Lore were in imaginative bliss living together as a family at Hidden Villa Ranch in California, and then there was the horror of being adopted, which snuffed out the Afrofuturistic glimmer of what they could be until they were nineteen-year-old adults. Postmemory realities impact identity.

Dynamic identity development is the focus of this chapter. I explore how Greta, Lilli, and Lore forged new identities and new lives and how the twins navigated new traumas once adopted. Did the ways Greta detached herself from her past in order to gain access to freedom contribute to the downward spiral Lilli and Lore experienced at this stage of their lives? Though Greta was able to access freedom for herself, the twins were not, as they were bound by absence, erasure, racism, emotional and physical assault. They were lost to the liminal space, the place in between, or as writer and film director Jordan Peele might say, trapped in the sunken place.[1]

RECLAIMED AND ABANDONED

What level of racism is enough to break familial bonds? Greta was free from her children for several months in 1955, living a life where the label "mother" did not define her, nor did the term *Negerhoren*. For nearly a year, Greta worked to establish a life and a new identity as an immigrant. In the months Greta was in California on her own, the twins still had a life in Germany. Lilli and Lore's day-to-day was akin to attending a boarding school, but they were fully integrated into German life, held German citizenship, and shared Greta's last name. The twins had friends and friendship networks, and despite living in a dormitory/orphanage, they also had family, an ideal held firmly by my great grandmother, Hermine. However, Hermine was undermined when, unbeknown to her, Greta worked covertly with the nuns at the orphanage to have the twins put on a plane to the US, permanently severing their

---

1. In Peele's *Get Out* (2017), Black bodies serve white people in a variety of capacities. The white patriarch of the film performs a procedure that transplants the brains of white clients into Black bodies. In this way, the white clients gain access to traits they lack (e.g., a healthy body and desired traits and skills) as well as a type of immortality. The Black victims are trapped in their own bodies, hypnotized and powerless, remaining partially conscious in the "the sunken place."

relationship with their grandmother. Lilli and Lore were to be reunited with their mother, but Hermine, who wanted and loved the girls, never saw the twins again.

On May 2, 1955, Lilli and Lore sat at an airport with an adult guardian who made sure they got onto the correct flight and buckled into their seats in anticipation of their first plane ride, which according to Lore was "full of other German children," many of whom were up for adoption. "I remember the plane load of children and adults singing happy birthday to Lilli and me. I remember we were given stuffed animals as presents; Lilli was given Donald Duck, and I received Mickey Mouse. It was all kind of surreal and overwhelming. Lilli was fine, but I had air sickness and vomited, I didn't know what was going on, so I couldn't enjoy the celebration. I just sat and clung to my stuffed animal." When the plane landed in California the next day, the twins were back in Greta's life. It is difficult to comprehend why Greta would arrange for her children to join her in her new life when she did not want to be a mother. Why would she want to bring her haunted memoried past forward, into the postmemory identity she was trying to create? Perhaps it was due to her belief that the United States was a place to begin again, that immigration would allow her to create new memories without being the target of racism. In the intersection of her memoried past and the new identity she was trying to create, immigrating to the US was the meeting point, the place between memory and creative imagining where Greta could compel a new life for herself, and temporarily for her twin girls.

Since the one-drop rule and Jim Crow would not be oppressions that affected Greta, the US could be a place of possibility. Perhaps the twins, who could pass as white without the label of *Besatzungskinder* (occupation children) or worse, could create new memories away from Germany as well. Maybe Greta discovered, in her absence from the twins, that she loved them and that Lilli and Lore filled a void. What I could discern from conversations with Greta was that visiting the twins became a more burdensome time commitment and a financial drain for the remaining family members in Germany, and in those financially difficult times during the postwar rebuilding era, the children were, after all, Greta's responsibility. For Greta's siblings, the twins became a chore, because they were primarily the ones who had to take care of Lilli and Lore. The siblings, who were working and of dating age, no longer wanted to take care of the twins because they had their own lives to live. Greta may also have been persuaded by the family who sponsored her in the US, since they did not judge Greta for having mixed-race children out of wedlock.

Greta, like many immigrants, established a foothold in the US through sponsorship. Greta's sponsors were Frank and Josephine Duveneck, a wealthy,

German-speaking Bostonian family who moved out west. Hidden Villa Ranch, located in Los Altos, California, was founded by Frank and Josephine, and they were not a family to sit on the sidelines when it came to social injustices. According to a biography of the Duvenecks I discovered on a tour of the ranch, Frank and Josephine were "legendary figures in the San Francisco Bay Area and have been mentors to thousands of people. Their concerns for education, social justice, and the environment made them instrumental in the founding of organizations which are still vital to our community today."[2] Hidden Villa Ranch was described as a "haven for many," as the Duvenecks assisted "European refugees in the 1930s and 1940s, Dutch sailors during World War II, Japanese-American returnees from" imprisonment in the US camps, "Cesar Chavez and Mexican-American farm workers, and Native Americans."[3] According to Mike Mackey's account of Duveneck in *Heart Mountain,* Frank became involved in assisting Japanese Americans when he discovered, walking through San Francisco, signs that were "posted on walls and telephone poles with directions and requirements for Japanese evacuees" to be removed from California and imprisoned: "My mind went back to similar notices that I saw in Germany some years ago," Duveneck said, "proclaiming restrictions against the Jews."[4] Mackey further relates that Frank noticed Japanese men wearing American legion caps, one of whom told him that he believed his US Army service in World War I "entitled him to stay in his home. Frank wondered how anyone could 'consider the color of a man's skin a test of his loyalty.'"[5] This kind of humanity was foundational to the concept of Hidden Villa Ranch.[6] According to a placard at the ranch, "the Duvenecks believed that building relationships between people would lead to a more peaceful and just society."[7]

In 1937 Hidden Villa became the "first youth hostel west of the Hudson River," and in 1945 the Duvenecks "started the first interracial summer camp in the [United States]," creating a place centered on "environmental awareness

---

2. Onsite placard at Hidden Villa Ranch.
3. Onsite placard at Hidden Villa Ranch.
4. Mackey, *Heart Mountain,* 16.
5. Mackey, *Heart Mountain,* 16.
6. On an earlier version of the website for Hidden Villa Ranch (ca. 2014), I found the following information: "Hidden Villa Ranch was founded by Frank and Josephine Duveneck who purchased the land in 1924 and offered it as a gathering place for discussion, reflection, and incubation of social reform. Over the following decades, the Duveneck's established the first hostel on the pacific coast (1937), the first multiracial summer camp (1945), and Hidden Villa's Environmental Education Program (1970). The Trust for Hidden Villa was established as a nonprofit in 1960" (Hidden Villa Ranch, "What Is Hidden Villa").
7. Onsite placard at Hidden Villa Ranch.

and multicultural understanding."[8] Being surrounded by such open and accepting people, Greta eventually told Frank and Josephine Duveneck that she had twin daughters, and the Duvenecks welcomed the family of three with open arms for three years, from 1955 to 1958. The Duvenecks even helped Greta obtain her first job in the US, as Greta shared, "working for a bakery. Mrs. Duveneck introduced me to the owner, and I got the job the next day." The freedom that Greta had, a life as a single person without the responsibility of children, evaporated, and the memory and the reality that she had to be the sole breadwinner haunted her. After working at the bakery, Greta said, "for approximately six months, through a customer contact at the bakery," she found a full-time office assistant job at a large firm and with better pay. To "catch a ride to work at [this firm], I walked down the same half-mile dirt road that the twins would in order to get to school," said Greta.

Hidden Villa Ranch was big enough to house Greta and the twins nine months out of the year, but because the ranch was a working ranch, hostel, and summer camp, during the summer months, Greta had to vacate her living quarters to paying renters, though the twins were allowed to remain since they joined the summer camp. A few times, when the hostel was full, Greta and the twins experienced transience, as Greta said, she "moved from house to house with the girls. We stayed with a variety of white families where they didn't charge us rent." The instability of this situation wore on Greta. She referred to this time in her life as "awful" and "stressful," because there were times when she did not know which friend might take them in, and as a new immigrant with few friends to guide her through new cultural norms, Greta navigated instability, uncertainty, and vulnerability. Greta tried, as much as she could, to avoid renting apartments or staying in hotels and motels because of the expense. In her new home, Greta discovered the tables were turned as it was she, and not the twins, who was without shelter for temporary periods when the hostel at Hidden Villa was full. While the apartment she shared with Hermine and her sisters in Germany was crowded, to be temporarily homeless was a new experience for Greta.

With the twins still residing in a German-speaking household and knowing very little to no English, Greta and the Duvenecks were the world for the girls. Lore said, "I thought they were our *oma* and *opa*. We loved them. We felt safe and secure. We had maids who would dress us, bathe us, and prepare our meals, and we had pet ducks whom we named Oskar and Oliver." They also had Greta full-time and no longer needed to vie for the nuns' attention at the orphanage. Instead of living in a dormitory that housed seventy

---

8. Hidden Villa Ranch, "Mission and History."

postwar children, they now had a large home and acreage to safely play in and explore. No longer did they carry the stigma of *Besatzungskinder,* and no longer did they have to go hungry or wait until the weekend to see their mother. "I remember running around on the ranch and having plenty of children to play with in the summer," Lore said. "I also remember these really long walks to get to school."

    Hidden Villa is nestled at the foothills of the Santa Cruz Mountains on "over 1600 acres," as I learned during a guided tour Greta and I took in 2013. Walking the grounds, I felt as if I had a window into the lives lived before me. As I followed the footsteps of the generations before me, I found myself wondering: Did the twins play in this spot? Did they have a favorite place on the grounds or a favorite nook in the house? As Greta and I walked through the large house, touring all the rooms, I saw the kitchen and dining room where she and the twins ate their meals and the rooms where Lilli and Lore slept. When she saw these memoried spaces, Greta said they "looked just like they did" when she and the girls lived there. At one point in the tour, I saw Greta take the arm of our guide, and then she told small portions of her story—leaving Germany, being sponsored by the Duvenecks, and coming to live in Hidden Villa. The details Greta chose to share with a stranger spoke to her nostalgia and how she saw her post-memoried version of herself; she foregrounded elements that cast her as a struggling immigrant and skimmed over elements that cast her as a struggling single mother. Two things stood out to me in this moment: First, I was able to hear how Greta presented herself and her life to others who were not family and did not know the intimate details of her life. Second, I was able to more intimately understand how, for the first time, Greta, Lilli, and Lore could be seen as neither hypervisible nor invisible but simply as German daughters living with their mother.

    In a new country, the twins found a sense of normalcy, and this included going to school. The twins were enrolled in and entered the US school system but could not speak English. There was no English as a second language (ESL) curriculum in their school, and the Federal Bilingual Education Act (which has since undergone revision) did not exist and was not passed until 1968. Excited to start at a new school and meet new children, children the twins thought would speak German, Lore said she ran up to a group of girls and excitedly "spoke to some other girls around my age, in German, and instead of the girls responding to me, one girl slapped me in the face." This was Lore's introduction to the California school playground. While I do not want to excuse the child's physical violence, the little girl who slapped her was likely confused and shocked by Lore's incomprehensible speech. Feeling silenced, Lilli and Lore had only one another to communicate with on the playground. The teachers, on the other hand, saw the twins as school novelties. Placed in the situation of being the hypervisible new foreign kids at school, at one point, Lore shared, "our school gathered an assembly where Lilli and I had to sing German songs. We had no idea what we were supposed to do, but we were standing on stage in front of the school and figured out the teacher wanted us to sing German songs, so we did." But at least Lilli and Lore had the safety of their mother as they began life in a foreign land. If anyone in their little family of three missed anything about Germany, nothing was shared or conveyed. The way Lore described Hidden Villa seems like imagined hope come to life, a kind of Afrofuturistic bliss. In fact, being at Hidden Villa with Greta could have been especially helpful for Lilli, who had a difficult time adjusting to life in the dormitory/orphanage in Mannheim. The back and forth between Greta's apartment and the difficult existence in the dormitory wore on Lilli, who began to act out in troubling ways and was constantly disciplined by the nuns with "no food, not being able to visit mom, constant time outs," as Lore recounted, and "coal in her stocking at Christmastime," chimed in Greta. Being with Greta, even out of their home country and familiarity, created new possibilities for stability for the twins.

The love the twins had for the Duvenecks was mutual, and the Duvenecks, who knew that Greta never wanted to be a mother, longed to adopt the twins. Oddly, when Frank and Josephine asked multiple times to adopt the twins, Greta turned down their requests. Greta said, "They wanted to adopt the girls, but I said no." Eventually Greta met a man, a white man, who became her boyfriend. Greta shared, "He was instantly smitten with me. I asked around about him and learned he was divorced with two daughters, but the daughters lived with their mother." Greta met this man at work, and the bachelor entered the lives of the twins. The girls spent time with him, and they became a family unit of sorts, going on "outings together and tucking the girls into bed," said Greta, and as Lore recalled, "reading us bedtime stories." Greta was particularly taken with this man because, she said, he "always accepted me and accepted my past. He never held that against me. He didn't mind that I was not a virgin." In this recollection, "past" becomes an enthymeme or a coded word for expected virginity for women, as well as a code for having children out of marriage, and *afrodeutsche Nachkriegskinder* at that. The social expectation that women remain chaste until marriage was one that Greta violated. To escape this shame, Greta left her country and home and traveled to a world where no one knew her, except the Duvenecks.

However, something happened, and for some reason, Greta and her boyfriend broke up. Greta said, "I was devastated. I couldn't be a single parent again." Whatever caused the breakup, Greta would not say. During this unstable period, Lilli acted out as well, starting a fire at Hidden Villa, which caused the Duvenecks to temporarily kick Greta and the twins off of the ranch, making them homeless and adding more instability to an already precarious situation. How long the breakup lasted was never revealed during the interviews. Recognizing that Greta's and the twins' lives were in a downward spiral, at some point the Duvenecks welcomed them back, but in 1958, two life-altering events occurred that would upend everything: (1) Hermine died, and (2) Greta received a proposal. Hermine died unexpectedly from a stroke, and her death presented Greta with a choice she had never had before: keep Lilli and Lore or have them adopted. Hermine's death opened up new possibilities for Greta and the twin's lives were to be forever changed. Also in 1958, Greta and her boyfriend reconciled, and he proposed. Greta's decision about what to do with the twins was made when the man presented his terms: "I'll marry you, but I don't want another man's children." Greta agreed. Greta was now about to be free of her daughters and be married to a wealthy man.

Learning about the engagement, the Duveneck family once again offered to adopt the twins. Inexplicably, again, Greta turned them down. It was curious that Greta passed up an opportunity to be free of her twins since she had wanted to have the twins adopted immediately after they were born, and now, Hermine was no longer an obstacle. Greta refused to answer why she did not want this German family, a family the twins loved, to adopt her children. Instead, Greta announced to the Duveneck family that she and her fiancée had begun parental rights termination paperwork, which they had already filed with the court; the twins would be entering the California orphanage/foster care system. Furious, recalled Greta, the "Duveneck family never spoke to me again. They never forgave me." As an insider and outsider to this story, I find Greta's refusal to be a selfish act. Greta could move on with her new life, and the twins could have as well, with the stability the Duveneck family provided, but Greta chose not to allow this. Perhaps having a German family adopt the children, a German family knowing Greta's shame, would have kept her secret alive. To begin again with new memories, Greta had to sever the old ones.

The parental rights termination papers were finalized in July 1958, and Greta was a married woman in October 1958. The push-pull of Lilli and Lore's existence had been decided. No longer was there a tug-of-war between Hermine's desire ("I don't want them to be adopted") and Greta feelings ("I don't want them in my life"). Greta reminisced, "We wanted to begin anew like any newly married couple." Ten-year-old Lilli and Lore were not invited to the wedding, and Greta began to make new memories as a married woman with no children in her new home with her new husband. This new life meant she did not have to work, could frequently travel, and had the luxury of a weekly housecleaner and gardener. Lilli and Lore in foster care became an afterthought whom Greta would visit monthly until their adoption, nearly two years later. As Lore shared, "Once having arrived in Ming Quong [the

FIGURE 5.1. In Greta's backyard in Los Altos, California, with Lore (*left*) and Greta (*right*). Lore is holding one of two abalone shells Greta placed beneath a tree in memory of the twins in 1958. Image taken by the author's father.

orphanage], I have fond memories of Mom's monthly visits [and her] taking Lilli and me for dental and hair appointments." She also recalled that Greta provided them "a living allowance at the orphanage" so they "would have spending money for candy or whatever we wanted." In honor of the twins, Greta planted a tree in her new yard and around the base of the tree placed two abalone shells containing artificial flowers, almost like a memorial to the dead (see fig. 5.1). Greta's daughters were remembered, but erased, having become the embodiment of the visible invisible. This is the furthest away the twins were from Greta until they were adopted and completely out of her life.

The representation of Lilli and Lore as inanimate objects places them beyond the space of liminality and into obscurity and secrecy. The "twins-as-shells" memorialization absolved Greta from her own complicity in the continued disruption of and eventual disappearance from the twins' lives. In Greta's postmemory imagining for her daughters, she made the argument that the girls could go on with new lives, without her, and begin anew, as she did, without the realization that they had been left behind. At ten years old, Lilli and Lore were stripped of another stable environment and became wards of the state in July 1958. They maintained their German citizenship until their German passports expired and were never renewed, at which point they became citizens of no country. Lilli and Lore were now fully integrated into the California orphanage system, and the Children's Home Society placed them in Ming Quong in Los Gatos, California, where they resided from 1958 to 1960 and where the twins were suddenly American, suddenly Black, and suddenly alone.

In 2013 I attempted to view and tour Ming Quong, but it no longer existed as a Children's Home, but in 2017, a museum installation about Ming Quong provided this summary:

> The Ming Quong Home, which translated to "Radiant Light," opened in 1915 in Oakland, [California,] and in 1936 in Los Gatos, [California,] and served Chinese American girls of all ages. The Home was the first institution of its kind in the United States to admit Chinese children. Ming Quong was part of a network of Presbyterian Mission Homes created in San Francisco in 1874, whose initial purpose was to intervene on behalf of young, Asian, immigrant females who had become vulnerable upon arrival into the United States. Although Ming Quong was referred to as an orphanage, it functioned more as a custodial home for girls with families that could not care for them financially or emotionally.[9]

Initially a home for children of Chinese descent, starting in 1953, Ming Quong actively operated as an orphanage for all children, Lilli and Lore among them.[10] It was here that liminality and a liminal existence began to enshrine Lilli and Lore, as they were haunted by their memoried German experiences of being left behind.

JUSTIFICATION AND ADOPTION

Justification

Greta reinvented herself as a thirty-six-year-old newlywed, and on September 24, 1959, became an American citizen (see fig. 5.2). The twins, however, were in a precarious situation, because their only documents, which they had no control over, were German passports. Since Lilli and Lore were not placed for adoption in Germany, the US viewed them as German citizens with German passports. Lilli and Lore, as ten-year-old children, did not understand

---

9. "Radiant Light."
10. Peterson, "Ming Quong."

FIGURE 5.2. Greta's US citizenship surprise party at work in Los Altos, California, with Greta centered and foregrounded in the image. Family photo, author's private collection, supplied by Greta.

the importance of citizenship and papers or being legally documented in their new country of residence. The twins were brought to a new country by means beyond their control; today they would be labeled Dreamers. When other postwar children were adopted out of Germany into international locales, the termination of their German citizenship was automatic and the application for citizenship in their new country began. However, this was not the case for Lilli and Lore, who were never available for adoption in Germany. When Greta surrendered the twins to the social worker in California, among their meager possessions were their German passports. When their passports expired, the people who adopted them never attempted to make Lilli and Lore naturalized citizens of the United States. In the simplest terms, Lilli and Lore were undocumented.[11]

---

11. Lille and Lore's situation was similar to that of Korean and other transnational adoptees in the US in that citizenship status is particularly precarious as a result of the complicated and exclusionary logics of racial identity and national belonging. See Kim and Park Nelson, "'Natural Born Aliens.'"

Undocumented immigrants are "foreign-born people who do not possess a valid visa or other immigration documentation, because they entered the US without inspection, stayed longer than their temporary visa permitted, or otherwise violated the terms under which they were admitted."[12] At times, transnational adoption results in adoptees becoming undocumented because adoptive parents have not followed the US naturalization process. Sometimes this is a result of adoptive parents wishing to keep the adoption a secret from the child in an effort to keep the memoried past sealed, hidden, and forgotten. As Rosemarie Peña explains, "All the [postwar] children [who were internationally adopted] were eligible for United States citizenship upon their arrival into the US, but individual testimonies reveal that not all families were properly informed of the naturalization procedure, or perhaps some just neglected to follow up. Thus, some children did not receive their US citizenship until much later, if at all."[13] Under Section 27 of the German Nationality Act, a minor who is a German citizen, when adopted by a foreign parent, will automatically lose their German citizenship, but *only* if they automatically acquire the citizenship of the adoptive parent. Peña shares that in her own situation, her parents wanted to conceal her adoption and did not initiate naturalization until she "was 12 years old, only after they received an official notification from the federal government threatening my deportation. Prior to that time, as I discovered much later, I had been legally *staatenlos* [stateless]."[14] Udo Ackermann, known as Rudi Richardson, reminisces that he was "born in a Bavarian women's prison in 1955. His mother, a Jewish woman named Liesolette, was serving a prison term for prostitution. His father, whom he never met, was an African-American serviceman named George. Rudi was given up for adoption."[15] Adopted as a toddler, Richardson/Ackermann's parents, as Siek notes, "never had him naturalized as a US citizen. He was told he'd get citizenship automatically after being honorably discharged from the Army, but it never happened. This caused problems for him three decades later, when he was deported to Germany in 2003 after spending time in prison for drug possession and petty theft."[16]

Like Peña's and Richardson/Ackermann's families, Lilli and Lore's adoptive family did not complete their naturalization paperwork until 1967, when they were nineteen years old, seven years after they were adopted and two years after their German passports expired, and only because they and the people

---

12. Washington State Department, "What's the Difference?"
13. Peña, "Stories Matter," 247.
14. Peña, "Stories Matter," 247.
15. Siek, "Germany's 'Brown Babies,'" para. 2–3.
16. Siek, "Germany's 'Brown Babies,'" para. 8.

who adopted them were deployed back to Mainz, Germany. *Staatenlos,* Lilli and Lore had no official paperwork at a state or national level (for example, a general ID, driver's license, or valid passport) noting who they were, and at least on paper, they did not exist. They once again resided in a liminal space.

As wards of the state, Lilli and Lore had to abandon any hope of creating a life with their mother by their side. The postmemory fantasies that Lilli and Lore may have had in their Afrofuturistic imaginings of being a family with Greta had to be rewritten as Greta wanted to dive forward into her own imagined future without them. At ten years old, being discarded broke Lilli, who began to act out, sleepwalk, and exhibit behavioral problems toward her new caregivers in the California foster care system. While the state wanted the twins adopted together, the social workers had to separate Lilli and Lore as roommates. Lilli saw Lore as a symbol of her past pain and her present abandonment and became violent, transferring all of the rage Lilli had for her mother to Lore. Lore said, "The social workers were afraid Lilli was going to physically harm me since she was so violent, so they separated us." Lilli's problems were doubtless reactions to trauma. But Lilli's sleepwalking, for example, instead of being seen as a sign that she was processing trauma and in psychological distress, was categorized as a child pushing the boundaries of authority. According to Katie Gerten, "kids in foster care suffer from PTSD . . . at almost twice the rate of returning war veterans."[17] Instead of receiving sympathy from the foster care system, Lilli was continuously punished for what they saw as misbehavior.

For the most part, Lore, as opposed to Lilli, was a rule follower, a trait that earned her praise from the nuns in Germany and Greta alike. As Greta recounted to Lore, "Lilli was such a difficult and selfish child. She would not help the family. [Do you remember you] and I were scrubbing the floor? [You were] such a good worker, but Lilli, she just sat there, watching. I asked Lilli, 'Don't you want to help us?' and she said, 'No.' She was always like that." This obedient manner served Lore well and into adulthood, as following rules allowed her to create order out of chaos, and it became a defensive measure. Because she followed authorities, Lore more easily adjusted to the familiar pattern of seeing Greta infrequently while in the California orphanage, as they had when they all lived in Germany. Lore said she began to make new relationships and had a fast friendship with her "best friend, Helen," who was Chinese American and lived at Ming Quong too. Lilli, on the other hand, became isolated, and through her anger and violence, she created another loss by forcing the separation of the twins for Lore's own safety. According to Peña,

---

17. Gerten, "9 Heartbreaking Facts."

While psychologists agree that a permanent home and caregiver is the preferred solution for parentless children over institutional and foster care placement, the adoptive child has still suffered emotional harm associated with the initial rupture. It is also generally assumed that a child who has experienced multiple placements will have more difficulty adjusting to a new family than one who was adopted directly from his or her mother, but this does not mean that the latter is a panacea.[18]

This separation would haunt the twin's relationship for the remainder of their adult lives and alter their relationship with one another, just as being left in the orphanage eventually severed their relationship with their mother. Greta, on the other hand, thrived in her new postmemory creation of life and the new identity she crafted for herself without the twins, enjoying her new life as a white US immigrant.

The construction of Greta's new identity meant she needed to move her German twins out of the space of whiteness and into a Black construct. The same twins who once went from *afrodeutsche Nachkriegskinder* to white were now Black again, because a white parent not wanting Black children (regardless of phenotypic hue) was something that could be understood in the US during the Jim Crow era. Effectively, the twins were now considered, as the California social worker said, "part Negro."[19] During our first meeting, Greta said, "I am surprised that racism happens in this day and age. I am sheltered from all that as you know. To me, a Negro is no different than anyone else." However, when Greta relinquished her parental rights, she showed that she *did* know about race, racism, and its toxic effects, particularly as related to herself and Blackness. Greta's denial is illustrative of Connerton's fourth type of forgetting, "forgetting that is constitutive in the formation of a new identity. . . . The emphasis here is not so much on the loss entailed in being unable to retain certain things as rather on the gain that accrues to those who know how to discard memories that serve no practicable purpose in the management of one's current identity and ongoing purposes."[20] Greta knew that denying race and racism was necessary if her white womanhood was to be restored, and she understood the transformative nature of forgetting. Working with the social worker, Greta vacillated on the question of the race of the father, from

---

18. Peña, "Stories Matter," 248.
19. The term *Negro* is a highly stigmatized word that is no longer used to refer to Black people in the United States. *Black,* which is used more as a diasporic term to refer to Black peoples worldwide, replaced *Negro* in the 1970s, while *African American* also became a popular term beginning in the 1990s.
20. Connerton, "Seven Types of Forgetting," 62–63.

"white to Native American to Negro," but ultimately she revealed that the father, Albert, may have been part Black American, which allowed for sympathy and understanding from social and government agencies that otherwise would have judged her harshly for having had premarital sex, let alone with a Black man.

The social worker now had a great deal of sympathy for Greta, who was saddled with what she called two "mistakes"[21] who, in the eyes of the US one-drop rule, were suddenly not just "part Negro" but Negro, forced into US race binaries and white supremacist divisions.[22] Examining the social worker's paperwork, I wondered what might be considered worse: sex with a married man or sex with a Black American GI? Clearly for the social worker, Albert being Black was all the justification needed to sever parental ties.

In assessing Greta, the social worker said she was impressed by her success in life: "She had the equivalent of two years of college, was a manager in [Germany], supervised all employees and earned a very good salary." She was impressed with Greta's "above-average intelligence" and that she "had a definite accent and good command of the English language." She was also impressed with her beauty, "[Greta] had a very fair complexion [. . .] and is attractive and capable." But most of all, the social worker was impressed that Greta took care of her twin ten-year-old daughters despite their biracial status and the challenges that came with it and was "working through her feelings of past experiences."[23]

The social worker's representation of Greta is inconsistent with how Greta characterized her class positionality in Germany as someone struggling to make ends meet with two jobs. Greta's composite story comprised the different narratives told, which served to illuminate how she crafted her now-immigrant story of survival. Perhaps Greta told different stories depending on the circumstance, emphasizing her working-class struggles when justifying casting off her children in Germany and emphasizing her middle-class identity when she sought affirmation in the United States. Because of this story of survival, Greta was afforded all the benefits of whiteness, including being ascribed beauty and intelligence. In Germany, Greta's white privilege would have been secure had she not borne biracial children. Had she fulfilled the prescripts of Hitler Maiden upbringing, her cultural value, worth, and status would have been confirmed, and therefore, the likelihood of her immigrating to the US would have been low. The children were the anchors weighing her down, preventing her from accessing white privilege.

---

21. Social worker, Children's Home Society of California, accessed 2012.
22. Social worker, Children's Home Society of California, accessed 2012.
23. Social worker, Children's Home Society of California, accessed 2012.

As the social worker noted, the downward spiral of Greta's life began when two biracial babies were born. According to the social work records, Greta's family had trouble accepting these postwar twins, and Greta's mother, in particular, had difficulty, asking Greta to move the babies out: "Your maternal grandmother . . . had difficulty accepting your racial diversity and requested your birth mother find another home."[24] This social worker quote contradicts the historical memoried narrative Greta shared, where Hermine appeared to be the *only* person in the family who wanted to keep the twins. Hermine, in Greta's postmemory revision, was now the person urging Greta to get rid of the twins. Further, Greta lived in the family home during the pregnancy and after; only the twins were displaced into the dormitory at the orphanage in Germany. The social worker took what seemed like evidence of unwantedness (the twins living in the Catholic home) as a fact of unbelonging and was also unaware of the housing crisis throughout postwar Germany that separated many families, not just mixed-race children and their families. The social worker thought the children were never accepted by anyone in the family given the postmemory narrative that Greta shared. There were no other adults who could cast doubt on the memories and experiences she shared, and the children had no credibility.

It can be argued that Greta manufactured accounts for various audiences to fit hegemonic norms in order to assimilate more easily in the US. First, Greta leveraged a "hard luck" immigration story, relying on one of the foundational narratives of the US—the "Horatio Alger myth," or the idea of pulling oneself up by your bootstraps. In the zeal to assimilate more easily into a new nation, immigrants may use that nation's stereotypes and prejudices in their own favor. Second, Greta admitted that she failed. Failure results in a loss of face. Greta was unable to measure up to the standard of what and who a good mother should be. Therefore, Greta gave herself the saddest backstory possible in order to evoke an emotional (pathetic) appeal. Third, Greta admitted that she not only failed but also violated societal expectations concerning virginity. Greta had evidence that she was a "naughty" or "bad" girl, and children were her punishment. In order to circumvent this loss of face, Greta showed that she had worked hard to change her course in life. The most dramatic evidence of change was letting go of what was weighing her down, in this case, children. Finally, Greta admitted that she violated societal standards regarding sexual relations with a "Negro." There was no greater sin a white woman at that time could commit than having sexual relations with someone who was not white. Greta never admitted she failed as a mother, because she never embraced the

---

24. Social Worker, Children's Home Society of California, accessed 2012.

label, but in the story she told the social worker, she readily admitted to violating two other norms. In this way, Greta persuasively and successfully leveraged her shame, her desire to save face, and her whiteness such that by the time Lilli and Lore entered the foster care system, they were the ones blamed for the struggles in Greta's life, not the other way around.

Adoption

Lilli and Lore were back in the space of liminality as they were thrust into the California foster care system. In this space, there was no Afrofuturistic moment of transitional possibility, because as children, they were still dependent on their mother, but she had no desire to bring them forward into her new life. Peña finds that "adolescence is . . . the time when most adoptees tend to struggle with issues of attachment and belonging."[25] Lilli and Lore thought they understood their place in the world with Greta but now reeled from a loss of not only culture, country, home, and language but also family. In referencing my mother grieving for her familial loss, the social worker noted: "[Lore] often mentioned [and]. . . . drew pictures of [her] birth mother."[26] But Greta never reclaimed the twins. Upon our first reunion after fifty-two years, Greta claimed the social worker had told her that if the twins weren't happy, they could come back to her: "The adoption agency lied. They said the girls were happy. The adoption agency refused to give the girls back. I was threatened with arrest if I took the girls back." This statement does not match the official state of California files. Rather, Greta's statement is a creative reimagining, perhaps driven by grief or embarrassment in the face of what actually happened when she dropped her twin daughters off at the orphanage. In Greta's account, she, not the twins, is the primary victim of the California foster care system.

What was apparent in the state of California files, however, was the racist reconstruction of the twins as Black, and Greta worked hard in her postmemory creation of self to distance herself from those revisions. The social worker declared the twins "Negro," which implied racist, negative phenotypical associations with the term. The files note, "there are language barriers for both" but then use language and record observations that echo the eugenics movement. In noting their skin color, the social worker said, "Lilli had a light complexion [with a] brighter rosy cast, and a round fat appearing face," whereas

---

25. Peña, "Stories Matter," 254.
26. Social worker, Children's Home Society of California, accessed 2012.

Lore had "a medium to dark complexion, thick lips, and a long narrow face." In commenting on their hair texture, the social worker said Lilli had "kinky textured light brown and blond hair," whereas Lore had "dark brown hair and less kinky textured hair." In referencing their intelligence, the social worker said Lilli "related easily, was outgoing and succeeded in being the leader," whereas Lore was "seriously thoughtful . . . (but) a slow learner. . . . [She] seemed to be well liked and accepted . . . but slow to be a leader." In remarking on their nationality, the social worker said Lilli "described herself as an American and a German but prefers to call herself an American," whereas Lore "was stubborn," indicating she refused the American label. In referencing "racial" categorization in the US, the social worker said, Lilli "cop[ed] with the recent information that her birth father was of Negro descent," whereas when Lore was "told of [her] part Negro heritage [she] reported [she was] German," thus embracing her liminal German identity.[27]

As can be seen in figure 5.3, the twins do not fit the social worker's minstrel description. In this image, Lilli and Lore are between five and seven years old and look like little girls who are coming from one of the Catholic churches near the Wasserturm, dressed in their Sunday best. Though of course phenotypic features such as full lips, melanin-rich skin, and tightly coiled hair are not undesirable (or exclusive to Black people), they do not apply to Lilli or Lore. Further, both the tone of the social worker's description and the fact that such terminology was deemed in any way relevant to a profile of the children become more sinister when considering her aim, which was to justify the adoption of a white woman's white-passing twin daughters. In doing so, the social worker relied on racist shorthand in order to reify the boundaries of whiteness, thereby using the California state foster care system to reinforce white supremacy.

Even at ten years old, Lilli knew what those in authority wanted to hear. Learning from the social worker that she was seen as the phenotypically preferred twin could have led to her being more willing to be labeled an American. Further, simply being told what her new identity was could have steadied her. Whatever the exact reason, Lilli was more willing to discard her German identity "in the formation of a new" one. The social worker is the example of Connerton's prescriptive forgetting, since she is the representative of institutional oppression, and though it may not be an individual racism that guides her actions but rather normalized parts of the institution, state, or nation (e.g., Jim Crow policies), the state engages in and implements policies that have a differential and/or harmful effect on marginalized children, in this case Lilli

---

27. Social worker, Children's Home Society of California, accessed 2012.

FIGURE 5.3. Twins Lilli (*left*) and Lore (*right*) at the Wasserturm (Water Tower) in Mannheim, Germany, which is a popular landmark in the city. Family photo, author's private collection, supplied by Lilli.

and Lore. Lilli's acceptance of her new label as an American resemble Connerton's "forgetting that is constitutive in the formation of a new identity."[28] Lore, on the other hand, loved Germany, loved her family, and most of all loved the nuns in Germany with whom she once lived. Lore was much more attached to Germany, as that country had stabilized her identity even if, at times, she had no system-approved foundation upon which to stand.

Years later, Greta still crafted narratives about the adoption of the twins in order to save face, though the story had changed. Two weeks after our first phone call with her in over five decades, Greta remarked that "the case worker said, 'I don't think you can give these girls up,'" implying that the social worker, despite her recommendation for adoption, perceived a strong maternal connection and thought Greta might be happier keeping the twins. Greta's

---

28. Connerton, "Seven Types of Forgetting," 61–62, 63.

revised memories belie the fact that she wanted to have the twins adopted immediately upon giving birth to them. Greta said she acquiesced to her caseworker's desires and justified the move to sever parental ties on economic grounds: "I did it so [the twins] could be in a home that was financially stable. But, I hung around the area just in case you [the twins] decided to come back." In crafting this postmemory account of placing the twins in the California foster care system and up for adoption, Greta places the onus for reuniting on the ten-year-old twins with the phrase "in case you decided to come back." But of course, the children had no power to return to their mother; only Greta had this power, and she is the one who put them in the state system in the first place. According to Lore, "I had no idea why mom left. She just left. I kept thinking everything was temporary and she would come back and get us, but she never did." Greta's final step was to say goodbye to the twins before they became wards of the state.

The social worker, in speaking with Lilli and Lore about their next steps in the California foster care system, told them that they were a problem for their mother's new marriage. According to the state of California records, the social worker wrote this recounting of the goodbye:

> [Your mother] married another and although she hoped to care for you after the marriage, she found it emotionally difficult to cope with the social intolerance of your bi-racial heritage and felt it interfered with her relationship with you. . . . (On the day she relinquished you) she met with you sensitively and sweetly and said her final goodbyes. She was emotional and this seemed to have meaning for you.[29]

Then the social worker had Greta come into the room with the twins to speak with them directly. The goodbye as Lore remembered it was also the complete antithesis of the goodbye as the social worker characterized it. According to Lore:

> I thought it was a visiting day. We were sitting outside on a bench at Ming Quong. My mother was very stoic. There was no handholding and no conversation. No motherly loving exchange. It was just a feeling of "let me get this off my chest and let me go." Greta said, "You know I am not coming back. This is the last time we are going to see each other." I stared at her, trying to read her. My reaction was, "She doesn't mean that. It couldn't be that." She always visited us in Germany and in Ming Quong. Then she left. Unbeknownst to us, she had already married and begun a new life.

---

29. Social Worker, Children's Home Society of California. Accessed 2012.

Maybe as an adult, Greta was emotionally distraught and could not say anything without crying, or perhaps since she was disconnected from motherhood, and because she only visited the twins in Ming Quong once a month, she felt like she was saying goodbye to relative strangers. A month between visits is a long span of time, particularly to children, so long in fact that Lore said, "Sometimes we wouldn't immediately recognize her."

Forgetting was a process that took many forms for Greta and her daughters. There was the forgetting required to create a new identity, in which facts and memories that did not serve a present purpose were deemphasized, but also more forceful, top-down erasures, like Greta's final, permanent goodbye. Though Connerton argues that the category of "repressive erasure" applies to "states, governments, and ruling parties" and typically involves physical acts of destruction (tearing down statues, scratching out engraved names), I suggest that Greta was an authority figure whose elective disappearance accomplished some of the same goals: "Repressive erasure can be employed to deny the fact of a historical rupture as well as bring about a historical break."[30] The historical rupture was the lost privilege of white womanhood, which Greta regained by leaving her children in the foster care system, and the historical break was severing the link between herself and the label and role of mother. There is also evidence of "meaningful memory" wherein "meaningful discourses, events, objects, and practices carry evocative, affective weight [and] create and/or sustain emotional affiliation."[31] This could be why Greta's twin daughters felt shock and emotional betrayal—their mother was permanently leaving (an event that sustained emotional affiliation for them)—whereas Greta had no tearful goodbye since she felt little maternal connection to them. For most rhetoricians, according to Blair et al., the notion of signification is of serious importance, for it suggests in what ways "discourses, events, objects, or practices might come to reference particular meanings."[32] The rhetorical signification for the twins was the presence (albeit inconsistent) of their mother throughout their lives. Even when placed in foster care, Lilli and Lore could cling to the notion that they had a mother and that had rhetorical meaning for them, because living outside the home was a memoried pattern and they still saw their mother, even if infrequently. For the social worker and Greta, the rhetorical signification was absence: Greta's absence visually signaled the justification to create new memories in a new life without her children. Haunted through historical memory, the twins were the last visual rhetorical symbol of the past while Greta's postmemoried future, her imagined, created future awaited.

---

30. Connerton, "Seven Types of Forgetting," 69, 60.
31. Blair et al., "Introduction: Rhetoric/Memory/Place," 3.
32. Blair et al., "Introduction: Rhetoric/Memory/Place," 3.

Somewhere in the depths of the memory lies the truth. Regardless of the disparities in the experience of the goodbye, the event resulted in adoption. In these varied recollections of the final goodbye, the memories function as a way to allow each person to go on with life. The social worker may recall the incident as one in which she conveyed an "adult truth" that ten-year-old children would not immediately understand: "Your biracial heritage interfered with a relationship with your mother." But for the twins, how could "the social intolerance of your bi-racial heritage" be too much? How can being who you are be too much? Lilli and Lore saw their mother inconsistently for the majority of their lives, yet Greta's "spoiled" virginity and sex with a Black man was what had to be erased, as did the visual signifier of that union, the twins. Lilli and Lore's memory is a goodbye told through a child's eye. The twins felt betrayed and did not understand why they were being abandoned. At first, they did not even fully understand that Greta was leaving forever, because in the past, she had always come back. Mourning, Lore drew pictures of her mother to keep her alive in her memory. Particularly during the onset of adolescence, as Peña observes "many adoptees begin to fantasize about their birthmothers and contemplate searching for and reuniting with their biological family members."[33] Greta-as-fantasy meant that there could potentially be a reunion, that Greta could change her mind and reclaim Lilli and Lore from the orphanage.

According to Greta and Lore, the twins had several offers of adoption from white families in the US, and Greta said the social worker allowed her to decline or accept these offers. In the case of white couples wanting to adopt the twins, Greta consistently said no. Lore recalled, "I remember white couples, Hawaiian couples . . . anyone but Black couples coming to look at Lilli and me. Families wanted to adopt us separately, but Ming Quong did not want to separate us." It was only when the social worker had an offer from a Black American military family that Greta approved placement. The adopting couple said they loved Germany and wanted daughters from that country. Why would Greta say "yes" to adoption by an African American couple but refuse offers from white families? This couple did not know the girls and did not speak German; they were complete strangers, as opposed to the Duvenecks who loved the twins.

Perhaps Greta made the choice based on the one-drop rule, thus legitimizing her desire to rid herself of her unwanted daughters without US societal judgment, or perhaps Greta saw the media campaigns in *Ebony* and *Jet* magazines or heard about Mabel Grammer's efforts. More likely, however, was that Greta had to abide by US adoption policy at the time, which placed African

---

33. Peña, "Stories Matter," 254.

American children with African American parents, white children with white parents, Chinese American children with Chinese American parents and so on. Following US adoption protocol meant that transracial adoptions were, for most of the twentieth century, rare.[34] Adoption matches and placement centered on things like race, ethnic group, and in the case of foreign children, Americanizing them. For Greta, this meant having Lilli and Lore adopted by a Black American family because of the twins' one drop of Black blood. In 1960, when Lilli and Lore were nearly twelve years old, a Black American family whom both twins described as "emotionally and physically abusive" adopted them. Greta, who never had any more children, was thirty-eight years old, married, and in a financially well-off, stable home environment.

ADOPTED INTO HORROR

Lilli and Lore had limited opportunities to meet with and spend time with the family who adopted them. Lore said she remembered that the "white family who ran Ming Quong wanted to adopt [her], but the social workers and Greta would not allow it." Lore recalled initial visits with the family who eventually adopted them as more like play dates away from Ming Quong, an afternoon where something different was happening. Soon, a judge asked Lilli and Lore if they wanted to be adopted by this family, and Lore responded with, "I guess, yeah sure." Their adoption by a Black American family fit the common pattern for *afrodeutsche Nachkriegskinder*. Peña finds, "Most Black German children were adopted by military families,"[35] particularly since many of the men were World War II veterans and were already familiar with Germany. Lilli and Lore were adopted by a military family, and the stability this adoptive couple was supposed to provide for the twins quickly crumbled when the couple took with the twins on a camping trip to Washington.

The husband made his first attempt to sexually assault Lore with his wife and Lilli sleeping next to them. Lore shared:

> We were all sleeping in the back of a station wagon. I was asleep and awakened when I felt this hand going up my leg. At first, I thought it was a wild animal since we were camping. And then I knew it wasn't. I sat up and snatched off the covers. His hand stopped momentarily. I stared him down and he stopped cold. I had my gaze drift over to his wife, and then I looked

---

34. See Herman, *Kinship by Design*.
35. Peña, "Stories Matter," 260.

back at him. I gave him the look of death that nonverbally said, "I'll scream, and I'll tell." He slowly backed his hand down my leg and the next morning acted like nothing happened.

But something had happened. Lore was a preadolescent girl who had not grown up with a father or father figure, and she suddenly had a "father" who touched her in the middle of the night. Lore survived this frightening and confusing attempt at sexual assault by this man. The twins' adoption was supposed to make them safer, but instead their new home became a place where memories of abuse were cemented and routinized, a reality that, according to Lore, "enhanced my sense of self-preservation."

Once home from the first camping trip, the twins lived in a world where they walked on eggshells, where a mere side-glance from the man or a glare from the woman let them know that their existence was precarious. In between the ballet and tap lessons the family paid for, there was psychological abuse to the extent that sometimes the twins could not sleep for fear they had done something wrong. There was emotional abuse, as Lore recounted, which involved screaming and yelling, and physical abuse, such as having their hands slammed in drawers. In one instance, the wife came up behind Lore, as Lore shared, "with a pair of scissors in her hands, holding me down and cutting off my long bangs." There was one last attempt to terrorize Lore when she was around fifteen years old. Lore said she was home alone from school, sick with strep throat, and the man "came home at lunch time. He never came home at lunchtime. None of us did. I was normally at school and he at work. I grabbed my heaviest schoolbook and hid behind my bedroom door. I screamed in my loudest, gruffest voice, 'Who's there?' Apparently, I was so loud and sounded [so] threatening that he panicked and left." To regain control of his power over Lore and recover from his humiliation after Lore successfully fended off his second attempted assault, the man punished Lore. Lore went from the focus of his desire to a girl who served him and his wife and the other children they adopted. In between these emotional and physical peaks of abuse, Lore and Lilli continued with their shared house chores, which included things like cleaning, cooking, and ironing. Lilli was also the target of this man's sexual violence.

The first time Lilli was raped, she was thirteen years old. Lilli and Lore shared a bedroom, and Lore awoke from her sleep to find the man in bed with Lilli. Lore said,

> He was on top of Lilli, who lay there quietly and cried. Awakened by her sobs and seeing what he was doing, I leapt out of bed and ran down the hall to

the bathroom and locked the door. [The man] then ran out of our room and went into his bedroom with his wife. Once I knew he was in his room, I ran back into our bedroom and ran to Lilli trying to comfort her. I said, "Let's tell [the wife]. Let's tell someone. Let's tell our teacher, let's tell the principal, let's go back to Ming Quong." But Lilli said, "No, why bother, I don't want to break up the marriage."

Lilli's response of "why bother" may sound defeatist, but in 1962, the systems for reporting child abuse and pedophilia were not set up in a way that valued the testimony of children. In addition, Lilli and Lore had no identification. The twins had no ID stating who they were and where they lived, no access to their German passports, and no US citizenship. Lore said the people who adopted them "kept all of our identification under lock and key. We didn't even know where those things were."

It's possible that if Greta had simply left the twins in Germany, they might have been better off. By 1961, when the twins were thirteen years old, German media had begun to write articles about the societal integration of *afrodeutsche Nachkriegskinder*. In one German magazine article, it was reported that,

> contrary to expectations, a nationwide survey aimed at gauging the accessibility of Negro children to local communities revealed the degree of their acceptance to be considerably higher in low-income and working class areas than in suburbs with well-to-do families. In Mannheim and Nuremberg-Fuerth, for instance, both industrial cities, the survey showed that hardly anyone turned around to look at a colored teen-ager. On the other hand, in Stuttgart, an elegant business town, or Lindau on Lake Constance, an exclusive vacation resort, the children were invariably eyed with "curiosity and amusement" by local residents.[36]

Sadly, it was too late for the twins to go back to Mannheim, Germany. The twins were in a panopticon of imprisonment. They were watched and kept by this abusive couple, trapped, invisible, and erased.

The second time Lilli was raped was on the floor of the family bathroom when she was sixteen years old, in 1964, and Lore was once again a witness. Lore said, "I heard Lilli screaming and snatched the bathroom door open. I found [the wife] holding Lilli down as [the husband] attempted to rape her. [The couple] screamed at me to 'get out' as Lilli's body was squirming trying

---

36. "Country has 6,000 Mixed Occupation Children," August 16, 1961, 103. Bundesarchiv, Koblenz, Germany. Archive Coordinates: Bestandssignatur: B/149, Archivsignatur: 8679, Standort 10, Magazin: 112B U.2.06, Reihen: 458, Regal: 0.

to avoid his touch. I stood there frozen. They pushed me out of the bathroom and slammed the door behind me." Lore was standing outside the bathroom door, with Lilli's cries heard on the other side. Twenty years later, Lilli told Lore what happened in the closed bathroom. The wife, who was not able to conceive, decided they would use Lilli as the vessel and forced surrogate. Lilli explained, "The cover for my underage pregnancy would be that I was boy crazy." Lilli luckily did not end up pregnant, but, already survivors, the twins continued to be vulnerable to sexual assault in the house, with no way out. Lilli's rape cleaved the twins, who up until that point in their lives had largely similar experiences.

The rhetorical and lived experience of "family," even simply the term, was one of extraordinary pain for Lilli. When I first heard this story, in addition to anger, flashes of *The Handmaid's Tale*[37] raced through my mind, as Lilli's experience parallels a dystopian scenario where girls and women have little control over their bodies and decision-making. The twins were survivors living among and through the physical and psychological trauma that binds all women who are raped, and I argue that despite the horror, both twins surviving all that they endured is a feat in and of itself. Afrofuturism is, in part, about agency and power. For example, Lore walking in on both instances of rape was brave and a testament to the power of the gaze—since Lore had no idea what she would encounter. The husband and wife did not stop when Lilli cried and writhed on the bathroom floor trying to dodge his penetration, but once Lore became a sixteen-year-old witness to this rape and not simply a newly adopted child who did not speak English well, the abusive couple knew that Lore would tell somebody, anybody, about what she witnessed, and he knew that would be the end of his military career. This was the last time he raped Lilli, instead watching and skulking from a distance until Lore moved out of the home in 1967 and Lilli in 1969.

Suddenly, in 1967, there was a flurry of paperwork and many trips back and forth to a California courthouse all involving the twins. This army family had been transferred to Mainz, Germany, and the adopted German twins existed without any paperwork. At nineteen years old, the twins were thrust back into visibility, only this time by the state of California, when the couple who adopted them back in 1960 had to finally file the necessary paperwork for their naturalized citizenship to be processed. Once the naturalized citizenship

---

37. *The Handmaid's Tale*, by Canadian author Margaret Atwood, was first published in 1985. In the novel, the United States is run by a radical, right-wing Christian theocracy in which women have little control over their lives. Essentially, they are property. Under this fundamentalist regime, the subjugated white women who are still fertile live as "handmaids" and are valued only for the potential fertility they offer.

was approved and their new US passports were in hand, the adoptive "family" all boarded a plane and landed in Mainz. I do not understand why the adoptive family took Lilli and Lore with them to Mainz, as according to Lore, "the [husband and wife] no longer wanted us" and were eager to place them outside the home permanently. The twins as adults were an inconvenience to the "family" who wanted to reimagine themselves and construct a new arrangement without two adult twins in their lives. As young adults, Lilli and Lore had run out their usefulness for the family, and the twins began to make their own space in the world. Both twins, as best they could, left the memories of emotional and physical abuse in the past in order to embark upon their creative imagining of what the future might bring, and only rarely looked back.

Lore's Escape from the Adoptive Household

Lore knew she had to escape the family whom she and Lilli had lived with for seven years. After living in Mainz for eight months, Lore said she "asked the neighbor, a woman, if she and her husband worked on base, and they said yes": "I asked her if she would take me to the military base so I could get my first job and take a civil service test. They agreed. I took my test and applied for a job at the base exchange. I felt like I was escaping a prison." This was the beginning of Lore's freedom from the adoptive couple. Lore was offered a job at the Mainz base exchange, which she accepted, and the adoptive family allowed her to take it since her employment and income meant she would be out of the family home. A week after accepting the job at the base exchange, Lore was offered a different job with the US Civil Service, which she accepted, giving up her base exchange position. Lore said at her Civil Service job, "[The adoptive father] watched me as I worked, telling people he was my father, and he just wanted to check up on me." Lore was now being stalked by the man who was emotionally and physically abusive. With this Civil Service position, Lore secured an apartment in Wiesbaden, Germany (about thirteen miles away from Mainz), in a building that was part of a hotel with a lobby, restaurants, and a club. The same building also had a residential side with a security lock, and these apartments were rented to women US federal employees only. Lore packed up her things, purchased a Volkswagen Beetle from the adoptive father, moved out of the family home, and drove to her new secure apartment, intent on creating new memories. The entire adoptive family came to Lore's new apartment to see where she lived, which meant now the adoptive father knew where she lived. While the adoptive family wanted the nineteen-year-old twins (legally adults) to move out of their home, they were simultaneously shocked by Lore's display of agency in moving out of the family home in Mainz so quickly. About a month later, the adoptive father went to her apartment. Lore said, "He patiently knocked on my door for approximately three minutes until he eventually left. I refused to open the door." Lore safely sat inside her apartment, and I imagine that the three minutes of knocking sounded like pounding in her ears. In Afrofuturistic terms, Lore was the victor because she survived, she escaped, and she had the power to choose whether to open the door. With the door firmly closed, Lore went on with her life in Germany, for the first time being able to exhale.

Lilli's Escape from the Adoptive Household

Lilli (see fig. 5.4) escaped the family home in Mainz, but it took her longer to do so. Rather than going the employment route, in 1969, at twenty-one years old, Lilli met a closeted gay man who was being stationed back in the US. Lilli said, "I offered to marry him as his 'beard,' so he would not have to come out to his family, and allay any suspicions his family had that he might be gay, and immediately divorce him upon landing back in the US if he agreed. He agreed. We were in New Jersey, and I filed the divorce papers and made my way back to California." Lilli, like Greta, looked at California as a place where she could begin anew, because she went back to California initially with no direction in mind. She did not share her address with her twin or anyone from the adoptive household.

My Encounters with the Adoptive Household

I met the people who adopted Lilli and Lore once when I was six months old, and again at fourteen years old at the woman's funeral. This was the first time I began to understand that there was a deep flaw and chasm in this adoptive "family." I remember standing next to the hospital bed of the dying woman, a relative stranger to me who once sent me a couple of letters and a gold bracelet with a heart charm, but I said my goodbyes. What I never forgot was the goodbye that I heard Lilli say to the woman who adopted her: "It's okay, you can go. If you need me to forgive you before you can go, then, fine. I forgive you." Standing next to Lilli, I immediately asked her why she was forgiving this woman, and Lilli said, "Not now, you're too young." I remember seeing the man (the adoptive father) once during the funeral, when he came out of his bedroom and walked down the steps of his house. He was a mystery to me,

FIGURE 5.4. Lilli after her return to the US. Family photo, author's private collection, supplied by Lilli.

because up until then I had not seen him, but all of us children were told to be quiet because of this mystery man located somewhere in the upper floors of the house. The man walked down the steps and stared down at me. I looked back up at him, and then he looked past me, saying nothing. Immediately behind me, with a protective hand on my right shoulder stood my mother, Lore, who stared back at him and guided me out of the house, into the rental car, and onto the beach where we stayed for the day. In reflecting back, what I read as a motherly gesture of love was also an act communicating power and control. In staring back at her abuser, in shifting the balance of power, the nonverbal action that Lore took—putting her arm on my shoulder—spoke loudly, and she once again denied her abuser any power over herself or her child. Lore left him standing alone on the staircase, impotent in humiliated silence, as she took us away from him and left. We returned from the beach later that evening, but I never saw the man again, and soon thereafter, we were on a plane back home.

One of the things that Lilli and Lore were looking for when we were at the man's house for the funeral were the hidden citizenship papers and the twins' photographs from Germany. Lilli received her box of childhood photographs, but Lore did not receive hers. According to Lore, she was told by the others in the adoptive household that they were "packed away and too difficult to get," and neither twin received any information about their German citizenship. In this man's last act of power and denial, Lilli and Lore remained in a liminal space of existence with few visual artifacts of their life together in Germany and their life with Greta. Another authority figure in their lives engaged repressive erasure, as the adoptive father treated them as "enemies" and saw that much of their past and "images of them were destroyed."[38] The man who adopted the twins became complicitous in the erasure of official, documented, memoried objects concerning the twins' origin story, a story they remembered and one about which he could have provided information but did not. Most important to the twins was the lingering question of their German citizenship. Lilli and Lore held German passports through 1965, but from 1965 to 1967, they were *staatenlos* until they received US naturalization in 1967. Haunted by the legacy of liminality, marginalization, racism, and erasure, Lilli and Lore's life journey, up until they were able to leave the adoptive household, had been largely a story of insurmountable obstacles and generational trauma.

AN EMBODIMENT OF TRANSNATIONALISM AND JIM CROW: A CONCLUSION

The twins' lives bear the marks of the transnationalism of Jim Crow, and these harsh realities make Afrofuturistic reimagining difficult, if not at times, impossible. Afrofuturism aims to reclaim the past and rewrite dominant narratives so that Black lives can be celebrated across time and productively imagined into the future. But the very real ways that Lilli and Lore's histories have been marginalized and erased shows just how difficult this can be. The legacy of anti-Blackness enveloped them, and they could not get out from under the racism sustaining white supremacy, erasure, and liminality; they could only survive. Subject to systems of white racism in both Germany and the US, the potential for an Afrofuturistic creative imagining of the self was all but impossible. The twins had no positive connections to Blackness. During their childhood in Germany, the stigma of being *afrodeutsche Nachkriegskinder* isolated them from their mother for reasons they did not understand. Once in the US, a Black identity was not only thrust on them in essentialist, racist terms but also was presented as the primary justification for their abandonment by

---

38. Connerton, "Seven Types of Forgetting," 60.

Greta and their adoption into a family who had no history of knowing or caring for them. These experiences were enduringly painful for the twins, especially as those who denied them access to a future defined by the hope and respect they deserved (Greta, the California foster care system, their adoptive parents) were those who should have been their advocates in the first place. Because transnational Jim Crow already wrote the story, Lilli and Lore were treated as estranged and outside the national vision of Germany, cast as Negro under Jim Crow and the one-drop rule in the US, erased out of existence by Greta, and abused by the people who adopted them. Nonetheless, they survived. This book is a testament to that fact and aims to bring their story into full visibility despite the many forces that sought to keep it, and them, hidden. Mine is an Afrofuturistic endeavor.

The intersectional threads of memory and postmemory met in 2012, when, given the indelible marks of race, racism, and Jim Crow on the twins, I asked Greta about how her ideas around race changed over time and she said, "A person is a person." This was a somewhat progressive idea Greta espoused as she looked back on the past she fled, and this was a sentiment that was hard to believe since race and racism ignited the generational trauma thrust onto Lilli and Lore, and Greta refused to acknowledge this. Greta and the choices she made in order to build her imagined future were the reasons we had arrived at this point. She created an identity in which she could be sheltered from, and keep a proper distance from, issues of race and racism. Based on what I came to know about Greta over the few years I was able to interact with her, I think she knew the politically correct thing to say about race and racism—"a person is a person"—but that openness did not extend to her daughters or to the Black mixed-race granddaughter interviewing her. It is one thing when issues of race and ethnicity are believed to exist only outside the family, but quite another when your secret "shame" knocks on your door and wants to talk to you about your past. My presence and my inquiries into her life were where the junctures between her memoried past and her imagined postmemoried future collided.

CHAPTER 6

A Family Reunion and Generational Trauma

A Conclusion

> There is so much more to tell, but I will respect your privacy and leave the decision in your hands for any future contact.... You are welcome to contact me at your discretion.
> —Lore's reintroduction letter to Greta, 2012

Contacting her mother was a way for Lore to access and evaluate her past. In utilizing this most foundational element of Afrofuturism, Lore engaged in postmemory by imagining a world, a future world, where she could have a relationship with Greta that could potentially bring about a different result, one in which she, Lilli, and their respective families were acknowledged and seen. By engaging in a familial search that began in 2010 and writing her letter to Greta in 2012, Lore grasped onto the Afrofuturistic concept of hope. Hope for imagining a new relationship, an adult relationship, with Greta. In hoping for a more positive contemporary relationship and outcome, Lore asked both Lilli and Greta to walk alongside her on this new familial journey once the memoried events of their lives were thoroughly brought to light. In bringing the twins' and Greta's pasts to light, Lore asked Greta to dismantle and reframe the creative imagining Greta had made use of in her own life, which had served as her guidepost when she dropped off the twins at the orphanage and relinquished her parental rights in 1958. Through the reunion, Lore asked Greta to confront and challenge the postmemoried narrative that had become cemented, ingrained, and imagined as a lived "truth" once the twins were adopted in 1960.

Reuniting with the past is not simply cosmetic, and there is no apt blanket apology for decisions made via exigence or convenience. The mere reappearance of Lore and her family in Greta's life signified much about who Greta's family was and who Greta had chosen to become. But I wanted our presence to be something more than a nonverbal signifier: I wanted a new relationship and a new future in which she would be accountable for her past actions. I was asking Greta to engage in a rhetoric of resistance toward her imagined life and the postmemory creative imagining of a postwar immigrant. I was asking her to re-remember her memoried self, through her daughters' lens and mine. Even if momentarily, I was asking her to engage in a form of inclusion that embraced us, saw us, and wanted us. Lilli and Lore's reemergence into Greta's life revealed the pains Greta had taken to hide and erase certain public memories as related to herself, her husband, and her imagined way of being.

My Afrofuturistic wish was for her to throw off the shackles of antiquated ideas of whiteness, white womanhood, and colorism. This chapter examines the process of reengaging with the memoried past as a way to challenge and solidify familial actions in the past as well as in the present. Greta's acknowledgment of her past was complicated further when her multiracial granddaughter also came to the reunion table, thus potentially upsetting any white-imagined future Greta may have had for Lore. In this chapter I ask why Greta opened the door to a reunion with the twins and met her granddaughter, only to then close the door and never publicly acknowledge either. The vastness of time coupled with generational trauma is explored.

PRE-REUNION: WHY ENGAGE

When I was a young girl, I imagined a life and a maternal history for Lore that did not exist. I have always known that my mother was adopted, and the absence of Greta and any history that came with it was painfully blank when I had to complete a genealogy assignment in elementary school. I sat through long stories other children shared about their historical pasts, and invariably half the class, it seemed, was related to Leif Erikson, had come over on the Mayflower, or was long-lost British royalty. When it was my turn to present my familial history, I faced a triple bind of being blocked from knowing much beyond one to three generations due to adoption, the enslavement of Black people, and Native genocide. Thus, with no way to surmount the white supremacist legacy and genocide within my own veins, I imagined who Greta might be. Looking back as an adult, sadly my childhood imagination resembled the postmemory imaginations that Greta crafted about her own identity in order to regain her white privileged standing. My creative memories mirrored Disney tales where the mean mother (Hermine) denies her daughter (Greta) the ability to be with the love of her life (Albert). I dreamed of Greta pining away locked in her castle tower, because Hermine was embarrassed and ashamed that Greta dated and had sex with a Black American. I imagined Greta forever bereft, denied her ultimate love, because of the racism of her mother. I imagined Greta overcome with grief about not knowing what became of her twin daughters after they were taken away. I imagined Greta filled with sadness because she had no knowledge of her granddaughter. I had to imagine Greta as the victim, because I could not imagine a mother denying her own children and willfully severing familial ties. My postmemory imaginations were shattered during my first conversation with Greta, when I learned some aspects of how she crafted her history and the rules with which she bound our relationship.

On July 13, 2012, Greta's first words on the telephone after fifty-two years were, "I always hoped you'd forgive me." After an hour on the phone, Greta suggested a reunion, and we met in person the weekend of Labor Day in California for a four-day visit. After July 13, we spoke most Sundays, and only on Sundays because Greta wanted to and needed to keep some routine and control in her life, after the disruption that our return had caused. Her daily schedule was this:

8 a.m.: Wake up
10 a.m.–12 p.m.: Errands and lunch
3–5 p.m.: Cook and eat
6 p.m.: An hour of rest
7 p.m.: Read the newspaper and/or work on cross-stitch/stitchery
8–10 p.m.: Two hours of television
10 p.m.: Get ready for and go to bed

At many points in my field notes I wrote, "I wish [Greta] was not so regimented with her time." Initially, I did not understand why someone would cling so rigidly to self-created rules, especially for family disconnected from one another for fifty-two years. But then I got to know Greta more and saw the tightrope walk of white racism she still chose to navigate for fear her postmemory creative imaginings might be exposed and her white womanhood once again revoked. On August 10, 2012, when I rang her on a Friday, she was out "running errands" when I called. My voicemail was not returned because I called her on the wrong day, off schedule. On August 17, for example, when we preinformed Greta that we would call her on a Friday instead of a Sunday at 1 p.m., she waited by the phone that day to tell Lore and me (since we phoned her together), "It's 1 p.m., but I am running errands and can't talk" and hung up. Greta had waited to receive the call only to scold us for violating her rules. Despite our rule violation, Greta later spoke with us on the phone for forty minutes that Friday, and after reminding us that we could only phone her on Sundays between 1 and 2 p.m., she surprisingly told Lore that she "loves her very much." I was on the other end of the phone line in the same room with Lore when I heard Greta finally reciprocate the "I love you," a phrase my mother had been saying to Greta since July 13, that up until then had not been uttered. In that conversational moment between mother and daughter, Greta loved Lore and loved the idea of learning what became of her. Visually, Lore radiated happiness upon hearing the first "I love you" from her mother in her adult life.

Conversations with Greta on July 13 and July 27, 2012, destroyed my childhood fantasies about Lilli and Lore's childhood and replaced them with the raw memoried and postmemoried events that left Lilli and Lore in the hypervisible/invisible space of liminality. The conversations were attempts to fill in the gaping holes of our erased familial past with generic references to various German family members, dates of births or deaths, and reasons why the twins were placed for adoption. We were supposed to be satisfied with Greta's answers to those questions in order to get to a place of equilibrium, where the superficiality of phatic communication (small talk) could reign. After August 3, these phatic patterns were difficult to break, since the majority of knowledge and power remained with Greta. Our conversation on August 3 covered these topics: How are you? How is your work? And how is your book coming along? There were also brief discussions about replacing lightbulbs and about workers from Mexico who, Greta said, "came to the house to do work, but don't speak English." There was no depth to the conversation beyond what one might share with a stranger, which is what we were, after just two weeks being back in one another's lives. At one point, we both shared that we loved the comedy television show *Modern Family* (2009–20), which I found ironic since it was a multigenerational show about love and family centering a gay couple and mixed-race and multiethnic families and even featured an adopted child. The most personal information I learned on August 3 was that "all members of the family have hearing problems." Greta shared, "Mine [diminished] in my twenties and thirties. I've had a hearing aid since my forties, and I just spent three thousand dollars on a state-of-the-art hearing aid." I wrote the following in my field notes about that conversation: "After 35 minutes on the phone there was continued avoidance about other [German] family members." When I asked her what they thought of the reunion, Greta replied, "I don't want to talk about it." My reflections in my field notes after this conversation were full of disappointment; I never imagined after fifty-two years there would be boundaries erected by Greta. I thought there would be relief, a chance for Greta to finally put aside the weight of the memoried past, but instead she chose to continue pushing Sisyphus's stone for eternity.

Within the first two weeks of reconnecting, Lore sent Greta pictures of herself and her husband. When Greta told me about this, she said, "[Lore's] always been a looker, even as a young child. I never looked as good as [she does]." I was thrilled Greta made this comment because it allowed me to ask about her physical features. Subsequently, I asked, "Does my mom favor you?" I imagined Greta looking one way in my head. Perhaps what visually existed with Greta also existed within me, a similarity that she would be unable to resist, because by doing so she would reject herself. Instead, Greta replied, "I don't want to talk about it."

"I don't want to talk about it" was Greta being vigilant in retaining the power and the ability to control her public performance of self. If she could manage her narrative fabrication, then she could publicly and privately manage the family who was now back in her life. If Greta failed at the public performance, her postmemoried world would unravel, and crashing down on her would be the memoried life she fought to erase and the reductionist, antiquated stereotypes that came with it (about premarital sex, biracial children, and loss of white privilege), which she imagined were still alive, haunting her. Thus, "I don't want to talk about it" was a successful rhetorical strategy that stopped conversations and questions.

August 17, 2012, was the last time I spoke with Greta before my arrival for the reunion. I tried calling Greta on August 24 (a Friday), but she did not answer the phone. Lore tried phoning Greta on August 29 (a Sunday), and she answered, and they spoke about our upcoming visit. In preparation for our arrival, Greta asked if Lilli was coming too. Lore said she did not know and that she'd had difficulty contacting Lilli about the reunion. Perhaps to preempt any potential rejection, Greta said, "Lilli had emotional issues. [I] have no desire to have contact with her." Greta closed the door on a reunion with Lilli early on, relegating Lilli to a past Greta did not want to remember. However, Lilli knew about our quest to find Greta and watched from the sidelines as Lore and I navigated international (Germany) and national (US) bureaucracies for two years. One week before our first visit to reunite with Greta, Lore heard from Lilli:

> LORE: Do you remember when I told you about our mom, Greta, and I read you the letter I wrote, and you weren't interested?

LILLI: Yes, I'm still not. And, I bet you never heard from her.
LORE: Well, I heard from her. [My husband] and I and Tracey [and her husband] are all going out to California to visit her next week.

After a brief moment of stunned silence, Lilli wept. Lore sighed and said, "Lilli wept uncontrollably for about five minutes. I said nothing. It broke my heart." With just over five decades of loss and memories released, Lilli, whose voice was weak, according to Lore, said she was "exhausted and getting a headache" and uttered these words: "I would like to go with you next time."

In the ensuing chaos that naturally comes with trips, Lore realized that she did not have any childhood photos, because unlike Lilli, Lore was never able to reclaim her baby photos from her adoptive family. The photos became an exigent signifier and important artifact for Lore in reclaiming her identity, a German identity, which had been denied and erased. Lore said, "I need these photos, so I have as much proof as necessary just in case Greta doesn't believe us or Greta's husband is skeptical for some reason." Lilli, as a way of participating in the reunion, reclaiming her German identity, and being present, sent Lore the only childhood photos that still exist for Lore to take to California and represent them both. These photographs most particularly allowed Lilli to be seen, even if liminally, because the images were evidence of life lived with and without Greta.

REUNION

The First Day: Lore's Reunion with Greta

Lore and her husband arrived in California on August 30, 2012, and present at this reunion were Greta and her husband, and to Lore's surprise, Greta's youngest sister (who used to babysit Lilli and Lore in Germany) and her husband. It was clear that Greta's youngest sister was there to support Greta, but it also meant that Lore, and by default, Lilli, were seen by at least one additional family member. When I asked my father about the reunion and their first day, he said, "Lore and Greta immediately embraced, the reunion was fantastic, and there is a family resemblance." Lore agreed with my father's assessment, but she provided the more subtle detail that only a family member, a daughter, might notice about her mother. The details a daughter who often lived with the fear of abandonment by her mother might pick up and retain. Lore tried to discern the verbal and nonverbal clues that might illuminate how the reunion was going and whether she and Lilli might be welcomed back into the family.

After the hellos, hugs, and kisses, there was a silence that Greta filled by asking, "Have you eaten?" A simple question that is often asked of visitors, but also a question nearly every mother asks their children when they first return home. Lore said she and my father replied "no," and so they were off to Greta's "favorite Chinese restaurant." Seated at the table were Greta and her husband, Greta's sister and her husband, and Lore and my father. An uncomfortable silence loomed as the group studied the menu. When I asked Lore about that silence, she said, "It was a nice reunion, but an out-of-body experience. It seemed just so civilized. It was quiet and respectful." What Lore is describing is a lack of the intimacy and warmth that often come with close relationships (e.g., inside jokes and verbal and nonverbal communication patterns that make sense to inside community members). As Michael Hecht and HyeJeong Choi explain, "identities have semantic properties that are expressed in core symbols, meanings, and labels."[1] As Lore had been an outsider to her German family for fifty-two years, an uncomfortable silence settled in. When I asked her how she felt about the reunion, Lore disclosed she was "in shock": "That is how I would describe it. This [reunion] was something [no one thought] would ever happen." The server was the person who broached the uncomfortable silence, Lore said, by "welcoming Greta and her husband by name." Greta never introduced Lore or her husband to the server, who clearly seemed to know the couple. Lore said, "I thought [Greta] would interject and say something, but she didn't. Greta kept her head down, and never introduced me as her daughter and family, nor my husband."

From Greta's perspective, having one daughter visually present invoked re-remembering a past that departed from her self-created present master narrative. Greta had no counterstory prepared to address the visual, in-person presence of Lore. Silence, in this case, was Greta's tool for retaining power and equilibrium in her life. In addition, Greta could not and would not reveal that Lore was her daughter, because doing so could disrupt the narrative Greta may have told the staff. At one point, Greta may have proclaimed to the server, as she had to other people, "I don't have any children." Technically, Greta was correct when she told people she had no children, as Greta signed away her parental rights in 1958. To have introduced Lore as her daughter would have disrupted the narrative of adoption and would have caused Greta to lose face for being caught in a lie. The postmemory creative reality that Greta spun exposed the fragile and precarious nature of her existence.

Further, for Greta to reveal that she had twin daughters would have meant an identity loss and an acknowledgement of her memoried self in relation

---

1. Hecht and Choi, "Communication Theory of Identity," 139.

to race, whiteness, and motherhood. Greta's responses to the group dynamics at the restaurant made Lore ponder the past: "I wondered if she was that way, eyes averted and head down, when she was with us in Germany?" Was Greta worried about the antiquated gendered expectations she violated (e.g., premarital sex, interracial sex) and white layers of her identity? Based on her communicative action of head bowed, gaze averted, and silence, Greta showed that even with postmemoried desires, and maybe a desire to know Lore as an adult, identities, as Hecht and Choi explain, "always are interconnected with each other, a quality that is labeled 'interpenetration.'"[2] Thus, Lore had little chance to begin anew with Greta because Greta closed any contradictory gaps that would have arisen for herself and settled into complementary interpenetration frames that erased Lilli and Lore from existence. Thus, Greta felt no obligation to answer the server's questions at the Chinese restaurant. Greta's only desire in that moment was for her and their connection to remain invisible.

When I asked Lore how she thought Greta acted with her, she said, "Withholding. That is how I would describe [Greta]. She was and is always on her guard no matter what." Identities are dynamic, but they are also "codes that are expressed in conversations and define membership in community,"[3] write Hecht and Choi. The server created an assumed collective identity that re-centered Lore as someone in Greta's life, thus bringing the outsider in. If Greta's creative imagining for her life was to retain credibility, Lore could not be an inside member. Therefore, Greta's response was a silenced panic. Greta used silence to manage the dynamism and chaos that Lore sitting at the table caused. The server awkwardly navigated the silence by taking the orders. Lore said, "I excused myself to go to the bathroom and wash my hands. To my surprise, Greta followed me." In doing the woman-bonding thing of going to the bathroom together, Greta re-engaged Lore in politeness, but that was it. There was no conversation about what happened at the table, just a heavy silence as the two were in the restroom. The two women then went back to the table, dinner was eventually served, and with the evening over, Lore and her husband went back to their hotel.

Greta's communicative strategy reminds me of manicured lawns in suburban neighborhoods; there is a story beneath the perfect lawns and the stuccoed houses, but no one dares to scratch the surface. It is likely that the server and other members of the wait staff would not have cared that Lore was Greta's daughter and instead would have said something like "Welcome,

---

2. Hecht and Choi, "Communication Theory of Identity," 140.
3. Hecht and Choi, "Communication Theory of Identity," 139.

enjoy your visit." However, Greta, haunted by the past, imagined a negative response based on her lived experience, perhaps anticipating more questions, like "Where have you been all these years?" or "I thought you had no children, Greta." Greta's possessive investment in her postmemory construction caused her to erase Lore's presence at the table, wielding silence to her advantage. Lore was once again walled off by Greta and placed into liminality—nothing was going to jeopardize Greta's carefully crafted life and certainly not a four-day reunion with her long-unacknowledged daughter.

Author's First Day: My Reunion with Greta

Nostalgia and curiosity led Greta to respond to us, and I had questions. Do we look like one another? Have similar habits? Share any medical conditions? Will she want and recognize us? Will the other members of the family want to meet us? My questions are all examples of critical imagination, a concept that rhetorical scholars Jacqueline Jones Royster and Gesa E. Kirsch discuss. Critical imagination allows for "seeing the noticed and the unnoticed, rethinking what is there and not there, and speculating about what could be there instead. . . . Critical imagination . . . is not an endpoint"[4] but rather an imagination of possibility, much like that offered through Afrofuturism. In juxtaposition, my father had a more general and superficial memory of the events of the reunion between Lore and Greta on that first evening, merely noting that the two "embraced" and that the reunion was "fantastic."

As an outsider to the complicated mother-daughter relationship, it makes sense that my father would not look for evidence of more subtle aspects of the past reemerging since he was looking for overt forms of rejection from Greta, for example, her being overtly rude or distant. None of these behaviors occurred. Rather, the opposite happened. My father said, "I thought she was nice. The family was nice, and they were nice and accepting of me too. Greta and the rest of the family hugged me." Being embraced was a nonverbal signal to my father that allowed him to see the overt behaviors of the reunion and the kind of nonverbal gestures family members made (e.g., hugs), but he missed the covert messages that Lore, even after more than fifty years, was keenly aware of. However, it was this positive, superficial rendering of my father's that caused me to write, "I hope I receive the same kind of reception" in my field notes.

---

4. Royster and Kirsch, *Feminist Rhetorical Practices*, 20–21.

It was decided from my first phone call with Greta that a reunion was in order, as Greta filled in some of the gaps of our German life and family. She said she and her husband would pick my husband and me up from the airport when we arrived because she wanted to see me immediately. It was then that Greta revealed that she "never learned how to drive an automobile," which was something she regretted: "I feel trapped with no freedom. In Germany we had such good public transportation, I never needed to learn how to drive." After this kind offer to pick us up, it dawned on me that we did not know what the other looked like. "How will she know I am who I say I am," I wondered, and so I sent a slate of images, according to my field notes, "so she would know what I looked like and there would be no surprise by the fact that I am part Black." Upon receiving the images, when we next spoke on July 26, Greta said, "My granddaughter is so beautiful! [Her husband] is handsome. So proud of her. She is so smart. Your picture is next to my telephone." I felt seen. The next week when we spoke, August 3, I called her *oma* (grandmother) for the first time, which Greta said, was "music to [her] ears." However, closing the familial gap linguistically did not mean that my questions would be answered. I continued to press for more answers to familial questions and details about our upcoming the reunion. I asked, "Will there be other family members at the reunion?" and "What do the other family members think about the reunion?" to which Greta's response was, "I don't want to talk about it." A week before we were set to arrive and meet Greta for the first time, the offer to pick my husband and me up from the airport was rescinded, and Greta withdrew this same offer to Lore. Instead, Greta told me the same thing she said to Lore, "You can go onto Google and get the directions. When you arrive at the hotel, call us, and we can get together then."

I could not help but wonder if the airport pickup was withdrawn because Greta's husband was in his nineties and California traffic is stressful for anyone, or if they decided not to pick us up because of what my father and I looked like, and the questions I asked about the past. In each phone conversation we had, I was able to ask the difficult questions Lore could not, because I had no past with Greta. Greta could cut off a conversation or stop speaking to me altogether, but I had nothing to lose because I was at the beginning of my relationship with her, not the end. The freedom to take communicative risks allowed me to temporarily embrace an Afrofuturistic reality where I was not constrained by the *afrodeutsche Nachkriegskinder* label, racism, and shame that clothed Lilli and Lore. I was able to foreground Greta, Lilli, and Lore's memoried past and deftly navigate the race shame Greta had, because she could not pinpoint me to that time. By countering her desire to constrain and mark my social identity, I was temporarily empowered and reversed the hegemonic order, because I had the power to pose questions. Through an Afrofuturistic lens, I was empowered to question because even as the legacy of Jim Crow and white racism washed over me, it was only Greta who attempted to constrain my identity and box me in. I, on the other hand, refused her categories and placed myself in the center. I was the embodiment of her genealogical future despite her imaginative attempts to disconnect from and move beyond her Black memoried past. I articulated a familial memory that was inclusive and placed myself as an insider in relation to her German identity, not an outsider. My linguistic choices of "our," "us," and "we" forced her to see me outside of the liminality she might have desired. Greta had limited power over me beyond familial historical knowledge. Greta's response to my temporary empowerment was to try to regain power and control. Greta provided vague answers to questions I posed or outright refused to answer them. Sometimes this took the form of not answering her phone. By elevating myself to familial insider, Greta's only move in this chess game was denial. Her sudden refusal to pick me up from the airport was a flex of power, reminding me that I was coming into her territory and her seat of power.

On the day of our arrival, once at the hotel, the first thing I did was call Greta. She did not answer her phone. Breakfast bled into lunch, and there was still no answer. Lore and I worried if we'd ever get together. I tried calling her again in the early afternoon, and she finally picked up. At last, we were given permission to come over to her house. In our home movies, what was captured that first day of our reunion was awkwardness, fear, nervousness, and love. As I recounted in my field notes, "I met Greta (my *oma*) for the first time in person today." As we pulled up to her house and got out of the car, Greta, according to my field notes, "immediately ran out and hugged me over and over again. She kept saying, 'my granddaughter' and then turned to [my husband] and said, 'now I have a grandson.' [My husband] looked absolutely thrilled." Neither my husband nor I had any living grandparents, so we were both elated by the joyful reception. We had a positive reunion full of hugs, kisses, smiles, and joy (see fig. 6.1). This was the kind of reunion that would be covered as a typical "feel good" story on the evening news.

After numerous hugs, which felt natural, photos, and simply taking in the sight of one another, to my surprise, I saw that Greta's youngest sister and her husband were also present. Greta's youngest sister and her husband came outside. Having never spoken with one another, we gave each other awkward hugs. I wanted to greet Greta and speak with her in German, but I was boxed out of speaking the language of my genealogy and had to default to English, even after I reminded her that I could speak in German if that were more

FIGURE 6.1. Tracey (author, *left*) and Greta (*right*) meet for the first time. Tracey had just stepped out of the car. Family photo, author's private collection.

comfortable. German felt like a language used only for familial insiders. I eventually hugged Greta's husband. Even though I spoke with Greta's husband on the phone, and he listened in on every telephone conversation I had with her, it felt strange to hug a man I had never met in person before, even one who the twins thought fondly of. We all continued to hug and talk as we ate cheesecake, had coffee, and ate an afternoon snack on her patio. Next, we transitioned into her home, where familial memoried histories were shared (see fig. 6.2).

Once inside Greta's house, I noticed that my photographs were not next to her phone like she had told me. I looked in the kitchen and saw images of her niece and nephew and their family covering her refrigerator, but none of Lore and me. I saw an image of US Olympic gold medalist gymnast Gabby Douglas on her refrigerator, but again none of her children or grandchild. I asked Greta about what happened to the images of us, and instead of answering my question, she talked about the great gymnastic talent of Douglas and ushered me out of the kitchen and into the living room where Lore was waiting. Greta sat us down on her couch and before any questions were asked said, "I thought if you were unhappy in your new home, you would be returned to

FIGURE 6.2. German family members reunite for the first time, eating cheesecake and drinking coffee. Lore (*left*), Tracey (author, *next to Lore*), Greta (*center*), and the author's father (*bottom right*). Family photo, author's private collection.

me. That's what the adoption agency said. They refused to give you back to me." Greta's words tumbled out uncontrollably, not allowing time for Lore or me to have any kind of verbal response. Greta then said, "The day that I found out I was pregnant was the worst day of my life." Silence. My mother and I had no words. The pregnancy, the twins . . . all of it unwanted. As Greta vacillated over the course of our visit from saying in one breath that the twins were desired and "not mistakes" and then in the next that they were undesired, it was clear the twins were born into liminality. They were only seen in relation to the pain they caused her physically and mentally.

In beginning to consider Greta's life without us, I stumbled upon our *Familienstammbuch* (family genealogy book), and as I exclaimed "Oh, wow" at finding such an important family document, Greta's youngest sister snatched the documents out of my hands and cried, "That book is only for family!" I told her, "I'm family." But to her, I was not. She then looked at my husband, pointed at him, declared, "Now he looks like a proper German," and placed the *Familienstammbuch* in his hands. My husband, with his pale skin, light brown hair, and blue eyes, was given access to look at a family document even though he has no biological connection to the family and could not translate the contents, as he cannot speak German, simply because of how he visually appeared. He was given the genealogical keys to my background because he was free of the racist entanglements my German family carried and that marked Lilli, Lore, and now me. In hovering over his shoulder, like an interloper in my own past, I saw the last two pages of the *Familienstammbuch* were reserved for Greta to enter Lilli's and Lore's names and their birth date, baptism date, and dates of marriage. She never did. Greta's sister's actions effectively erased me from the *Familienstammbuch* too, because visually I did not look like I belonged to a family that privileged whiteness yet declared they were nonracist because Greta had a picture of Gabby Douglas on her refrigerator. My white German family could cheer for Douglas because there is no biological connection, but they could not cheer for or acknowledge two biological children and a grandchild, because we were tainted with white supremacist imaginings of inferiority and shame. Greta seemed to relate to my father in a similar way: because he was not a biological relation but had only married into her German family, he was placed in the same category as Gabby Douglas—outside of the family and therefore no threat.

Later in the day, we went for dinner at a seafood restaurant where, when the server asked, "Are you celebrating anything?" I immediately responded, "Yes, a family reunion." Greta said nothing. I did not realize it initially, particularly since I was not at the Chinese dinner, but during all our restaurant dinners, Greta displayed the same pattern of embarrassment, shame, and silence. When he asked if we were all from California, Greta answered and said, "We are," pointing to herself and her husband. The server, filling the conversational gap stated, "Oh, visitors!" to the rest of us at the table and asked all the questions Greta never offered: "Where are you visiting from?" "How long will you be here?" and "How do you know one another?" Lore answered the first two questions. It was the third question, "How do you know one another?" that stopped the questioning and conversation, since Lore said, "I'm visiting my mother." Greta looked down and never responded. Again, Greta employed the communicative strategy of silence. As Cheryl Glenn notes, "rhetorical power is not limited to words alone. . . . The silence of those with power and authority over us, or with the power and authority invested in them by the institutionalized structures, which govern and control society . . . , often works to intensify our anxiety and our frustration. . . . When silence is a means for exerting control and managing the situation, silence originates with the dominant party, stimulating the subordinate party to explore options for breaking the silence."[5] The drowning silence filled the space. Lore said, "The entire table was silent for fear of saying anything that Greta might not want known.

---

5. Glenn, *Unspoken*, 23, 32.

Greta's life and the whole point of the family was secrecy," so Greta employed silence as her form of communication with the server, because answering his question would be the beginning of the end in terms of her new identity and identity management.

Greta was the one person at the table most concerned with managing how she appeared to others. Greta's silence nonverbally signaled that the server was an outside member not worthy of a response to what she sees as an insider, and therefore, intimate question. Greta's management of the delicate dance required to maintain her identity performance recalls Hecht and Choi's notion that identities "are . . . constituted in relation to others and performed."[6] In Greta's case, her identity performance included avoidance (ignoring the question), nonverbal avoidance (head down, gaze dropped), and silence. In my Afrofuturistic revisioning, I tried to reclaim myself as an insider in my German family, and at the conclusion of the dinner and my first day meeting Greta, when we were back at her house wondering about the remainder of this visit, I asked, "Will there be a reunion with the whole German family?" Greta's youngest sister replied, "Let's see how this turns out and how we all feel about one another, and we may have a family reunion." In keeping with Greta's schedule, we were back at our hotel by 8:45 p.m.

REMAINDER OF THE REUNION

For the remainder of the reunion, we settled into a familiar pattern where I called Greta, waiting until she gave us a designated time to come over. Sometimes Greta answered the phone immediately and other times not for hours. Arriving at her house, we would say our hellos and give hugs and then look through decades of photographs and listen to her stories. During our visit, we learned we were essentially unwanted and learned about a life that had not included us for fifty-two years. Questions like "Was Lilli and Lore's and biological father Black?" went ignored and unanswered. Instead, there were days spent looking at her award-winning stitchery, which, according to Greta, was "perfect. You can't tell what is the front and what is the back." Her stitchery was indeed perfect (see fig. 6.3), and she had cultivated an amazing talent first developed while making the twins baby clothes with her mother, Hermine. Greta took Lore and me through each stitch, pattern, and thread over the remaining days of our visit. Her artwork was framed all over the house, and she showed off her artistic talent the way a parent shows off pictures of their

---

6. Hecht and Choi, "Communication Theory of Identity," 138.

FIGURE 6.3. Greta (*right*) showing Tracey (author, *left*) her award-winning stitchery. Family photo, author's private collection.

child or their child's achievement. But I wondered, in my field notes, if Greta's stitchery was a hobby to "fill the void of the twin's absence from her life once the twins were adopted?"

Greta took us through the chronological events of her memoried past with and without the twins as featured players, and she spent hours sharing each and every detail of her nieces' and nephew's lives. As I recounted in my field notes, "It is painful seeing the happy pictures of Greta's life with her nieces and nephew and her husband's daughters." Despite being my own Afrofuturistic hero in centering myself in Greta's world when we talked on the phone, it was painfully obvious that Lilli, Lore, and by default myself, were erased from her postmemory present. We were like statues from a bygone era, razed and replaced with the acceptable, modernized, and convenient images of her stitchery and nieces and nephew. Greta divulged that any images she'd had of Albert were "thrown away. Some images are just too painful." I eventually found the images of me that she had said were proudly displayed next to her phone instead hidden on her crowded bookcase slightly sticking out from between two books. I never found Lore's images. Later, when I visited Greta the next year, I sent more images of myself right before the trip. When I was at her house, in the kitchen, I went to throw an item away, and sitting in her trash bin were the photos I had just sent. Did she want me to see the destroyed photos? Was she sending me a message? I never asked her. I was too afraid she would close the door to any relationship with me if I asked. Because I saw the second set of photos I sent her destroyed, I never sent her photos of myself again. I thought "Why bother?" but more significantly, I was crushed, because I learned, like Lilli and Lore, that I, too, was disposable. While I had the power to center myself in my own creative imagining, that did not mean that Greta centered me. In my field notes, I wrote, "I don't think Greta ever thought she'd have her daughters back in her life." The ripples of unbelonging splashed onto me just like they had for Albert, Lilli, and Lore. In order for Greta to have some modicum of control in the chaos our visual presence caused, we had to be razed, our images thrown away and relegated to the trash.

Greta was forthcoming with many aspects of her past that filled in many historical, memoried gaps, but learning about her life with Albert or anything about Albert was incredibly difficult, until the last day of our visit, when it was just us girls—Greta, Lore, and I—out shopping. The shopping mall was a nice respite from the photo albums, stitchery, and the supervising gaze of Greta's youngest sister, who was there for the entire reunion, because Lore and I were able to create our own living memories with Greta rather than merely looking at a static visual history that excluded us. Macy's was chosen because Greta loved to shop, and she declared, "I am looking forward to shopping, but I am not getting in one of those pushcarts! I want to walk." And so, she did. The slow pace of shopping created an intimate space, where finally, temporarily, Lore and I were granted access into her memoried world. "I know you want to know," said Greta to both Lore and me about our continued questions about Albert, "I just don't want to talk about this in front of [my husband]. It's embarrassing." Greta had resisted being forthcoming about Albert because she did not want to present herself as a sexualized being with a sexual past that predated her relationship with her husband. In addition, she never had any privacy on the phone in talking with us, because her husband was always listening on the other end. Her evasiveness and repetition of "I don't want to talk about it" in this instance made sense. In preparing to share intimate details about the man she called "the love of her life," Greta stated, "[My husband] never asked me about my past, and I never asked him about his. He is learning a lot about me now."

In this moment of inclusion and visibility, I felt love for Greta, and I felt seen and acknowledged until we went to the bathroom. Standing at the sink washing our hands stood three generations of Germans: *oma*, mother, and granddaughter, who would react very differently to what happened next. As we turned to leave the bathroom, with Greta holding onto Lore's arm and me immediately behind them, a stranger exclaimed, "Oh, how beautiful! Mother and daughter together shopping! How wonderful! You two look just like each other!" Erased, I was not seen as part of the familial group because of my brown phenotypic hue in juxtaposition to Greta's translucent white skin and Lore's own light hue. Forced to out myself, I said, "I'm with them! I'm the granddaughter." The stranger looked at me, hesitated, and said, "Oh, have fun shopping." I immediately felt a deep sadness and sense of unbelonging. Unable to look past my color to see a family resemblance, phenotypically I was seen as an outsider in relation to both Greta and Lore. In the moment of being recognized as Greta's daughter, Lore proudly said to the stranger, "Yes, this is my mom" and looked at Greta. Greta said nothing orally but dipped her head down, once again, and let go of Lore's arm. Lore said, "I felt her let go of my arm. As I looked over at her, I saw embarrassment." Greta's nonverbal response was the embodiment of embarrassment and shame. Following the stranger's recognition of a family resemblance, Greta's nonverbal reaction washed Lore and I in shame. Her silence seemed to call up the racism she experienced in Mannheim as a mother to mixed-race twin daughters, but her refusal to acknowledge Lore and I as family left us feeling as if we were drowning.

In this moment, Lore and I had become the hypervisible signifiers of familial entanglement, and therefore Greta felt "outed." Lore and I were the visible embodiment of her humiliated silence. As Connerton notes, humiliation is "so difficult to forget. It is often easier to forget physical pain than to forget humiliation. . . . Confronted with a taboo, people can fall silent out of terror or panic or because they can find no appropriate words."[7] The acknowledged, visible, and physical presence of her daughter and granddaughter brought Greta's humiliation to the surface. Silence accompanied by a bow of her head was Greta's survival strategy, and it served her well while transitioning out of Germany and into the US; her desire for silence ultimately led to dropping her twins off at the orphanage. It was these silences that successfully allowed Greta to bring her postmemory self into being, because acting, communicating, and moving silently, reflects Connerton, "can . . . be a form of survival, and the desire to forget may be an essential ingredient in that process of survival."[8] This was the last day of our reunion, and Lore and I never addressed or processed what happened in Macy's with Greta, because there was no point. Her nonverbal communication of embarrassment, shame, and her desire to make us invisible said everything. After shopping, we went to dinner together, and then after dinner we were back at her house, taking a final look at albums and listening to her final stories. One story involved Greta's nieces and nephew

---

7. Connerton, "Seven Types of Forgetting," 67–68.
8. Connerton, "Seven Types of Forgetting," 68.

receiving one item of her prized stitchery. I asked about the possibility of Lore and I receiving three pieces of her cross-stitch (one for Lilli, Lore, and me) and was ignored. Gifts of Greta's artwork signified being loved, being seen, and being family, and at that time, we did not warrant possession of such an artifact. At the end of this first trip, back in our liminal spaces, we said our goodbyes and left her house.

Post-Reunion Rejections for Lilli, Lore, and Me

When she first received Lore's reintroduction letter, Greta said she "dropped the letter and collapsed onto the floor" and then immediately contacted Lore in an effort to see what had become of her daughter's life. However, after that first reunion, Lilli and Lore never saw Greta in person again. A number of firsts in the initial year of our reunion went unmarked. Lore and I both sent Christmas cards, birthday cards, letters, and gifts to Greta and cards to her youngest sister, but only Lore's efforts were reciprocated; my attempts went unanswered. It became apparent that the initial reunion was likely all that was going to occur and had been enough to satisfy Greta and her youngest sister. During the Christmas holiday in 2012, we had a Skype reunion with Greta, and we were led to believe there would be more family members on the call, like the nieces and nephew and even Greta's middle sister. Instead, we met with only Greta and her husband and Greta's youngest sister and her husband once again. Instead of facilitating a meeting with other members of the family, they held up photos of the family Christmas they'd had with one another without Greta's twin daughters and granddaughter.

To Greta, in our phone call the following Sunday, I said, "I was disappointed that we did not have an opportunity to talk with [other members of the family] via Skype on Christmas. I was led to believe that we would. Do [you and your sister] not want us to meet them? Is [your youngest sister] embarrassed by us and our reunion?" Greta replied, "Yes," followed by a heavy silence. Greta then broached the silence with, "I will talk with [my middle sister] and tell her about the reunion and tell her to be really honest. I will tell you what she says." The phone call ended with Greta saying, "We are so connected, Tracey. I just love you so much. When you come and visit in March, we are just going to talk, your husband too. I think he's great. He's connected to me. I feel like I know him from before."

It was the end of this phone call, not the rejection, that stood out to me in the moment: the rhetorical power of connection. When I heard the word "connected" coupled with "love," I thought my Afrofuturistic dream had come true. *Connected* implied a relationship. Connection to my husband seemed like a given, since he was included by Greta's youngest sister merely due to how he phenotypically presented. However, a rhetorical connection with me signaled an open rebellion against her youngest sister's shame. Love and connection meant that my days spent "closeted" might end, because Greta might feel compelled to leverage her rhetorical power and open the door, reframing how the rest of my German family was to behave and treat us in the future. It did not dawn on me until later that Greta could end a phone call with promises of love and connection, without judgment, since we were on the phone, and I could not see her in person. There was no visual risk of shame and condemnation from her sisters and no stranger present to cause her discomfort. Based on the power of those two words, I thought Greta was ready to make a radical shift in her thinking and carve out a new world where Lilli, Lore, and I were seen as family and insiders, and because of those two symbolic words, I was inspired to plan our second reunion.

SECOND REUNION

I was the only one present for the second visit in March 2013, and I pressed on with trying to fill in the gaps of our genealogy, asking more questions about family stories and genealogy in hopes that greater knowledge of our German family might mean being centered in it. In late 2012 I had sent private Facebook messages and pictures of our first reunion to my third cousins (the children of Greta's nephew) as proof of our shared familial existence only to receive silence in return. On December 28, 2012, I wrote:

> Dear [Cousins],
> This may seem odd, but my name is Tracey Patton and I am your cousin. I am a professor at the University of Wyoming. Greta is my grandmother. Your grandmother is my great aunt. My family and I were lucky enough to find Greta and this September we were reunited after many years of searching. I'm really hoping to get to know you both in the future. I hope to hear back from you both soon.
> Your cousin, Tracey

Then on January 19, 2013, I wrote:

> Dear [Cousins],
> I sent a message previously about our family lineages. I am hoping I have the right people. I think I do based on the multiple images that my great aunt, [her husband], and Oma Greta have shown me. Here are some family pho-

tos of our reunion over Labor Day weekend 2012. It would be great to get to know the rest of my extended family.

Your cousin, Tracey

In looking at the situation through their eyes, I can see how an unsolicited Facebook message from a stranger might elicit an immediate call to their mother or their grandmother (Greta's youngest sister) rather than a reply to a stranger (me). But, given that our existence had often been met with forced invisibility, erasure, and silence by Greta and her youngest sister, the cousins' response followed a familiar pattern. Greta was the only person who could change the response and narrative, but she had no desire to do so. Just as Greta did not want to admit her middle sister's racism toward the twins, because it embarrassed Greta, she also likely did not want to take the same risk with her youngest sister's extended family. As someone who avoided negative and racist situations, Greta likely avoided this confrontation as well, because her created identity was at stake. Instead, Greta put a barrier around those she had the most control over, her twins and granddaughter.

In my field notebook, I wrote, "This relationship is unsatisfying as-is. I am tired of following all of Greta's [and her youngest sister's] restrictions, only to be pushed off, hidden, and denied when convenient." In hoping to delve more deeply into the issue and persuade Greta to reveal our existence to other German family members, one month prior to my arrival, I broached this topic of invisibility with Greta and spoke openly about my frustration.

> TRACEY: I get the feeling that [your youngest sister] does not care for me, that she does not like me. To tell you the truth, it really bothers me. It is like you all are embarrassed by me, by Lilli and Lore for some reason. I can't help that Lilli and Lore were mistakes. If Lore wasn't born, I wouldn't be here. You show us pictures of family members, but never show them images of us.
>
> GRETA: I'm in agreement with my sister. You can't force relationships.
>
> TRACEY: I agree with that, but you can't force relationships when the people don't even know you exist.
>
> GRETA: We're embarrassed! I'm sorry I have such a crummy family. To me, people are people.

Clearly Lilli, Lore, and I were more than just people; we were ghosts from a memoried past that Greta and the rest of my German family had long relinquished. With the cloud of embarrassment hanging over me, my goal for the second trip to California in 2013 was twofold: develop a stronger relationship with Greta and fill in my understanding about life for the twins at Hidden Villa and at the Ming Quong orphanage. Greta agreed to help.

Lilli and Lore did not attend this second in-person reunion. Lore said, "I didn't want to look at anymore photo albums and stitchery," since those were all examples of Greta's postmemoried life created without the twins. Lore's decision not to attend a second reunion was her exercising her power, choice, and agency. Similar to the representational goals of Afrofuturism, Lore chose when she did and did not want to be made invisible. By choosing absence, Lore sent a message that her postmemoried life was worth protecting and was more important than a mother who was still ashamed of her presence all these decades later. At the close of my three-day visit with Greta and her husband, Greta showed me more examples of her prized stitchery, and I hinted that I would like to take home some examples of her art. Greta again ignored me. I asked more overtly a second time about receiving some of the prize art that her siblings, nieces, and nephew had received but the twins and I had not. Greta ignored my question a third time, and finally her husband impatiently barked, "Just give her some stitchery!" to which Greta responded by grabbing two tablecloths and placing them in my hands. In that moment, only Greta's husband saw my desire to be included in the family tradition. Not fully appreciating Greta's invisible familial border, Greta's husband crossed the dividing line of "insider" versus "outsider," a line that meant everything to her and nothing to him. Giving me Greta's cross-stitch meant an end to my questioning about such an important family heirloom.

Upon receiving the stitchery, feeling like a temporary insider, I crossed the dividing line and once again pressed for a reunion of all the family members. I wanted Lilli, Lore, and I to be visible and not closeted. To my request, Greta responded, "You are a wonderful granddaughter, too bad you're the wrong color." I was gutted, shocked, and shamed. No words came out of my mouth when I opened it—my head simply dropped. In Greta's mind, I existed wrongly and was outside of her world. I, not Lilli or Lore, was the person who had pushed for a reunion and visible recognition by the rest of our German family. The fact that Lilli and Lore did not push for a reunion or visibility speaks to the harm and continued erasure they already knew was inevitable because they had lived through it twice: first when they were put out of their home and lived in the dormitory/orphanage in Germany, and again when they became wards of the California state foster care system. The twins had already traveled this route of desiring to be seen and instead being relegated to the margins earlier in their lives. About my continual push for acceptance, Lore said, "Those people are ignorant. They believe they are above us, that they are better than we are. They are not. I want to protect you from them."

What I failed to understand at the time is that the familial and public acknowledgment of Lilli, Lore, and I was not a simple matter. Even basic introductions could not occur without a radical shift in the identities the entire German family had constructed. Greta's erasure of the twins and whatever postmemoried lives they created had to stand, because she and her youngest sister were not willing to acknowledge, in Connerton's words, a "historical rupture"[9] in their own postmemory identity construction. Greta was not willing to risk any other relationships with insider family members, as she had not been close to her middle sister since 1948. "I talk with her via Skype at Christmas and that's it," she said. Like an adult version of the game telephone, all other conversation between the two sisters "went through [the youngest sister]." A memory of the twins could exist via the abalone seashells, but their physical presence and inclusion into Greta's deliberate reconstruction of a life without them could not. There was no ability to negotiate a different outcome, because we were outside the familial compact of remembrance and were therefore outsiders who just happened to share DNA.

REUNION TO REJECTION: RELATIONSHIP DISSOLUTION

Greta reopened what I thought was a closed door to any future familial reunions in April 2013, when she surprisingly told Lore she was "excited" to plan a third reunion "in Las Vegas." Everyone who attended the first reunion would be invited, with additional invitations extended to Lilli and all members of the German family. According to Lore, "[Greta] requested that I contact her [youngest sister] since 'she'll make all of the plans.'" I, too, was fully in support of a third reunion and encouraged the event planning. I did not initiate the idea, Greta did, yet I found out I was scapegoated for it. Shocked about a possible third visit, Greta's youngest sister asked Greta about it and then called Lore. Lore recalled her conversations with both Greta and Greta's youngest sister: "Greta became very defensive and said, 'It is all Tracey's idea.'" Greta's youngest sister declared to both Greta and Lore, "We need to cut out these visits." Whereas the first visit encompassed anxious joy and the second visit was tolerated, the possibility of a third reunion was met with ire and then canceled. Initially, the cancelation was blamed on Greta's mental state, as according to Greta's youngest sister, Greta didn't know what she was saying and had "a touch of dementia." Lore countered and said that Greta "seemed pretty sharp." Greta's youngest sister concluded the conversation by telling

---

9. Connerton, "Seven Types of Forgetting," 60.

Lore, "The trip with Tracey and going back to the [Hidden Villa Ranch] are bringing up too many memories," memories that were supposed to remain confined to the past. We never returned to Greta's home, because as ghosts from Greta's memoried past, we were not eligible to remain in her present, even if that meant Greta would be alone.

In the fall of 2013, Greta's husband died. Her life was in transition as she moved out of their home and into a senior living community. Ironically, Greta complained to Lore about "being lonely, being forced to make new friends, and only seeing her youngest sister once a week to every couple of weeks." I offered to go and visit her, but Greta said, "The only person who should visit me is Lore." When Lore offered to visit, Greta asked Lore to move into the senior living community with her: "Lore, the room next door to me is vacant. Wouldn't it be nice if we could be neighbors?" The offer to be neighbors, and not mother and daughter, revealed how Greta might have imagined her post-memory life *with* Lore—friendly, with no mother-daughter intimacy. Greta conveniently forgot that Lore had created her own life, without her centered, that included a husband and daughter. When Lore declined Greta's offer, Greta did not extend it again, and Lilli did not offer to go at all. When I asked Greta if her new neighbors knew about the twins and me, she replied with her familiar refrain, "I don't want to talk about it." In January 2014, I called and offered once again to visit Greta, and she hung up on me. The more I pushed for a relationship with her, the more our relationship deteriorated, to the point that she stopped answering the phone during my designated 1 p.m. Sunday phone calls. The only form of communication available to me was to send Greta a letter, which I did the next month, including my contact information for her once again. I wrote:

> Dear Greta,
> It's your granddaughter, Tracey. . . . I miss our weekly conversations, but after our extremely short conversations in mid-January, I thought I would try writing [to] you instead. When I last rang you, you hung up and ended our conversation after only 1 minute and 8 seconds. This abbreviated conversation made me wonder if you still want to talk and continue our relationship.

My letter went unanswered, and our weekly conversations became even more sporadic.

In the summer of 2014, when I temporarily moved to Berlin for research on this book, I contacted Greta's middle sister via letter in hopes of meeting in person. Given the strained relationship Greta recounted, I knew any contact was unlikely, and indeed, my letter was met with silence and my request to meet went unanswered. During this same summer, Greta, on the other hand, took a family cruise with her youngest sister and their family. There would never be a family reunion that included Lilli, Lore, and me, and none of our German family members outside those I had directly contacted would ever know of our existence. Rather, Greta and the family members who had joined her on the cruise sent a large, framed portrait showing who they considered to be their family—it included aunts, uncles, and in-laws. Lilli, Lore, and I were not invited on this family cruise and only learned about the vacation after the fact. Upon my return to the US, I attempted to resume my weekly phone calls with Greta, but she rarely answered. Greta maintained some semblance of weekly phone calls with Lore, but her conversation with me only continued via indirect communication through Lore, and she still had not spoken to Lilli since 1958.

In spring 2015, Greta died. In a birthday/bereavement card sent to Lore that was accompanied by the aforementioned 2014 family cruise photo, Greta's youngest sister wrote:

> Dear Lore, We wish you a happy birthday! We hope you enjoy the picture, it was taken in 2014 August. We are so sorry for your loss, we all miss Greta very much. Love, [Greta's youngest sister] and family.

When Greta died, symbolically, so did Lilli, Lore, and I. Greta's youngest sister telephoned Lore (who informed Lilli and me) about Greta's death, and almost immediately Lilli, Lore, and I began to make plans to attend the funeral. However, Greta's youngest sister said there was not going to be any funeral. As Greta had told me in our last conversation, "I want to go out the same way I came in, without any fanfare." There was no funeral, but there was a memorial. We were not invited to the memorial and assumed that the flowers we sent were also hidden. Lore said, "I don't think the flowers we sent were displayed." Lore is likely correct because up until the very end, the family was concerned about appearance. Greta's youngest sister made sure that they would not have to explain the large bouquet from Lilli, Lore, and me or answer inconvenient questions like, "Who are Lilli, Lore, and Tracey? What do you mean by her children and grandchild? Where have they been all this time?" Even after her death, maintaining Greta's postmemoried identity, how she had come to present herself to the world, took precedence. The fear of what others would say, coupled with the vast wealth the other family members inherited, were the driving factors. Maintaining the invisibility of Greta's twin daughters and her granddaughter became paramount.

Lilli and I had no contact with Greta's youngest sister, and the little contact Lore had with her all but stopped within a year, but not before Greta's youngest sister told Lore they were taking some of the inheritance from Greta and "taking a family trip to Hawaii." Without Greta there to renew family ties, there was no longer a reason for the twins and I to remain connected with the German family, and besides, Greta's youngest sister saw to keeping that door closed. At a crossroads in forming a new family identity without Greta, it was convenient for them to bury our narratives and postmemoried identities at the same time they buried Greta.

I had joined Lilli and Lore in a space of liminal existence. I was told Greta loved me, but I was never acknowledged or introduced as her granddaughter; I always had to "out" myself. In signaling memoried and antiquated racist views about interracial coupling and mixed-race children, Lilli and Lore's beginnings and my phenotypic hue prevented any familial acknowledgement beyond those present at the initial reunion. I suspect the reasons we were continually excluded were due to shame and racism. Greta did not give birth to me, so there should be no shame. But alas, shame and racism remained. As time went on, it became painfully obvious that the twins and I, even five decades later, were their embodiment of *Toxi*, having shown up on their doorstep and disrupted the family identity they had crafted and cultivated. One reunion was enough for them, but I kept returning in search of more inclusion.

Why open the door to a reunion only to close it? Our vision of what was possible failed to account for Greta's deep-rooted desire to remain as she was. Our Afrofuturistic hope had imagined a world in which Greta might reimagine her family so that we could be imperfectly together again in a place of forgiveness and renewal and walk forward into the unknown together as a family. Instead, the stigma and legacy of interracial sex, embarrassment, adoption, and erasure proved we were no match for the white racist ideas about Blackness they had carried with them since postwar Germany, ideas that became cemented by the racist structural formations of the Jim Crow US. Our hope for an imagined familial future ended. Issues of race, racism, and societal shame superseded family and kept us hidden from view.

GENERATIONAL TRAUMA MEETS AFROFUTURISM

Sitting in the stillness of our destined fate, Lilli, Lore, and I visually signal relational flows and our positionality as temporary. Examining memory and postmemory as they ripple through the generations allows various patterns to emerge, as the knowledge and understanding gained can reinterpret our understanding of an historical event or interrupt what we imagined could be possible over time. Through our reunion one consistent theme for Lilli, Lore, and I was generational trauma. Peña remarks that "disrupted childhoods are always traumatic and inevitably have lifelong implications. Whether a child is adopted at six days, six months, or 6 years of age, he or she has experienced abandonment, separation, and loss, and will suffer emotionally from the experience in some way and at some time in his or her life."[10] The vastness of time, which was too wide to be bridged, and resistance made transitioning out of liminality impossible for Lilli, Lore, and me. Instead, we are examples of the cross-generational trauma engendered by anti-Blackness and the legacy of Jim Crow. Our location "here" in real life, and not as some mirage from the past, created a temporary sense of belonging that withered.

Greta experienced the first wave of trauma that would later crash down on and drown three of us out of existence in our own family. Greta, after being rejected by her boyfriend, Albert, experienced the trauma of forced single motherhood and racism from her middle sister and Germany. In order to ensure her survival, she freed herself of what she perceived as encumbrances (the twins and her native country). But more than five decades later, Greta still retained feelings of embarrassment and shame, which were exposed when we arrived back on the shores of her life. Only Greta could hear the imagined taunts and cries of white womanhood denied, which she thought she would risk again if Lilli and Lore were recognized. The granddaughter that Lore brought with her into the future, by default, was in the past as well due to Greta's antiquated notions about race. There could be no shifting of the ground as it related to race and visibility for the family Greta birthed. For Greta, the line was drawn in 1960 at the Ming Quong orphanage, and there was no way to alter the foundation she built and the past she wanted to leave behind. She never reclaimed Lilli, Lore, or me beyond a glimpse to see what had become. The twins and I were birthed into a static and racist imagining of Blackness that prevented us from simply being. As one of my closest and most trusted friends said, "Greta is confused. Is she happy to have you in her life, but ashamed [too], so she wants you on the down low?" The answer is yes, and both emotions are possible. Shame coupled with embarrassment and then shrouded in racism become powerful emotions. Greta wielded these emotions and then weaponized them. She had the power to control Lilli's, Lore's, and my erasure even as we saw ourselves. What we had the power to claim was

---

10. Peña, "Stories Matter," 248.

how we engaged with our collective loss and the pain of living outside the postmemoried ideal we created upon Greta's initial response to Lore's letter. After we had peeked through that door and onto imagined hope and a future, the cross-generational trauma of rejection returned, drowning Lilli, Lore, and me, and it was Greta who controlled the floodgates. I suspect that over the decades, Greta was proud of the foundational deception she had crafted in order to support her postmemoried identity. What I might experience and see as lies and erasure was, for Greta, the "truth," and it set her free.

THIRD TIME'S A TRAUMA

What does it mean to examine concepts of trauma and repetition? Lilli and Lore were left twice, first in Germany and then at an orphanage in California. I am the one who pressed to open the door for the trauma of abandonment to be repeated a third time. I could not conceive of a reality where, after fifty-two years, the twins and I would be so easily removed. Because Greta answered the letter, I never thought that we would *not* be insiders, filling an absence that I imagined had plagued Greta all these decades. I never conceptualized how our return to Greta's life would affect her. I never imagined that our largely joyous reunion, forever recorded on video as a homage, would usher in, once again, erasure. Against rootlessness, in the way that Afrofuturism can offer, Lilli, Lore, and I sought a new multiracial creation of family that would have cast off our shackles of otherness and thrust Greta and her past into visibility, and by default, the twins and I permanently into her life. But, she refused. At the initial reunion, Greta lifted the veil of family just long enough for us to see through the opaqueness and learn and see what she had stolen from us. We heard the details of a life that unlocked a part of me I did not even know existed, longing for the unknowable unknown. Lilli, Lore, and I were denied the love Greta heaped onto her nieces and nephew and the love she poured into her stitchery. Greta passed on the generational trauma of rejection that made her flee Germany, and this ripple effect lives in us.

Greta never asked about our lives or how her disappearance and rejection wounded us. There were no apologies necessary in her world because that would have acknowledged how her acts of self-preservation had caused generational trauma. Therefore, there was only recognition of how she had succeeded and overcome for her own individual gain. There was nothing that Lilli, Lore, or I had to offer that Greta was willing to sacrifice her postmemoried status for, and I as the granddaughter of the next generation was a visual signifier of her legacy of shame. There were times when Greta loved me, and I reciprocated that sentiment. I loved having an *oma* in my life, and I imagined the possibilities that might bring about as her only grandchild, but the Jim Crow ideas that had clothed the twins were draped heavily over me as well. This confinement to white racist stereotypes of Black people left me no ability to permanently grasp the buoy of Afrofuturism in order to create an imagined space of belonging within our family. It was impossible to disrupt the flow of white racism and the more than fifty years of comfortable living without us.

Conditioned from their memoried experiences to expect disappointment from Greta, Lilli and Lore were not surprised by her resistance. Lilli anticipated the rejection immediately and chose not to participate in the reunion. Lore held out hope and was more willing to forge into the future. Hope is a powerful emotion in Afrofuturism, because at its core is the possibility for a new beginning and the ability to imagine a different kind of future, but sometimes moving forward necessitates letting go of the past altogether, because despite your best efforts, the past is still being rewritten in order to leave you out, as was the case for Lilli and Lore. I, on the other hand, was shocked. Never having experienced rejection from my parents or my paternal grandmother, I sought to continuously ameliorate issues and dead ends that slowed relationship development and formation. I interpreted all rejections and rebuffs as temporary, and because I did, I was complicitous in the cycle of rejection that held Lilli, Lore, and me captive. I thought I was immune to the memoried past, but the legacy of German racism against Black Germans and US Jim Crow lived on my body, within my body, and around my body. There was no way for me to ever get rid of this racist stench. As Greta's youngest sister said to me, "The twins were a mistake, so therefore you are a mistake." At that definitive moment, I realized that I was the next victim and survivor of Greta's cross-generational trauma, embarrassment, and shame, because, in keeping with white racist beliefs, in their minds, once you are anything Black, nothing else about who you are matters.

DREAM DEFERRED: A CONCLUSION

Afrofuturism argues for a positive approach to the future and is intentionally designed to be a movement infused with Black joy, in juxtaposition to the white supremacist past and present, but Albert, Lilli, Lore, and I are examples of how Afrofuturism can fall apart when our imagined hopes are still tethered to resistant entities who have no desire to change an outcome that benefits them. Afrofuturism that never arrives is like a dream deferred.[11] Greta's static

---

11. See Hughes, "Harlem."

FIGURES 6.4A AND 6.4B. Comparing a photo of Lilli (*left*) and Lore (*right*) and a photo of the author at the Wasserturm in Mannheim, Germany. Family photo, author's private collection. The image on the left was supplied by Lilli, and the image on the right was supplied by the author.

view of embarrassment, shame, and race caused me to wonder if the initial joy of finding one another was fictive. There was no postmemory opportunity for me to stand within the Afrofuturist imaginings I longed for and tried to create despite Greta's resistance. I found myself back in Germany walking the same streets in Mannheim that she and the twins did. I saw the same Catholic church generations of my family attended, and I even visited the Wasserturm, recreating the image that was taken of Lilli and Lore all those decades ago (see figs. 6.4a–b).

Lilli never reunited with Greta or the rest of the German family; her last time seeing Greta was in 1960 at the Ming Quong orphanage in California, when Greta said goodbye. Unlike Lore, Lilli never lost her German accent. Lilli had a difficult adult life, one that repeated the patterns of abuse that characterized her early existence and which included abusive romantic partners and drug addiction, something she later overcame. Lilli even mirrored Greta's patterns of absence and disappeared from Lore's and my life for twenty-two years, but later she grasped at her Afrofuturistic possibility and reemerged happy and with a desire to make a good life with her twin and me. Lilli died in 2018 due to complications from early onset dementia, and in the last year of her life, she stopped speaking English. Lore said, "The nurses at the nursing

FIGURE 6.5. Tracey (author, *left*) and Lore (*right*). Family photo, taken by former student and photographer Canaan Hurst, used with permission.

home called me and said that Lilli was speaking some kind of foreign language. I told them Lilli and I are German. Lilli was speaking German." At the end of her life, the language Lilli went back to was German, and in her mind at times, perhaps she was back in Germany, the country of her birth and her lost citizenship.

I studied communication and German at university, but Lore was the first person who taught me German as a child, and even though we still say things like *tschüß* (goodbye) and use phrases like *ich liebe dich* (I love you) and *schlafen schön* (sleep pretty), at some point Lore stopped speaking German, which for her was a language of pain, oppression, and rejection. Lore, who is slow to trust and an incredibly private person, wrote to Greta that "family commitments and work took front-and-center [in my life]. I am a proud wife and mom married now 43 years." In these words, Lore revealed that she had built a vibrant career and created the stable family life she lacked in her youth and was now the loving, engaged mother she never had (see fig. 6.5). The family Lore created and the career she had were her Afrofuturistic hopeful beginnings.

How does one navigate a public narrative about having no children that, when one digs a little deeper, falls apart? How did Greta navigate her decision in the 1960s to drop off her children at an orphanage because of an invisible one drop of Black blood, a decision that earned her praise and sympathy then but that today would earn her condemnation? Lilli's and Lore's lives were hardly emblematic of a Disney fairytale, but their experience is unique because few children from postwar Germany who were adopted internationally have been able to find their biological parent(s). My family's story in the history of *afrodeutsche Nachkriegskinder* is also unusual because the twins were adopted later in life, as preteens who were able to remember and tell their own stories. What binds our three generations of women together? Why did Greta open that door, only to insist that we remain invisible? The pressure of societal shame due to racism coupled with gendered expectations for women, first in postwar Germany and then as the albatross Greta could not shake, were insurmountable barriers for my family. Our story reaffirms how racist forms and systems keep knocking Black people down and allow cover for those who are able to access and benefit from the power of white privilege. It is a story that goes beyond the people it directly involves and references a larger narrative about Germany, World War II, the United States, race, and citizenship.

An unsatisfactory, liminal, and erased identity was not what we imagined for ourselves. We know our German family exists, but since our existence revealed what Greta sought to keep hidden, we were given no choice but to move on without her and the remainder of the German family. At some point, we had to consider whether it was worth forcing ourselves into a family defined by loss, pain, racism, and generational trauma. As I uncovered, through my research on this project, the German foundations that sought to deny our existence as well as the transnational effects of race, racism, and Jim Crow, we began to understand the stereotypical ways in which we were understood by our family. No longer fighting to prove we belonged, we decided to make ourselves whole by becoming the arbiters of our own fate. In testing the boundaries of our own fate, with an Afrofuturistic imagining in mind and a desire not to stay mired in erasure, embarrassment, racism, and shame, we shaped a new postmemory, a post-Greta identity. Lilli, Lore, and I endured even if our relationship with Greta and the rest of the family did not survive. We endured even if our time together ended. Armed with hope, Lore and I carry Lilli's spirit with us as the two of us go forward, once again, on our own.

BIBLIOGRAPHY

Agamben, Giorgio. *Remnants of Auschwitz: The Witness and the Archive*. New York: Zone Books, 1999.

Ahmed, Sara. *The Cultural Politics of Emotion*. 2nd ed. New York: Routledge, 2014.

Aitken, Robbie. "Making Visible the Invisible: Germany's Black Diaspora, 1880s–1945." Sheffield Hallam University Research in Action Projects, October 10, 2019. https://www.shu.ac.uk/research/in-action/projects/being-black-in-nazi-germany.

Aitken, Robbie, and Eve Rosenhaft. *Black Germany: The Making and Unmaking of a Diaspora Community 1884–1960*. Cambridge, UK: Cambridge University Press, 2013.

Amanpour, Christiane. "Janelle Monáe: 'Erasure Is Happening Right under Our Noses.'" CNN, May 13, 2022. Interview, 6:22–6:34. https://www.cnn.com/style/article/janelle-monae-memory-librarian-christiane-amanpour/index.html#:~:text=%E2%80%9CThese%20are%20real%20experiences%20for,it's%20being%20done%20through%20lawmaking.%E2%80%9D.

Anderson, Benedict. *Imagined Communities: Reflections on the Origin and Spread of Nationalism*. Rev. ed. New York: Verso, 2016.

Anderson, Reynaldo. "Afrofuturism 2.0 & The Black Speculative Arts Movement: Notes on a Manifesto." *Obsidian* 42, no. 1/2 (2016): 228–36. https://www.jstor.org/stable/44489514?seq=1.

Armada, Bernard J. "Memory's Execution: (Dis)placing the Dissident Body." In *Places of Public Memory: The Rhetoric of Museums and Memorials*, edited by Greg Dickinson, Carole Blair, and Brian L. Ott, 216–37. Tuscaloosa: University of Alabama Press, 2010.

Ashcraft, Karen L., and Michael E. Pacanowsky. "A Woman's Worst Enemy: Reflections on a Narrative of Organizational Life and Female Identity. *Journal of Applied Communication Research* 24 (1996): 217–39.

Associated Press. "German Soccer Team Kneels in Solidarity with the N.F.L. Players' Protests." *New York Times*, October 14, 2017. https://www.nytimes.com/2017/10/14/sports/soccer/german-soccer-team-kneels-in-solidarity-with-nfl-players-protests.html.

Axster, Felix. "'... Will Try to Send You the Best Views from Here': Postcards from the Colonial War in Namibia (1904–1908)." In *German Colonialism, Visual Culture, and Modern Memory*, edited by Volker M. Langbehn, 55–56. New York: Routledge, 2010.

Baldwin, James. "Autobiographical Notes." In *James Baldwin: Collected Essays*, edited by Toni Morrison. Library of America, 1998.

Barbeau, Arthur E., and Florette Henri. *The Unknown Soldiers: African-American Troops in World War I*. Boston, MA: Da Cap Press, 1996.

Beevor, Antony. Introduction to *A Woman in Berlin: Eight Weeks in the Conquered City; A Diary*, xiii–xxi. Translated by Philip Boehm. New York: Picador, 2000.

Biddiscombe, Perry. "Dangerous Liaisons: The Anti-Fraternization Movement in the U.S. Occupation Zones of Germany and Austria, 1945–1948." *Journal of Social History*, 34, no. 3 (2001): 611–47.

Black, Edwin. *War against the Weak: Eugenics and America's Campaign to Create a Master Race*. Washington, DC: Dialog Press, 2012.

Blackler, Adam. "After the Herero 'Uprising': Child Separation and Racial Apartheid in German Southwest Africa." *Age of Revolutions*, March 30, 2020. https://ageofrevolutions.com/2020/03/30/after-the-herero-uprising-child-separation-and-racial-apartheid-in-german-southwest-africa/#_ftnref4.

Blair, Carole, Greg Dickinson, and Brian L. Ott. "Introduction: Rhetoric/Memory/Place." In *Places of Public Memory: The Rhetoric of Museums and Memorials*, edited by Greg Dickinson, Carole Blair, and Brian L. Ott. Tuscaloosa: University of Alabama Press, 2010.

Blakely, Allison. "The Emergence of Afro-Europe: A Preliminary Sketch." In *Black Europe and the African Diaspora*, edited by Darlene Clark Hine, Trica Danielle Keaton, and Stephen Small. Urbana: University of Illinois Press, 2009.

Blumberg, Rhoda Lois. *Civil Rights: The 1960s Freedom Struggle*. New York: Twayne, 1991.

Boehling, Rebecca. "Gender Roles in Ruins: Local Politics under American Occupation, 1945–1955." In *Gender and the Long Postwar: The United States and the Two Germanys, 1945–1989*, edited by Karen Hagemann and Sonya Michel, 51–72. Washington, DC: Woodrow Wilson Center Press, 2014.

Breitenbach, Dagmar, and Zulfikar Abbany. "Black or White." *Deutsche Welle*, January 13, 2012, https://www.dw.com/en/berlin-theater-surprised-by-bitter-dispute-over-blackface-actor/a-15660982.

Brinkman, Svend, Michael Hviid Jacobsen, and Søren Kristiansen. "Historical Overview of Qualitative Research in the Social Sciences." In *The Oxford Handbook of Qualitative Research*, edited by Patricia Leavy. Oxford: Oxford University Press, 2014.

Bultman, Lori. "Remembering the Service of the Fifth Army's 92nd Infantry Division." US Army, February 18, 2021. https://www.army.mil/article/243460/remembering_the_service_of_the_fifth_armys_92nd_infantry_division#:~:text=For%20their%20accomplishments%2C%20the%2092nd,Division's%20World%20War%20II%20association.

Burke, Kenneth. *Language as Symbolic Action: Essays on Life, Literature and Method*. Berkeley: University of California Press, 1966.

Burleigh, Michael, and Wolfgang Wippermann. *The Racial State: Germany 1933–1945*. Cambridge, UK: Cambridge University Press, 1991.

Campt, Tina M. "Converging Specters of an Other Within: Race and Gender in Prewar Afro-German History." *Callaloo* 26, no. 2 (Spring 2003): 322–41.

———. *Other Germans: Black Germans and the Politics of Race, Gender, and Memory in the Third Reich*. Ann Arbor: University of Michigan Press, 2005.

———. "Pictures of 'US'? Blackness, Diaspora, and the Afro-German Subject." In *Black Europe and the African Diaspora*, edited by Darlene Clark Hine, Trica Danielle Keaton, and Stephen Small. Urbana: University of Illinois Press, 2009.

———. "Reading the Black German Experience: An Introduction." *Callaloo* 26, no. 2 (2003) 289–90.

Chávez, Karma R. *The Borders of AIDS: Race, Quarantine, and Resistance*. Seattle: University of Washington Press, 2021.

Chin, Rita, and Heide Fehrenbach. "Introduction: What's Race Got to Do with It? Postwar German History in Context." In Chin, Fehrenbach, Eley, and Grossman, *After the Nazi Racial State*, 1–29.

Chin, Rita, Heide Fehrenbach, Geoff Eley, and Atina Grossman, eds. *After the Nazi Racial State: Difference and Democracy in Germany and Europe*. Ann Arbor: University of Michigan Press, 2009.

Colley, David P. *Blood for Dignity: The Story of the First Integrated Combat Unit in the U.S. Army*. New York: St. Martin's Press, 2003.

Collins, Patricia Hill. *Black Sexual Politics: African Americans, Gender, and the New Racism*. New York: Routledge, 2004.

———. "Learning from the Outsider Within: The Sociological Significance of Black Feminist Thought." *Social Problems* 33, no. 6 (October–December 1986): 14–32.

Condit, Celeste M., and John L. Lucaites. *Crafting Equality: America's Anglo-African Word*. Chicago: University of Chicago Press, 1993.

Connerton, Paul. "Seven Types of Forgetting." *Memory Studies* 1, no. 1 (January 2008): 59–71. https://doi.org/10.1177/1750698007083889.

Constitution of the German Reich. Available from the Cornell University Library, https://digital.library.cornell.edu/catalog/nur01840.

Davis, Diane. *Inessential Solidarity: Rhetoric and Foreigner Relations*. Pittsburgh, PA: University of Pittsburgh Press, 2010.

Davis, James F. *Who Is Black? One Nation's Definition*. University Park: Pennsylvania State University Press, 2001.

"Declaration Acquisition." Bundesverwaltungsamt. Accessed August 20, 2021. https://www.bva.bund.de/DE/Services/Buerger/Ausweis-Dokumente-Recht/Staatsangehoerigkeit/Einbuergerung/EER/01-Informationen_EER/01_01_EER_was_ist/01_02_EER_was_ist_node.html.

Dei, George J. Sefa. *Reframing Blackness and Black Solidarities through Anti-Colonial and Decolonial Prisms*. New York: Springer, 2017.

Denzin, Norman K. *Interpretive Ethnography: Ethnographic Practices for the 21st Century*. Thousand Oaks, CA: Sage 1997.

Dery, Mark. *Flame Wars: The Discourse of Cyberculture*. Durham, NC: Duke University Press, 1994.

Diedrich, Maria I. "From American Slaves to Hessian Subjects: Silenced Black Narratives of the American Revolution." In *Germany and the Black Diaspora: Points of Contact, 1250–1914*, edited by Mischa Honeck, Martin Klimke, and Anne Kuhlmann, 92–112. New York: Berghahn, 2013.

Elia, Adriano. "The Languages of Afrofuturism." *Lingue e Linguaggi* 12 (2014): 83–96.

El-Tayeb, Fatima. "'If You Can't Pronounce My Name, You Can Just Call Me Pride': Afro-German Activism, Gender, and Hip Hop." In *Dialogues of Dispersal: Gender, Sexuality, and African Diasporas*, edited by Sandra Gunning, Tera W. Hunter, and Michele Mitchell. Malden, MA: Blackwell Publishing, 2004.

———. *Schwarze Deutsche: Der Diskurs um Rasse und Nationale Identität 1890–1933*. Frankfurt: Campus, 2001.

Eshun, Kodwo. "Further Considerations on Afrofuturism." *CR: The New Centennial Review* 3, no. 2 (Summer 2003): 287–302. https://www.jstor.org/stable/41949397.

"Executive Order 8802: Prohibition of Discrimination in the Defense Industry, 1941." Milestone Documents, June 25, 1941. https://www.archives.gov/milestone-documents/executive-order-8802.

"Executive Order 9981: Desegregation of the Armed Forces." Milestone Documents, July 26, 1948. https://www.archives.gov/milestone-documents/executive-order-9981.

Fehrenbach, Heide. "Black Occupation Children and the Devolution of the Nazi Racial State." In Chin, Fehrenbach, Eley, and Grossman, *After the Nazi Racial State*, 30–54.

———. *Race after Hitler: Black Occupation Children in Postwar Germany and America*. Princeton, NJ: Princeton University Press, 2007.

Fenner, Angelica. *Race under Reconstruction in German Cinema: Robert Stemmle's* Toxi. Toronto: University of Toronto Press, 2011.

Fiske, John. *Media Matters: Race and Gender in U.S. Politics*. Minneapolis: University of Minnesota Press, 1996.

Fitzpatrick, Matthew Peter. "The Threat of 'Wooly-Haired Grandchildren': Race, the Colonial Family, and German Nationalism." *History of Family* 14, no. 4 (2009): 356–68.

Flores, Lisa A. "Creative Discursive Space through a Rhetoric of Difference: Chicana Feminists Craft a Homeland." *Quarterly Journal of Speech* 82, no. 2 (May) 1996: 142–56. https://doi.org/10.1080/00335639609384147.

Florvil, Tiffany N. *Mobilizing Black Germany: Afro-German Women and the Making of a Transnational Movement*. Champaign: University of Illinois Press, 2020.

Geist, Patricia, and Lisa Gates. "The Poetics and Politics of Re-Covering Identities in Health Communication." *Communication Studies* 47, no. 3 (1996): 218–28.

Gellately, Robert, and Nathan Stolzfus. "Social Outsider and the Construction of the Community of the People." In *Social Outsiders in Nazi Germany*, edited by Robert Gellately and Nathan Stolzfus. Princeton, New Jersey: Princeton University Press, 2001.

"German Brown Babies." Black German Cultural Society. Accessed December 15, 2014, http://afrogermans.us/german-brown-babies-2/.

"German Unwed Mothers Face Tough Problem Suing Yanks." *Overseas Weekly*, July 17, 1955.

Gerten, Katie. "9 Heartbreaking Facts on Foster Care." Youth Dynamics, January 16, 2022. https://www.youthdynamics.org/9-heartbreaking-facts-on-foster-care/.

Glenn, Cheryl. *Unspoken: A Rhetoric of Silence*. Carbondale: Southern Illinois University Press, 2004.

Goedde, Petra. *GIs and Germans: Culture, Gender, and Foreign Relations, 1945–1949*. New Haven, CT: Yale University Press, 2003.

Gordon, Avery F. *Ghostly Matters: Haunting and the Sociological Imagination*. Minneapolis: University of Minnesota Press, 2008.

Grossman, Atina. "The 'Big Rape': Sex and Sexual Violence, War, and Occupation in German Post-World War II Memory and Imagination." In *Gender and the Long Postwar: The United States and the Two Germanys, 1945–1989*, edited by Karen Hagemann and Sonya Michel, 31–50. Washington, DC: Woodrow Wilson Center Press, 2014.

Haas, Francois. "German Science and Black Racism—Roots of the Nazi Holocaust." *The FASEB Journal* 22 (2008): 332–37.

Hagemann, Karen, and Sonya Michel. "Introduction: Gender and the Long Postwar: Reconsiderations of the United States and the Two Germanys, 1945–1989." In *Gender and the Long Postwar: The United States and the Two Germanys, 1945–1989*, edited by Karen Hagemann and Sonya Michel, 1–27. Washington, DC: Woodrow Wilson Center Press, 2014.

Halbwachs, Maurice. *On Collective Memory*. Translated, edited, and with an introduction by Lewis A. Coser. Chicago: University of Chicago Press, 1992.

Hartman, Saidiya. *Wayward Lives, Beautiful Experiments: Intimate Histories of Riotous Black Girls, Troublesome Women, and Queer Radicals*. Reprint ed. New York City: W. W. Norton, 2020.

Hawley, Charles. "'African Village' Accused of Putting Humans on Display." *Spiegel International*, June 9, 2005. https://www.spiegel.de/international/german-zoo-scandal-african-village-accused-of-putting-humans-on-display-a-359799.html.

Herbst, Philip. *The Color of Words: An Encyclopaedic Dictionary of Ethnic Bias in the United States*. Yarmouth: Intercultural Press, 1999.

Hecht, Michael L., and HyeJeong Choi. "The Communication Theory of Identity as Framework for Health Message Design." In *Health Communication Message Design*, edited by HyeJeong Choi, 137–52. Los Angeles: Sage Publications, 2012.

Herman, Ellen. *Kinship by Design: A History of Adoption in the Modern United States*. Chicago: University of Chicago Press, 2008.

Hervieux, Linda. *Forgotten: The Untold Story of D-Day's Black Heroes, at Home and at War*. New York: HarperCollins Publishers, 2015.

Hidden Villa Ranch. "Mission and History." Accessed 2014. Updated page content currently found at https://www.hiddenvilla.org/about-us/mission-history/.

Hidden Villa Ranch. "What Is Hidden Villa." Accessed 2014. Updated page content currently found at https://www.hiddenvilla.org/about-us/.

Hirsch, Marianne. *The Generation of Postmemory: Writing and Visual Culture after the Holocaust*. New York: Columbia University Press, 2012.

Höhn, Maria. *GIs and Fräuleins: The German-American Encounter in 1950s West Germany*. Chapel Hill: University of North Carolina Press, 2002.

———. "Love across the Color Line: The Limits of German and American Democracy, 1945–1968." In *Germans and African Americans: Two Centuries of Exchange*, edited by Larry A. Gree and Anke Ortlepp. Jackson: University Press of Mississippi, 2011.

Höhn, Maria, and Martin Klimke. *A Breath of Freedom: The Civil Rights Struggle, African American GIs, and Germany*. New York: Palgrave MacMillan, 2010.

Honeck, Mischa, Martin Klimke, and Anne Kuhlmann. Introduction to *Germany and the Black Diaspora: Points of Contact, 1250–1914*, edited by Mischa Honeck, Martin Klimke, and Anne Kuhlmann, 1–18. New York: Berghahn, 2013.

hooks, bell. "The Oppositional Gaze: Black Female Spectator." In *Black Looks: Race and Representation*, 115–32. Boston, MA: South End Press, 1992.

Hügel-Marshall, Ika. "Crossing Borders, Overcoming Boundaries." In *Children of the Liberation: Transatlantic Experiences and Perspectives of Black Germans of the Post-War Generation*, edited and translated by Marion Kraft, 171–81. Oxford: Peter Lang, 2020.

Hughes, Langston. "Harlem." In *The Collected Poems of Langston Hughes*, edited by Arnold Rampersad and David Roessel. Annotated ed. New York: Vintage Books, 1995.

Hyslop, Jonathan. "White Working-Class Women and the Invention of Apartheid: 'Purified' Afrikaner Nationalist Agitation for Legislation against 'Mixed' Marriages, 1934–9." *Journal of African History* 36, no. 1 (1995): 57–81.

Jackson, Michael. *Paths toward a Clearing: Radical Empiricism and Ethnographic Inquiry*. Bloomington: Indiana University Press, 1989.

Jacobson, David. *Place and Belonging in America*. Baltimore, MD: Johns Hopkins University Press, 2002.

Johnston, Carolyn Ross. *My Father's War: Fighting with the Buffalo Soldiers in World War II*. Tuscaloosa: University of Alabama Press, 2012.

Jones, Jeannette Eileen. "'On the Brain of the Negro': Race, Abolitionism, and Friedrich Tiedemann's Scientific Discourse on the African Diaspora." In *Germany and the Black Diaspora: Points of Contact, 1250–1914*, edited by Mischa Honeck, Martin Klimke, and Anne Kuhlmann, 134–52. New York: Berghahn, 2013.

Kantor, Jodi. "Story of Survival." *CBS This Morning*, aired May 20, 2021, 7:00–7:30, 8:23–9:50. https://www.cbsnews.com/video/investigative-journalist-jodi-kantor-talks-to-her-grandmother-hana-about-surviving-holocaust.

Kaplan, Paul H. D. "The Calenberg Altarpiece: Black African Christians in Renaissance Germany." In *Germany and the Black Diaspora: Points of Contact, 1250–1914*, edited by Mischa Honeck, Martin Klimke, and Anne Kuhlmann, 21–37. New York: Berghahn, 2013.

Kim, Eleana J., and Kim Park Nelson. "'Natural Born Aliens': Transnational Adoptees and US Citizenship." In *Adoption across Race and Nation: US Histories and Legacies*, edited by Silke Hackenesch, 61–84. Columbus: The Ohio State University Press, 2022.

Kirchner, Walter. "The Academic Success of *Negermischlinge* ['Mixed-race Negroes']." German History in Documents and Images. https://ghdi.ghi-dc.org/sub_document.cfm?document_id=4563.

Kirkpatrick, Clifford. "Recent Changes in the Status of Women and the Family in Germany." *American Sociological Review* 2, no. 5 (1937): 650–58.

Kirsch, Gesa E., and Jacqueline J. Royster. "Feminist Rhetorical Practices: In Search of Excellence." *National Council of Teachers of English* 61, no. 4 (June 2010): 648–56.

Kirsch, Gesa E., and Liz Rohan, eds. *Beyond the Archives: Research as a Lived Process*. Carbondale: Southern Illinois University Press, 2008.

Koller, Christian. "The Recruitment of Colonial Troops in Africa and Asia and Their Deployment in Europe during the First World War." *Immigrants & Minorities: Historical Studies in in Ethnicity, Migration, and Diaspora* 26, no. 1–2 (2008): 111–33.

Kuhlmann, Anne. "Ambiguous Duty: Black Servants at German Ancien Régime Courts." In *Germany and the Black Diaspora: Points of Contact, 1250–1914*, edited by Mischa Honeck, Martin Klimke, and Anne Kuhlmann, 57–73. New York: Berghahn, 2013.

Lee, Ana Paulina. "Memory and Non-Place: Visual Testimonies of Japanese American Internment during World War II." *Journal of Latin American Cultural Studies* 28, no. 1 (January 2019): 97–111. https://doi.org/10.1080/13569325.2018.1528441.

Lemke Muniz de Faria, Yara-Colette. "'Germany's "Brown Babies" Must Be Helped! Will You?' U.S. Adoption Plans for Afro-German Children, 1950–1955." *Callaloo* 26, no. 2 (Spring 2003): 342–62.

Lewis, David Levering, ed. *W. E. B. Du Bois: A Reader*. New York: Henry Holt Books, 1995.

"Life for Women and the Family in Nazi Germany." BBC News, 2021. https://www.bbc.co.uk/bitesize/guides/zxb8msg/revision/3.

Littlejohn, Stephen W. *Theories of Human Communication*. 5th ed. Belmont, CA: Wadsworth Publishing Company, 1996.

Lowe, Kate. "The Black Diaspora in Europe in the Fifteenth and Sixteenth Centuries, with Special Reference to German-Speaking Areas." In *Germany and the Black Diaspora: Points of*

Contact, 1250–1914, edited by Mischa Honeck, Martin Klimke, and Anne Kuhlmann, 38–56. New York: Berghahn, 2013.

Lusane, Clarence. *Hitler's Black Victims: The Historical Experience of European Blacks, Africans and African Americans during the Nazi Era.* New York: Routledge, 2003.

Mackey, Mike. *Heart Mountain: Life in Wyoming's Concentration Camp.* Powell, WY: Western History Publications.

Martinez, Aja Y. "A Plea for Critical Race Theory Counterstory: Stock Story versus Counterstory Dialogues Concerning Alejandra's 'Fit' in the Academy." In *Composition Studies* 42, no. 2. 2014.

Michaels, Jim. "Emerging from History: Massacre of 11 Black Soldiers." *USA Today,* November 7, 2013. https://www.usatoday.com/story/news/nation/2013/11/07/wereth-black-soldiers-battle-of-bulge-army-world-war-ii-history/3465059/.

Milloy, Courtland. "Liberators Worth Seeing." *Washington Post,* May 29, 1994. https://www.washingtonpost.com/archive/local/1994/05/29/liberators-worth-seeing/9c39cd6b-2463-4680-9416-1f0467d30297/.

Mjagkij, Nina. *Loyalty in Time of Trial: The African American Experience during World War I.* Lanham, MD: Rowman & Littlefield, 2011.

Motley, Mary Penick. *The Invisible Soldier: The Experience of the Black Soldier, Word War II.* Detroit, MI: Wayne State University Press, 1987.

Moyd, Michelle A. *Violent Intermediaries: African Soldiers, Conquest, and Everyday Colonialism in German East Africa.* Athens: Ohio University Press, 2014.

Murphy, Alexandra G. "Hidden Transcripts of Flight Attendant Resistance." *Management Communication Quarterly* 11, no. 4 (May 1998): 499–535.

"Muted Group Theory." In *A First Look at Communication Theory,* edited by Em Griffin, Andrew Ledbetter, and Glenn Sparks, 409–20. 10th ed. New York: McGraw-Hill, 2019.

Naranch, Bradley. "Global Proletarians, Uncle Toms, and Native Savages: Popular German Race Science in the Emancipation Era." In *Germany and the Black Diaspora: Points of Contact, 1250–1914,* edited by Mischa Honeck, Martin Klimke, and Anne Kuhlmann. 170–71. New York: Berghahn, 2013.

"Nationality Law Changed." Bundesverwaltungsamt. Accessed August 20, 2021. https://www.bva.bund.de/DE/Services/Buerger/Ausweis-Dokumente-Recht/Staatsangehoerigkeit/_documents/Meldung/Meldung_Gesetzesaenderung.html.

Noakes, Jeremy. "Social Outcasts in the Third Reich." In *Life in the Third Reich,* edited by Richard Bessel, 83–96. Oxford, UK: Oxford University Press, 2001.

"Obtaining German Citizenship." Germany.info. Accessed April 11, 2021, https://www.germany.info/us-en/service/03-Citizenship/german-citizenship-obtain/919576.

Oguntoye, Katharina, May Optiz, and Dagmar Schultz, eds. *Showing Our Colors: Afro-German Women Speak Out.* Translated by Anne V. Adams. Amherst: University of Massachusetts Press, 1992.

Okuefuna, David, dir. *Hitler's Forgotten Victims.* United Kingdom: SpiritWorld Entertainment, 1997. TV movie.

Olick, Jeffrey K. Introduction to *States of Memory,* edited by Jeffrey K. Olick, 1–16. Durham, NC: Duke University Press, 2003.

Oliveres, Jordi. "Watch: What Is Afrofuturism?" *The Root,* April 20, 2016. https://www.theroot.com/watch-what-is-afrofuturism-1790855036.

Partridge, Damani J. "Occupying American 'Black' Bodies and Reconfiguring European Spaces—The Possibilities for Noncitizen Articulations in Berlin and Beyond." *Transforming Anthropology* 21, no. 1 (2013): 41–56.

Pascoe, Peggy. *What Comes Naturally: Miscegenation Law and the Making of Race in America.* Oxford, UK: Oxford University Press, 2009.

Patton, Tracey Owens. "I Want to Show You My New Family: Race, Rejection, and Reunion in Postwar Germany." In *Adoption across Race and Nation: US Histories and Legacies,* edited by Silke Hackenesch, 150–73. Columbus: The Ohio State University Press, 2022.

Peña, Rosemarie. "Stories Matter: Experiences of Black German Adoptees in the U.S." In *Children of the Liberation: Transatlantic Experiences and Perspectives of Black Germans of the Post-War Generation,* edited and translated by Marion Kraft, 243–81. Oxford: Peter Lang, 2020.

Peterson, Judy. "Ming Quong: Once an Orphanage Now Modern Treatment Refuge." *Mercury News,* May 25, 2017. https://www.mercurynews.com/2017/05/25/lighting-the-way-orphanage-for-young-sex-slaves-is-now-modern-treatment-refuge/.

Phillips, Kendall R. "The Failure of Memory: Reflections on Rhetoric and Public Remembrance." *Western Journal of Communication* 74, no. 2 (2010): 208–23.

Pierre, Nora. "General Introduction: Between Memory and History." In *Realms of Memory: Rethinking the French Past.* Vol. 1, *Conflicts and Divisions,* edited by Lawrence D. Kritzman, 1–20. Translated by Arthur Goldhammer. New York: Columbia University Press, 1996.

Pile, Steve. "Skin, Race, and Space: The Clash of Bodily Schemas in Frantz Fanon's *Black Skins, White Masks* and Nella Larsen's *Passing.*" *Cultural Geographies* 18, no. 1 (2011): 25–41. https://doi.org/10.1177/1474474010379953.

"Population in the Former Territories of the Federal Republic of Germany and the German Democratic Republic from 1950–2016." Statista, June 21, 2022. https://www.statista.com/statistics/1054199/population-of-east-and-west-germany/#:~:text=During%20the%20German%20partition%2C%20the,16.4%20million%20during%20this%20time.

Pugach, Sara, David Pizzo, and Adam Blackler. *After the Imperialist Imagination: Two Decades of Research on Global Germany and its Legacies.* New York: Peter Lang, 2020.

Quahie, Kevin. *Black Aliveness, or A Poetics of Being.* Duke University Press, 2020.

"Radiant Light: Memories from the Ming Quong Home in Los Gatos." Accessed June 5, 2017. http://www.museumsoflosgatos.org/site/wp-content/uploads/2012/02/Ming-Quong.pdf. Page no longer available. Please see https://www.numulosgatos.org/exhibitions-2/2017/4/21/radiant-light-the-story-of-eastfield-ming-quong for more information.

Raphael-Hernandez, Heike, and Pia Wiegmink. "German Entanglements in Transatlantic Slavery: An Introduction." *Atlantic Studies: Global Currents* 14, no. 4 (2017): 419–35. https://www.tandfonline.com/doi/pdf/10.1080/14788810.2017.1366009.

Renes, Martin. "The Stolen Generations: A Narrative of Removal, Displacement, and Recovery." In *Lives in Migration: Rupture and Continuity,* edited by Martin Renes, 30–49. Barcelona: University of Spain, 2011.

Ricoeur, Paul. *Memory, History, Forgetting.* Translated by Kathleen Blamey and David Pellauer. Chicago: University of Chicago Press, 2004.

Roseman, Mark. *Lives Reclaimed: A Story or Rescue and Resistance in Nazi Germany.* New York: Metropolitan Books, Illustrated Edition, 2019.

Royster, Jacqueline Jones, and Gesa E. Kirsch. *Feminist Rhetorical Practices: New Horizons for Rhetoric, Composition, and Literacy Studies.* Carbondale: Southern Illinois University Press, 2012.

Timsit, Annabelle. "The Blueprint the US Can Follow to Finally Pay Reparations." *Quartz,* October 13, 2020. https://qz.com/1915185/how-germany-paid-reparations-for-the-holocaust/.

Schilling, Britta. *Postcolonial Germany: Memories of Empire in a Decolonized Nation.* Oxford, UK: Oxford University Press, 2014.

Schmidt, Nadine, George Engels, Stephanie Busari, and David McKenzie. "Germany Will Pay Namibia $1.3bn as It Formally Recognizes Colonial-Era Genocide." CNN, May 28, 2021. https://www.cnn.com/2021/05/28/africa/germany-recognizes-colonial-genocide-namibia-intl/index.html.

Schultz, Dagmar, dir. *Audre Lorde—The Berlin Years 1984–1992*. Written by Dagmar Schultz, Ika Hügel-Marshall, Ria Cheatom, and Aletta von Vietinghoff. Germany, 2012.

Siek, Stephanie. "Germany's 'Brown Babies': The Difficult Identities of Post-War Black Children of GIs." *Speigel Online*, October 13, 2009. https://www.spiegel.de/international/germany/germany-s-brown-babies-the-difficult-identities-of-post-war-black-children-of-gis-a-651989.html.

"Sixteen Get Bronze Stars." *America's Historical Newspapers*. Accessed March 24, 2021. Newspapers.com.

Skundrick, Seth, dir. *The Third Reich: The Rise and Fall*. Brooklyn, NY: New Animal Productions, 2010. DVD.

Small, Nancy. *A Rhetoric of Becoming: US American Women in Qatar*. Anderson, SC: Parlor Press, 2022.

Sollors, Werner. *The Temptation of Despair: Tales of the 1940s*. Cambridge, MA: The Belknap Press of Harvard University Press, 2014.

Steinmetz, George. *The Devil's Handwriting: Precoloniality and the German Colonial State in Qingdao, Samoa, and Southwest Africa*. Chicago: University of Chicago Press, 2007.

Stemmle, Robert A., dir. *Toxi*. Hamburg, Germany: Fono Film, 1952. DEFA Film Library, University of Massachusetts Amherst.

Stoecker, Helmuth. *German Imperialism in Africa: From the Beginnings until the Second World War*. London: Hurst, 1987.

Sturken, Marita. "Absent Images of Memory: Remembering and Reenacting the Japanese Internment." *Positions* 5, no. 3 (Winter 1997): 687–707.

Taylor, Howard Rechavia. "US Court Hears Case against Germany over Namibia Genocide." *Aljazeera*, July 31, 2018. https://www.aljazeera.com/news/2018/07/court-hears-case-germany-namibia-genocide-180731201918543.html.

Teo, Hsu-Ming. "The Continuum of Sexual Violence in Occupied Germany 1945–1949." *Women's History Review* 5, no. 2 (1996): 191–218. https://doi.org/10.1080/09612029600200111.

"Three Little Young Negroes . . . There Are 42 Colored Children in the City of Bamberg and Its Environs." Translated by Thomas Dunlap. *Neues Volksblatt*, no. 8, January 20, 1951.

Trigg, Dylan. "The Place of Trauma: Memory, Hauntings, and the Temporality of Ruins." *Memory Studies* 2, no. 1 (January 2009): 87–101.

van Dijk, Teun A. "New(s) Racism: A Discourse Analytical Approach." In *Ethnic Minorities and the Media: Changing Cultural Boundaries*, edited by S. Cottle, 33–49. Buckingham, UK: Open University Press, 2003.

Van Maanen, John. "An End to Innocence: The Ethnography of Ethnography." In *Representation in Ethnography*, edited by John Van Maanen, 1–35. Thousand Oaks, CA: Sage, 1995.

Victoria and Albert Museum. "The Adoration of the Magi (lower part of a rood screen)." vam.ac.uk, July 13, 2007, "Historical Context" section. http://collections.vam.ac.uk/item/O137359/the-adoration-of-the-magi-panel-unknown/.

Washington State Department of Social and Health Services. "What's the Difference between Legal and Undocumented Immigrants?" https://www.dshs.wa.gov/faq/what%E2%80%99s-difference-between-legal-and-undocumented-immigrants.

Weheliye, Alexander G. "My Volk to Come: Peoplehood in Recent Diaspora Discourse and Afro-German Popular Music." In *Black Europe and the African Diaspora*, edited by Darlene Clark Hine, Trica Danielle Keaton, and Stephen Small, 161–79. Urbana: University of Illinois Press, 2009.

Westover, Tara. *Educated: A Memoir*. New York, Random House, 2018.

Wigger, Iris. *The Black Horror on the Rhine*. London: Palgrave Macmillan, 2017.

———. "'Black Shame'—The Campaign against 'Racial Degeneration' and Female Degradation in Interwar Europe." *Race & Class* 51, no. 3 (2010): 33–46.

Wildenthal, Lora. *German Women for Empire, 1884–1945*. Durham, NC: Duke University Press, 2001.

———. "Race, Gender, and Citizenship in the German Colonial Empire." In *Tensions of Empire: Colonial Cultures in a Bourgeois World*, edited by Frederick Cooper and Ann Laura Stoler, 263–86. Berkeley: University of California Press, 1997.

Woodward, C. Vann. *The Strange Career of Jim Crow*. Oxford, UK: Oxford University Press, 2001.

Wright, Michelle M. *Becoming Black: Creating Identity in the African Diaspora*. Durham, NC: Duke University Press, 2004.

"WWII Draft Registration Cards for Florida, 10/16/1940–03/31/1947." The National Archives in St. Louis, Missouri. Record Group: Records of the Selective Service System, 147; Box 145. St. Louis, Missouri.

Yates, Frances A. *The Art of Memory*. Chicago: University of Chicago Press, 1966.

Zantop, Susanne. *Colonial Fantasies: Conquest, Family, and Nation in Precolonial Germany, 1770–1870*. Durham, NC: Duke University Press, 1997.

Zelizer, Barbie. "Reading the Past against the Grain: The Shape of Memory Studies." In *Critical Studies in Mass Communication* 12, no. 2 (June 1995): 214–39.

Zimmerer, Jürgen. "Krieg, KZ, und Völkermord in Südwestafrika: Der erste Deutsche Genozid." In *Völkermord in Deutsch-Südwestafrika: Der Kolonialkrieg (1904–1908) in Namibia und seine Folgen*, edited by Jürgen Zimmerer and Joachim Zeller, 45–63. Berlin: Links, 2003.

INDEX

abolitionists, 36

abortion, 101–2, 112

absent presence, 6

Ackermann, Udo (Rudi Richardson), 156

Adenauer, Konrad, 54

adoption: of children of rape, 141–42; and citizenship, 121, 155–56; and dynamics of belonging, 132–34, 161; and foster care system, 152–54, 157–65; German-Danish coordination, 137; German-US coordination, 130–31, 133–34, 137; marketing campaigns, 4, 78, 123, 124–25, 166; marriage requirements, 135; racial matching in US adoption policy, 166–67; in West German nation-building ideology, 130, 134–35

Africa, German colonization of, 38–45, 47

African Americans. *See* Black American families; Black American soldiers

African soldiers: *askaris,* in German East Africa, 39; French colonial, in Rhineland occupation, 45–47, 68, 69, 91–92, 94–95, 129. *See also* Black American soldiers

Afro-American (newspaper), 78

afrodeutsche Nachkriegskinder: adoption of (*see* adoption); archival record of, 17, 55–56; child support for, 135–36; citizenship of, 21, 121, 135, 154–57, 169, 170–71, 173–74; integration of, 136–37, 169; as label, 2, 3; liminal existence of, 5, 120, 126–27, 132–33, 141, 157, 174, 188; recovering voices of, 25–26; scientific experiments on, 127–29; statistics, 125–26; as threat to white German purity, 113–14, 123–24, 129–30; visas for, 131

Afrofuturism: acts of engagement with, 58–59, 61, 67, 74, 78, 87, 120, 170, 172, 185–86, 197, 205–7; as analytical framework, 8, 9, 10–11, 15–18, 30–32, 60; limitations of, 127, 146, 174–75, 201, 203–5

Agamben, Giorgio, 7–8

agency, Black. *See* Afrofuturism

Ahmed, Sara, 13

Aitken, Robbie, 37, 39, 47, 51, 90–91

Albert: composite narrative of, 73–74, 78–79; Greta's description of, 61–63, 83, 85, 105, 106, 107; marriage, 108–9; military record, 63–64

alienizing logic, 76, 129

American Revolution (1775–83), 35–36, 65
Anderson, Benedict, 130
Anderson, Reynaldo, 10
anthropological studies, 127–29
anti-Blackness, Germany: colonial-era, 38–45, 90; Enlightenment-era, 35–37; modern-day, 57–58; Nazi-era, 51–54, 69–73, 96; postwar-era, 55, 98–101, 127–29; Weimar-era, 45–49, 91–92, 94–95
anti-Blackness, United States: absent father stereotype, 133; and civil rights movement, 74, 78, 87, 137; and cognitive dissonance of democracy ideal, 55, 65, 85, 87, 137; in foster care system, 158–62; influence on Third Reich, 71–72, 75; in military culture, 55, 75, 76, 78, 83–85, 98–99, 103–4; one-drop rule, 3, 71, 123, 159, 166; and racial matching in adoption policy, 166–67; violence against veterans, 86; in wartime propaganda campaigns, 65–66, 75, 92–94, 93 fig. 3.1
Anti-Defamation League, 77
archival preservation, 17, 55–56
Armada, Bernard J., 118
askaris (African soldiers), 39
assimilation, 57, 70, 129, 134, 160. *See also* integration and desegregation
Atwood, Margaret, *The Handmaid's Tale*, 170, 170n37
autoethnographic methodology, 18–20
Axster, Felix, 40, 42

Baker, Audrey, 33, 34
Baldwin, James, 61
Barnes, John, 143n82
BDM (Bund Deutscher Mädel), 50–51, 72, 73 fig. 2.2, 100
Berliner Konferenz, 38
biracial children. See *afrodeutsche Nachkriegskinder*; mixed-race children
Bismarck, Otto von, 38
Black, Edwin, 52–53
Black American families: adoption campaigns directed at, 130, 133–34; culture shock of adopted children in, 137; and racial matching in US adoption policy, 166–67

Black American soldiers: and absent father stereotype, 125, 133; adoption campaigns directed at, 78, 123, 125; and blood purity, 128; and child support, 135–36; liminal existence of, 84; in postwar Germany, 83–85, 98–100, 102–4; rape charges, 140–41; service in American wars, overview, 64–65; as signifiers of German defeat, 82; in World War I, 65–67; in World War II, 73–78, 77 fig. 2.3. *See also* interracial relationships
Black Codes (1865–66), 71n27
Black German postwar children. See *afrodeutsche Nachkriegskinder*
Black Germans: assimilation of, 57, 70, 129, 134; and Hitler Youth, 72; liminal existence of, 10, 57–58, 70–71, 91; military service, 71. *See also afrodeutsche Nachkriegskinder*; anti-Blackness, Germany
Black Lives Matter, 58
blackface, 33, 124, 125 fig. 4.4
Blackler, Adam, 38, 39–40, 41
Blackness: and civil rights movement, 74, 78, 87, 137; in medieval visual imagery, 32–35. *See also* Afrofuturism; anti-Blackness, Germany; anti-Blackness, United States
Blair, Carole, 8, 9, 22, 107, 165
Blakely, Allison, 57–58
Boehling, Rebecca, 99
Brinkman, Svend, 21
Buchenwald concentration camp, 76–77
Bultman, Lori, 78
Bund Deutscher Mädel (BDM), 50–51, 72, 73 fig. 2.2, 100
Burke, Kenneth, 124
Butler, Ethel, 134
Butler, Octavia, *Kindred*, 31

Campt, Tina, 12, 14, 43, 44, 46, 50–51, 91, 92, 94–95, 96, 132
Cardwell, Daniel, 133
Casey, Edward S., 22
Catholic housing facilities, 78, 102, 121–22, 132, 151
Chávez, Karma, 9, 76, 129, 143

INDEX • 221

"chocolate soldiers" (*Schokoladensoldaten*), 83, 124
Choi, HyeJeong, 182, 183, 190
citizenship, German: and adoption, 121, 155–56; dual, 22; and interracial relationships, 21, 47n62, 51; of mixed-race and *afrodeutsche Nachkriegskinder*, 21, 40, 47, 91, 121, 135, 155, 169, 173–74; and passport expiration, 153–54, 155; and whiteness, 21, 38, 40, 90
citizenship, US naturalization process, 155–57, 170–71. *See also* immigration
civil rights movement, 74, 78, 87, 137
clubs, integrated, 103–5
collective cultural frameworks, 12
Colley, David, 65, 75
composite narratives, 60, 67–69, 73–74, 78–82, 107–8, 159
Compulsory Service Act (Germany, 1935), 71
concentration camps, 52, 53 fig. 1.4, 54, 76–77
connection, rhetorical, 194–95
Connerton, Paul, 14, 16–17, 56–57, 62, 107, 109, 118, 129, 139, 143n82, 158, 162–63, 165, 193, 198
constitutive forgetting, 88, 158, 163
counterstory, 19
critical fabulations, 107
critical imagination, 184
Crusade-era Europe, 32–35

Dachau concentration camp, 52, 53 fig. 1.4, 76
das Volk vs. *ein Volk*, 50
Davis, Diane, 61
decolonialism, 17
democracy, and racial in/equality, 55, 65, 85, 87, 130, 137
Denmark, adoption coordination with Germany, 137
Dery, Mark, 15–16
desegregation and integration, 84–85, 103–5, 136–37, 169
Dickinson, Greg, 8, 22
Diedrich, Maria, 35–36
discursive space, 120
Displaced Person Act (Germany, 1948), 131

divorce law, 81
Double Victory campaign, 74, 78
dual citizenship, 22
Duveneck, Frank and Josephine, 147–49, 151–52

Ebony (magazine), 4, 5 fig. 0.2, 72n29, 78, 166
ein Volk vs. *das Volk*, 50
Elia, Adriano, 30
El-Tayeb, Fatima, 38, 47, 57
emotional health rhetoric, 102
England, in World War II, 74–75
English as a second language (ESL), 150
Enlightenment era, 35–37
erasure: and absent presence, 6; and archival preservation, 17, 55–56; and generational trauma, 5–6, 202–3; in "official history," 12–13; repressive, 56–57, 129, 165, 174; and silence, 62, 109–10, 118, 180, 182–83, 189–90, 192. *See also* forgetting; postmemory
Erinnerungskultur (culture of remembrance), 79–80
Eshun, Kodwo, 10, 58, 67
eugenics, 46, 52–54, 96, 127–29
Executive Order 8802 (US, 1941), 74–75
Executive Order 9981 (US, 1948), 84

Familienstammbuchs (family genealogy books), 22, 23 fig. 0.3, 188–89
Federal Bilingual Education Act (US, 1968), 150
Fehrenbach, Heide, 55, 83, 85, 99, 101–2, 113, 130–31, 135
Fenner, Angelica, 127
Fiegert, Elfie, 123
1st SS Panzer Division, 76
Fisher, Eugene, 53
Fitzpatrick, Matthew Peter, 43
Flores, Lisa, 120
forced forgetting, 10, 16–17
forgetting: constitutive, 88, 158, 163; forced, 10, 16–17; prescriptive, 14, 69, 107, 139, 162; repressive erasure, 56–57, 129, 165, 174; structural amnesia, 88, 109, 143
foster care system, 152–54, 157–65

Franklin, Benjamin, 65
Frederick II, Holy Roman Emperor, 35

Gellately, Robert, 50, 52
gender. *See* Black American soldiers; interracial relationships; sexuality; white womanhood; women, Black; women, white German
generational trauma, 5–6, 201–4
German identity. *See* anti-Blackness, Germany; Black Germans; citizenship, German; white womanhood; whiteness
German Nationality Act, 156
Germany: colonial, 38–45, 90; Enlightenment, 35–37; medieval, 32–35; Weimar Republic, 46–47, 91–92, 94–95. *See also* Third Reich Germany; West Germany
Gesellschaft für Christlich-Jüdische Zusammenarbeit (Society for Christian-Jewish cooperation), 82–83
Gibson, William, 30
Gilges, Hilarius "Lari," 70
Glenn, Cheryl, 109–10
Goebbels, Joseph, 75, 139
Goedde, Petra, 121
Gordon, Avery, 5
Grammer, Mabel, 78, 131–32, 133, 137, 166
Greta, 104 fig. 3.3, 116 fig. 4.2, 126 fig. 4.5; confrontation with postmemoried creative imaginings, 107, 176–77, 180, 182–84, 185–86, 189–93, 197–98, 200–201; death of, 200; description of Albert, 61–63, 83, 85, 105, 106, 107; description of Robert, 67, 80–81, 82, 115; employment in Germany, 100, 117, 137–38, 140; employment in United States, 149; forced motherhood, 114–19; and generational trauma, 5–6, 201–4; in Hitler Maidens, 50, 72; identity reconstruction and reclamation, 14, 107–8, 112, 122, 143–44, 158–61; immigration to United Sates, 138, 142, 146; parental rights termination, 152–53, 159, 163–67, 182; post-reunion interactions with Lore and author, 198–200; pregnancy, 108–9, 110, 112, 114; reunions with Lore and author, in-person, 4 fig. 0.1, 62–63, 153 fig. 5.1, 181–84, 186–94, 187 fig. 6.1, 188 fig. 6.2, 191 fig. 6.3, 195–98; reunions with Lore and author, phone conversations, 178–80, 185, 194–95, 196; sponsor family, 147–48, 149, 151–52; US citizenship, 154, 155 fig. 5.2; view of Hitler, 49
Grossman, Atina, 138

Hagemann, Karen, 139
Halbwachs, Maurice, 13
Harlem Hell Fighters, 369th Infantry Regiment, 66
Harmon, Ernest, 83
Hartman, Saidiya, 107
Hawley, Charles, 37–38
Hecht, Michael, 182, 183, 190
Herbst, Phillip, 121n11
Herero people, 41–42, 44–45
Hermine, 116 fig. 4.2; death of, 152; relationship with Greta, 115–16; relationship with Lilli and Lore, 114, 116, 119, 121, 143, 146–47, 160; relationship with Robert, 80–81, 115
Hervieux, Linda, 74
Hidden Villa Ranch, Los Altos, California, 148–50, 151–52
Hirsch, Marianne, 13
Hitler, Adolf, *Mein Kampf,* 49, 72. *See also* Third Reich Germany
Hitler Maidens, 50–51, 72, 73 fig. 2.2, 100
Hitler Youth Group, 50, 72, 73 fig. 2.2
Höhn, Maria, 55, 76, 84, 86, 87, 95, 101, 103–4
Holocaust, 52, 53 fig. 1.4, 54, 76–77
homophobia, 101
Honeck, Mischa, 32, 34–35
Hügel-Marshall, Ika, 136
Humboldt, Alexander von, *Essai politique sur L'isle de Cuba,* 36
humiliated silence, 62, 118, 193
Hyslop, Jonathan, 40

identity management theory, 182–83, 190
immigration: and assimilation, 160; and dynamics of belonging for *afrodeutsche Nachkriegskinder,* 132; naturalization process, 155–57, 170–71; and sponsorship, 147–48; undocumented, 155–57, 169; visas, 103, 131
Indigenous people, as term, 29n1

insider/outsider status, 98, 124, 130, 182–83, 186, 189, 190, 197–98
integration and desegregation, 84–85, 103–5, 136–37, 169
interpenetration, 183
interracial relationships: bans on, colonial-era, 39–40, 47n62, 90; bans on, in United States, 54, 109, 135; bans on, Nazi-era, 53, 96–97, 97 fig. 3.2; and citizenship law, 21, 47n62, 51; in colonial propaganda campaigns, 42–43, 43 fig. 1.2; in postwar West Germany, institutional and ideological constraints, 99–103; in postwar West Germany, spaces for, 103–6, 105 fig. 3.4; *Verkafferung* label, 42; in Weimar propaganda campaigns, 46–49, 48 fig. 1.3, 94–95; white women stigmatized for, 100, 101, 110, 113, 121, 131–32. See also *afrodeutsche Nachkriegskinder*; mixed-race children
invisibility. *See* erasure

Jacobs, Gunter, 77
Jacobsen, Michael, 21
Jacobson, David, 72–73
Jedelhauser, Luis, 135
Jet (magazine), 4, 78, 166
Jewish Holocaust survivors, reparations for, 54–55
Jim Crow culture. *See* anti-Blackness, United States
Johnston, Carolyn, 66, 77
Jones, Jeannette, 37
Juana of Castile, 33
Jugendamt (Youth Welfare Office), 17, 17n44, 55, 122, 141

Kaepernick, Colin, 58
Kantor, Jodi, 55
Kaplan, Paul, 32–33
Kirchner, Walter, 127, 128, 129
Kirkpatrick, Clifford, 81
Kirsch, Gesa E., 18, 19, 184
KKK, 83
Klimke, Martin, 32, 34–35, 76, 84, 87
Kristiansen, Søren, 21
Kuhlmann, Anne, 32, 33, 34–35

Law for the Encouragement of Marriage (Germany, 1933), 81
Law for the Prevention of Hereditarily Diseased Offspring (Germany, 1933), 52, 53
Lee, Ana, 7–8
Lemke Muniz de Faria, Yara-Colette, 22, 131, 134
Lewis, David Levering, 69
Lilli and Lore, 115 fig. 4.1, 119 fig. 4.3, 126 fig. 4.5, 136 fig. 4.6, 163 fig. 5.3, 173 fig. 5.4, 205 fig. 6.4a, 206 fig. 6.5; birth of, 114–15; in Catholic dormitory/orphanage, 121–22, 126, 127–28, 151; citizenship and immigration status, 154–56, 169, 170–71, 173–74; divergent life paths, 120, 170, 171–72, 205–6; in foster care system, 152–54, 157–65; and generational trauma, 5–6, 201–4; immigration to United States, 146–47; Lilli's views on reunion with Greta, 180–81; Lore's post-reunion interactions with Greta, 198–200; Lore's reunions with Greta, in-person, 4 fig. 0.1, 62–63, 153 fig. 5.1, 181–84, 186–94, 188 fig. 6.2; Lore's reunions with Greta, phone conversations, 178–80, 185; upbringing in adoptive American family, 78–79, 166–70; upbringing in German family, 116, 117–20, 126–27, 143, 146–47; upbringing in Hidden Villa Ranch, 149–52
liminal existence: of *afrodeutsche Nachkriegskinder*, 5, 120, 126–27, 132–33, 141, 157, 174, 188; of Black American soldiers, 84; of Black Germans, 10, 57–58, 70–71, 91; and discursive space, 120; and generational trauma, 5–6, 201–3
Lorde, Audre, 51
Lore. *See* Lilli and Lore
Lowe, Kate, 33, 35
Lusane, Clarence, 69–70, 71

Mackey, Mike, 148
magi visual imagery, 33–34
marriage: and adoption requirements, 135; and divorce, 81; licenses denied for Black American soldiers, 102–3. *See also* interracial relationships
Marriage Law (1938), 81
Martinez, Aja, 19

masculinity: Black, 76; white, threatened by Black soldiers, 47, 91, 92. *See also* sexuality

Massaquoi, Hans, 72

Maurice, Saint, 33, 34

McNarney, Joseph, 83

meaningful memory, 165

medieval Europe, 32–35

Mellinkoff, Ruth, 34

memory: as analytical framework, 9; and *Erinnerungskultur,* 79–80; and fear of remembering, 56; meaningful, 165; "official" representations of, 11–13. *See also* erasure; postmemory; trauma

men. *See* interracial relationships; marriage; sexuality; soldiers; white womanhood; women, Black; women, white German

Mengele, Josef, 54

Michel, Sonya, 139

military. *See* African soldiers; Black American soldiers; soldiers

Ming Quong Home, 152–53, 154, 157, 164, 165, 166, 167

mixed-race children: citizenship of, 21, 40, 47, 91, 121, 135, 155, 169, 173–74; from rape, 101–2, 138, 140–42; as threat to white German purity, 40, 42–43, 46, 90, 113–14, 123–24. See also *afrodeutsche Nachkriegskinder*

Mjagkij, Nina, 65

Monáe, Janelle, 59

Moyd, Michelle, 38–39

NAACP, 78, 136

Nama people, 42, 44–45

Naranch, Bradley, 41

naturalization process, US, 155–57, 170–71

Nazi era. *See* Third Reich Germany

new racism, as concept, 98

nightclubs, 103–5

92nd Infantry Division, American Expeditionary Force, 66, 76, 77–78, 77 fig. 2.3

Nora, Pierre, 34

Nuremberg Laws, 51–52, 53, 71

Nuremburg Rally (1936), 51

"official history," 11–13

Ogungbure, Adebowale, 58

Oguntoye, Katharina, 51, 95, 96

Olick, Jeffrey, 7

Oliveres, Jordi, 16

one-drop rule, 3, 71, 123, 159, 166

183rd Engineer Combat Battalion, 76–77

Opitz, May, 51

orphanages, 102, 121–22, 123, 124–25, 127–28, 132, 151, 152–54

Ott, Brian L., 8, 22

outsider/insider status, 98, 124, 130, 182–83, 186, 189, 190, 197–98

Overseas Weekly (newspaper), 135, 136

Peele, Jordan, 146

Peña, Rosemarie, 22, 25, 134, 137, 156, 157–58, 161, 166, 167, 202

Penick, Frank, 140

Pershing, John J., 66

Philips, Kendall, 22, 56

postcards, 40–43, 41 fig. 1.1, 43 fig. 1.2

postmemory: and Afrofuturism, 17–18; as analytical framework, 13–15; composite narratives in, 60, 67–69, 73–74, 78–82, 107–8, 159; confrontation with creative imaginings in, 107, 176–77, 180, 182–84, 185–86, 189–93, 197–98, 200–201; and counterstory, 19; identity reconstruction and reclamation in, 14, 107–8, 112, 122, 143–44, 158–61. *See also* erasure; memory

post-traumatic stress syndrome (PTSD), 82, 157

power: rhetorical, 189, 194–95; silence as, 62, 109–10, 118, 180, 182–83, 189–90, 192. *See also* Afrofuturism

prescriptive forgetting, 14, 69, 107, 139, 162

pronatalist policies, 51, 81, 96

propaganda campaigns: colonial postcards, 40–43, 41 fig. 1.1, 43 fig. 1.2; in Weimar Republic, 46–47, 48 fig. 1.3, 91–92, 94–95; in World War I, Germany, 65–66; in World War I, United States, 92–94, 93 fig. 3.1; in World War II, 75, 138, 139

PTSD (post-traumatic stress syndrome), 82, 157

Puerto Rican soldiers, 75, 105

Quashie, Kevin, 16

race and racism. See *afrodeutsche Nachkriegskinder*; anti-Blackness, Germany; anti-Blackness, United States; interracial relationships; mixed-race children; white womanhood; whiteness
rape, 101–2, 129, 138–41, 167–70
Raphael-Hernandez, Heike, 36
Reichstag debates (1912), 43–44
Renes, Martin, 44, 128, 129
reparations, 45, 54–55
repressive erasure, 56–57, 129, 165, 174
Revolutionary War (1775–83), 35–36, 65
rhetorical power, 189, 194–95
rhetorical theory, 7–8, 18, 19
Rhineland occupation, 45–47, 68, 69, 91–92, 94–95
Richardson, Rudi (Udo Ackermann), 156
Ricoeur, Paul, 6
Robert, 68 fig. 2.1, 80 fig. 2.4; composite narrative of, 67–69, 79–82; Greta's description of, 67, 80–81, 82, 115
Rohan, Liz, 18
Rohrbach, Paul, 39–40
Roosevelt, Franklin D., 74
Roseman, Mark, 14, 24–25
Rosenhaft, Eve, 37, 39, 47, 51
Roth, Friedrich, 135
Royster, Jacqueline Jones, 18, 184
Rukoro, Vekuii, 45
Russian soldiers, 101–2, 138–39, 140, 141

Schilling, Britta, 38, 42
Schokoladensoldaten ("chocolate soldiers"), 83, 124
Schultz, Dagmar, 51
scientific experiments, 127–29
segregation, 55, 71n27, 75, 84–85, 98–99, 113, 124, 137. *See also* desegregation and integration
761st Tank Battalion, 76–77, 78, 84
sexual assault and rape, 101–2, 129, 138–41, 167–70
sexuality: of Black men as threat to white purity, 39, 46–48, 48 fig. 1.3, 95, 101, 140; of Black women as threat to white purity, 43–44, 90; double standards, 47, 51; of white women, stigmatized for interracial relationships, 100, 101, 110, 113, 121, 131
shame, 73, 96–97, 110, 122, 133, 143–44, 160–61, 185, 193, 201, 202
Sieg, Rudolf, 128, 129
Siek, Stephanie, 133, 156
slavery: and abolition, 36; in medieval Europe, 34–35; and rape, 129
Society for Christian-Jewish cooperation (Gesellschaft für Christlich-Jüdische Zusammenarbeit), 82–83
soldiers: Black German, 71; white German, 35–36, 67–68, 76, 79. *See also* African soldiers; Black American soldiers
Sollors, Werner, 113, 124–25
Sömmerring, Samuel Thomas, 35; *Über die körperliche Verschiedenheit des Mohren vom Europäer*, 37
Soviet Union, 139
sponsorship, and immigration, 147–48
sterilization, 46, 52, 53–54, 96
Stoecker, Helmuth, 38
Stollenwörthweiher See ("Sex Lake"), 105–6, 105 fig. 3.4
Stolzfus, Nathan, 50, 52
structural amnesia, 88, 109, 143
Sturken, Marita, 6

Third Reich Germany: anti-Blackness in, 51–54, 69–73, 96; marriage law, 81; racial purity ideology, 50–51, 71, 72, 96–97
333rd Field Artillery Battalion, 75–76
369th Infantry Regiment, Harlem Hell Fighters, 66
Till, Emmett, 70
Toxi (film), 123–24, 125 fig. 4.4
trauma: generational, 5–6, 201–4; and language, 7–8; PTSD, 82, 157. *See also* liminal existence

Trigg, Dylan, 7–8
Trinidad, 74–75
Trotha, Lothar von, 41–42
Truman, Harry S., 84
Tuskegee Airmen, 76, 78

undocumented immigrants, 155–57, 169
United States: adoption coordination with Germany, 130–31, 133–34, 137; eugenics movement in, 53–54; foster care system, 152–54, 157–65; interracial relationships banned in, 54, 109, 135. *See also* anti-Blackness, United States; Black American soldiers; immigration

Verkafferung label, 42
Volk, das vs. *ein*, 50
Voste, Jean (Johnny), 52, 53 fig. 1.4

War Brides Act (US, 1945), 103
Weheliye, Alexander, 50
Weimar Republic, 46–47, 91–92, 94–95
West Germany: adoption coordination (*see* adoption); anti-Blackness in, 55, 98–101, 127–29; nation-building ideology, 117, 130, 134–35; reparations to Jewish survivors, 54–55; stipends for Russian rape survivors, 138, 139, 140
Westover, Tara, 21
white womanhood: challenged, in postmemoried creative imaginings, 107, 176–77, 180, 182–84, 185–86, 189–93, 197–98, 200–201; protection rhetoric, 47–49, 48 fig. 1.3, 92–94, 93 fig. 3.1, 99; racial purity rhetoric, colonial-era, 44; racial purity rhetoric, Nazi-era, 50–51, 72, 96–97, 138; racial purity rhetoric, postwar-era, 100–102; racial purity rhetoric, Weimar-era, 46–48, 48 fig. 1.3, 91, 94–95; rebellion against, 100, 105–7; reclamation of, 107–8, 112, 122, 144, 158–61
whiteface, 123–24

whiteness: and citizenship, 21, 38, 40, 90; and cognitive dissonance, 29–30; in colonial visual imagery, 40–43, 41 fig. 1.1, 43 fig. 1.2; and phenotypic hue, 3; purity concerns, colonial-era, 39–40, 42–44; purity concerns, Nazi-era, 50–54, 138; purity concerns, postwar-era, 113–14, 123–24, 129–30; purity concerns, Weimar-era, 46–49, 48 fig. 1.3, 91–92, 94–95; and scientific gaze, 128; and US military culture, 75, 76, 78, 83–85; and US propaganda campaigns, 92–94, 93 fig. 3.1. *See also* white womanhood

white-passing, 138, 140, 162
Wiegmink, Pia, 36
Wiesel, Elie, 76
Wildenthal, Lora, 90
Wolfram von Eschenbach, *Parzival*, 33
women, Black: erasure of, 88; rape of enslaved, 129; as threat to white German purity, 43–44, 72, 90, 100
women, white German: and marriage law, 81, 135; and maternal rights, 135; in postwar nation-building ideology, 117; rape of, 101–2, 138–41; recovering voices of, 23–24; reproductive health care for, 101–2; stigmatized for interracial relationships, 100, 101, 110, 113, 121, 131–32. *See also* white womanhood
Woodson, Carter, 66
World War I: Black American soldiers in, 65–67; postwar Rhineland occupation, 45–47, 68, 69, 91–92, 94–95; propaganda campaigns, 65–66, 92–94, 93 fig. 3.1
World War II: Black American soldiers in, 73–78, 77 fig. 2.3; propaganda campaigns, 75, 138, 139
Wright, Michelle, 10

Yates, Frances, 12

Zantop, Susanne, 38
Zelizer, Barbie, 14, 22
zoo exhibitions, 37–38

INTERSECTIONAL RHETORICS
KARMA R. CHÁVEZ, SERIES EDITOR

This series takes as its starting point the position that intersectionality offers important insights to the field of rhetoric—including that to enhance what we understand as rhetorical practice, we must diversify the types of rhetors, arguments, frameworks, and forms under analysis. Intersection works on two levels for the series: (1) reflecting the series' privileging of intersectional perspectives and analytical frames while also (2) emphasizing rhetoric's intersection with related fields, disciplines, and research areas.

A Nation's Undesirables: Mixed-Race Children and Whiteness in the Post-Nazi Era
    TRACEY OWENS PATTON

Inscrutable Eating: Asian Appetites and the Rhetorics of Racial Consumption
    JENNIFER LIN LEMESURIER

Constellating Home: Trans and Queer Asian American Rhetorics
    V. JO HSU

Inconvenient Strangers: Transnational Subjects and the Politics of Citizenship
    SHUI-YIN SHARON YAM

Culturally Speaking: The Rhetoric of Voice and Identity in a Mediated Culture
    AMANDA NELL EDGAR

www.ingramcontent.com/pod-product-compliance
Lightning Source LLC
Chambersburg PA
CBHW020651230426
43665CB00008B/386